STAGING COYOTE'S DREAM

An Anthology of First Nations Drama in English

STAGING COYOTE'S DREAM

An Anthology of First Nations Drama in English

edited by

Monique Mojica

and

Ric Knowles

Playwrights Canada Press
Toronto • Canada

Playwrights Canada Press
54 Wolseley St., 2nd floor Toronto, Ontario CANADA M5T 1A5
416-703-0013   fax 416-703-0059
orders@playwrightscanada.com • www.playwrightscanada.com

Playwrights Canada Press acknowledges the support of
the taxpayers of Canada and the province of Ontario through
The Canada Council for the Arts and the Ontario Arts Council.

Cover Painting: "el sueño del coyote" [Coyote's Dream] by Oswaldo DeLeón Kantule "Achu". Oil on canvas 20" x 16". www.deleonkantule.net
Cover Design/Production Editor: Jodi Armstrong

National Library of Canada Cataloguing in Publication

Staging coyote's dream

Plays.

ISBN 0-88754-625-0

1. Canadian drama (English)—Indian authors. 2. American drama—Indian authors
I. Mojica, Monique, 1954- II. Knowles, Richard. 1950-

PS8309.I53S72 2002   C812.008'0897   C2001-902765-6
PR9196.7.I53S72 2002

First edition: May 2003.
Printed and bound by AGMV Marquis at Quebec, Canada.

TABLE OF CONTENTS

INTRODUCTION TO *STAGING COYOTE'S DREAM: AN ANTHOLOGY OF FIRST NATIONS DRAMA IN ENGLISH*

"STAGING COYOTE'S DREAM:" The title invokes the dream world, that realm of intangible reality in which the ethereal and the material coexist and are co-extensive. It also invokes, as Coyote—one embodiment of the Sacred Clowns, Tricksters, and Contraries of so many different First Nations cultures who enter sacred ceremony to scandalize, scare, ridicule, frighten, and make people laugh— the outlaw, the critic, the teacher, the disturber, the cultural hero and the buffoon. The trickster, variously called (among other things) Coyote, Weesageechak, Nanabush, Raven, Rabbit, Spider, Monkey, Agouti, or Koshare, serves as a source for a wide variety of First Nations theatre artists creating bodies of work that reflect the experience of being Aboriginal in the contemporary world. Coyote's dream opens up the realm of possibilities, gives permission to Native theatre artists themselves to dream, and to use theatre to materialize that dream – to envision, to give body and form to the unseeable and/or the differently seen. Coyote allows Native theatre artists to examine and reveal the realities of First Nations people who are forced to exist in a hostile environment. This is extraordinarily important, because so much of Native peoples' experience today is devalued and invalidated, to the degree that many Native people find it difficult not to invalidate themselves. But Coyote exists as the entirely mutable creative force who holds up the mirror and whose energy gives permission to make theatre that makes change.

Staging Coyote's Dream, then, is our title, and it signals what we hope this collection of plays will do. Our subtitle, *An Anthology of First Nations Drama in English,* tries to delineate our topic, and we have structured this introduction as an explication of its terms: "an anthology," of "First Nations" "Drama" "in English." To divide the topics up in this way is convenient, of course, but also problematic, in that it invokes categories and taxonomies rooted in Western European ways of knowing – ways of dividing, conquering, and disciplining the world that are foreign to, and have contributed to the subjection of, Native peoples throughout the Americas (and the land they inhabit). And of course such divisions and categories are also artificial: what we have to say here about each of these terms impinges upon, connects to, and overlaps with the other categories in ways that Coyote would recognize as entirely subversive of the cultural authority of the categories themselves. But the categories, are, nevertheless, useful, if only as necessary fictions, and there are choices and terms that have to be used.

"AN ANTHOLOGY..." This is "an" anthology," not "the" anthology: it is a collection of plays that appeals to and challenges us as editors. It is neither all of what's out there nor "the greatest hits." Nor can it claim to be representative of all the Nations, regions, cultures, spiritualities, or styles of performance that together constitute contemporary "First Nations Theatre" – or even to be representative of the "best" or most characteristic work of the playwrights whose work is published here. It is an eclectic selection of plays that emerge from a family of theatre artists who share certain aspects of their heritage and certain experiences of the contemporary world.

"**...OF FIRST NATIONS...**" *Staging Coyote's Dream* is the first collection of Native plays to be published in the land that is now called Canada, but it is not an anthology of "Canadian Plays," nor have we chosen to identify the plays collected here as "Native." The decision to use the term "First Nations," and the decision not to restrict the plays included to those produced within the geopolitical boundaries of Canada, makes two implicit claims. The first claims the right of First Nations peoples not to be subject to the political or legislative regimes of later-day nations; the second lays claim to a history that long precedes contact or colonization, that has not been superseded, and that cannot be circumscribed.

But what constitutes a "First Nations play"? In his introduction to *All My Relations: An Anthology of Contemporary Canadian Native Fiction*, Thomas King says that "Native literature is literature produced by Natives." But how do you define or identify a Native? Clearly, as King says, being Native is something less transitory than, say, being Canadian: "one can become a Canadian writer... without having been born in Canada, but one is either born an Indian or one is not."

> This definition... however, makes a rather large assumption.... It assumes that the matter of race imparts to the Native writer a tribal understanding of the universe, access to a distinct culture, and a literary perspective that is unattainable by non-Natives. In our discussions of Native literature, we try to imagine that there is a racial denominator which for full-bloods raised in cities, half-bloods raised on farms, quarter-bloods raised on reservations, Indians adopted by white families, Indians who speak their tribal language, Indians who speak only English, traditionally educated Indians, university-trained Indians, Indians with little education, and the like all share. We know, of course, that there is not. (x-xi)

As Monique said on a panel on "Women's Voices in Native American Theatre" at Miami University, Oxford, Ohio in 1997: "We are different and we are profoundly related, from our origin stories and the oral histories of the migrations of the people, we are relations. To what we share in our experiences of invasion, colonization and ongoing genocide, we are family. We are different and we are alike. More different than alike? Or more alike than different? Is the glass half full or half empty? Are you an Indian first or a woman first? What do you do with the non-Native part of your heredity when you identify yourself as a Native person? These questions are an exercise in reducing us to bite-sized pieces that make us more palatable to Western tastes, more acceptable to the foreigner's mindset. How many white artists are called upon to justify their influences? How many of them acknowledge or are even aware of how they have been influenced by us? The truth is that after 500 years of forced 'influence,' of being denied the right to declare who we are, and learning how to deny it ourselves, we are greater than the sum of our parts" (Mojica).

"**...DRAMA...**" Although performance has always been a fundamental aspect of First Nations cultures, drama and theatre as they are currently understood are European forms. They are not indigenous to Turtle Island, and they are not traditional performative forms for First Nations peoples. The act of writing and staging "plays," then, necessarily involves Native theatre artists in simultaneous activities of protection and translation; but this is why theatrical forms are so useful and necessary for contemporary First Nations artists.

To take protection first, while it is true that ceremonial healing and performance are fundamental qualities of the trickster and the cultures which the trickster inhabits, the ongoing challenge of Native theatre artists is to respect and protect what is collectively private within their cultures, while creating theatre rooted in aboriginal world views and sensibilities. In "staging Coyote's dream" we are not talking about re-creating specific rituals and ceremonies for the stage – Western culture willingly rewards the Native person for taking some sweetgrass or sage and recreating "authentic" rituals for a non-Native gaze. In creating theatre the First Nations artists represented in this collection are drawing on a known and lived sense of what is essentially ritualistic. They know that in all theatre there's a healing that takes place on the stage, in the audience, and between the stage and the audience, a healing that is part of the mutability of Coyote, part of the humour, and part of the ritual.

But when you call upon Coyote through ritual, when you call upon the ancestors, someone's going to show up. It becomes necessary to create a space, a container that tells the spirits that it's play, in order to respect and protect the culture and the people who are embodying the spiritual elements of that culture.[1] That container is theatre.

In Western European traditions, theatre is fiction, "just stories," and most recently, particularly in large commercial theatre operations, it has become just entertainment, packaged like other products for audiences understood to be consumers. In First Nations cultures, stories are never "just stories." They are essential ways of communicating memory, history, belief, and tradition, and they require what Ojibway critic Christine Lenze has called "response-ability" (51) to material that is not understood to be "just" fictional. To use theatre for a First Nations artist, then, is always to be translating, transforming, transposing (in terms of the integrity of the work itself), and negotiating, or accommodating (in relation to external contexts).

One of the tasks of First Nations theatre artists, and one of the subjects of most of the plays in this collection, *is* translation, broadly understood: translation between cultures and world views; translation between the unseen and the material worlds; translation between interior and exterior realities; translation between languages and discourses, including the values and ideologies they embody; and translation of the ways in which First Nations peoples navigate identity. Because most Native peoples in the contemporary world *live* in translation, and theatre can provide the opportunity to envision and embody— to materialize and give form to—the unseeable, the differently seen, and the interior experience of Native peoples. It allows First Nations artists to examine, show, and validate their experience of living in a hostile environment. It allows them to take the risk of turning that experience inside out—a kind of voluntary disemboweling—so that people can see what it feels like on the inside, and so that the healing can begin.

"...IN ENGLISH." Of course the most obvious act of translation in First Nations theatre takes place between languages. The plays in this collection are published in English, which is of course, together with French and Spanish (which we have not attempted to represent here), the language of conquest, the language that Native people were brutalized into speaking. The artists published here, by necessity, are "reinventing the enemy's language" (Harjo). For some, this involves a literal act of translation, conceiving the plays first in (say) Cree or Ojibway and moving them to English (occasionally with fragments or passages in their own languages) in order to reach their Native and non-Native audiences alike. Others, for whom English is all they have, engage in a different, more subtle kind of translation. These writers, like many Native members of their audiences, are quite literally living in translation, their heads and mouths filled with words and ways of thinking (and therefore perceptions, values, and ideologies) that are not their own – but filled, too, with perceptions, values, and patterns that *are* theirs, but that they don't feel the right to claim because the proper words for them don't exist in the only language they have. And English, as many elders and speakers of First Nations languages have taught, is a very poor medium for expressing First Nations cultures. There is, then, a lived gap, an interruption, that causes Native people who speak only English to translate constantly from a language that they don't inhabit.

But even for these writers, their own languages perhaps inhabit them. Troy Richardson, a North Carolina Tuscarora linguist who studied at the University of Pennsylvania and subsequently began teaching at Harvard, suggests that there is a way that many Native peoples speak English that is specific, in much the same way that African American English has been said to inscribe in its rhythms and syntax elements of ancestral African languages. He finds in Native writing in English sentence structures and syntactical elements from indigenous languages that are unknown to the writer but that nevertheless inhabit their bodies and speak through them. When Native writers translate from the inside out in that act of evisceration we have described as fundamental to much First Nations the-atrical production, what comes out may be traces of a language they don't speak. Their writing, *as* translation, may become an entity unto itself, a third thing, but one which represents most truly where they live in the contemporary world.

For these reasons, too, First Nations plays are most often structured differently from other plays. There are differences in the content (of the stories), in the cultural contexts within and through which the plays are produced and out of which they emerge, and in the plays' inclusion of the unseen worlds of these cultures, and of course these differences are legible in a multiplicity of structural differences, large and small. This, too, is partly a question of language. Cree, the first language of Tomson Highway, for example, is a much more musical and poetic language than is English, and this, together with Highway's training and experience as a classical musician, informs not only the sentence-by-sentence rhythms of his plays, but also their larger shapes and structures. And there is an element of translation here too, as Native theatre artists, adopting and adapting European dramatic forms and infusing them with elements of Native performance traditions, try to find structures within which to navigate, negotiate (often within themselves), and theatrically embody the experience of living in translation. Finally, in their different ways, many First Nations playwrights, employing traditional Western performance frames ranging from naturalism and realism through to the minstrel show, the pageant, the Indian Medicine Show, and the sitcom, use the master's structures to dismantle the master's structures in a kind of active perversion of the very forms that have been used against them as ways of "containing" their experience.[2]

But there is no one form. What this collection participates in and illustrates is a community working together on and towards a body of work. These plays are not simply part of, and assimilable by, a Western dramatic tradition; they constitute and participate in a history of their own. That history includes, of course, traditional Native ritual forms. It also includes a long tradition of oration, of pageantry, of auto-performance by figures such as poet Pauline Johnson, of performance in wild west shows, medicine shows, circuses, and rodeos (and these are some of the forms cited and perverted by contemporary artists). But most notably, that history consists of a tradition of contemporary theatrical performance that grew out of the activist Native political, cultural, and spiritual movement of the late 1960s and early 70s, in part a movement of cultural preservation that paradoxically, in the case of theatre, meant creating something that didn't exist before. And the "pioneers" of that movement are still active. The first Native theatre companies in what is now North America, the Native American Theater Ensemble and Spiderwoman Theater, were formed in 1972 and 1975 respectively. In Canada, Native theatre artists only began taking control of their own representation on stage in the late 1970s and 1980s at such places as Northern Delights in Sioux Lookout, Native Earth Performing Arts in Toronto and De-Ba-Jeh-Mu-Jig Theatre Group on the Wikwemikong Unceded Reserve, Manitoulin Island. And the artists who started these theatres and others across the continent continue to work together, acting in or directing one another's shows, listening to one another's voices, learning from and influencing one another, and teaching new generations of Native theatre artists at such institutions as The Institute of American Indian Art in Santa Fe, or the Centre for Indigenous Theatre in Toronto. They are still very much inventing themselves as Native theatre artists, and inventing and evolving, through plays such as those published here and many others, a powerful tradition of Native theatre, a way of staging Coyote's dream.

NOTES

¹   As Lloyd Kiva New argued in 1969, "we believe that an exciting American Indian theatre can be evolved out of the framework of Indian traditions. We think this evolution must come from the most sensitive approaches imaginable in order not to misuse or cheapen the original nature of Indian forms, most of which are closely tied to religion" (qtd in Geiogamah 12).

²   Among the things that Native theatre artists must contend with that can "contain" their work and limit the possible evolution of new forms are material conditions, economic, organizational, and cultural, that determine which types of work are produced and which are not. Given funding constraints, for example, it is not surprising that much Native women's theatre consists of one-woman shows, but this does not mean that the one-woman show is a form peculiarly suited to the expression of Native women's lives. The organizational, processual, and professional bottles into and out of which everything must be poured in the contemporary theatre world, too, impose systemic constraints that are inimical to certain methods of creation and modes of delivery. Many performance venues are available for some types of theatre and not others. Culturally, too, First Nations artists are rewarded for certain kinds of story—creation myths, comically self-deprecating tales, or "rez" stories of alcoholism, welfare, or drug abuse, for example—while other styles and stories—stories that challenge the power structure, challenge the continuing colonization of Native peoples, or make white people uncomfortable, excluded, or simply puzzled—are less welcome. Similarly, First Nations artists who try to describe culturally specific experience are subject either to the lethal embrace of inclusivity and identification—"we know exactly how you feel"—or to exclusion from the map of contemporary theatre because their work is insufficiently "universal" (which in practice means too difficult to assimilate, too far outside of Western norms).

WORKS CITED

• Geiogamah, Hanay. "Indian Theatre in the United States 1991: An Assessment." *Canadian Theatre Review* 68 (Fall 1991): 12-14.
• Harjo, Joy. *Reinventing the Enemy's Language: Contemporary Native Women's Writings of North America.* NY: Norton, 1997.
• King, Thomas, ed. *All My Relations: An Anthology of Contemporary Canadian Native Fiction.* Toronto: McClelland and Stewart, 1990.
• Lenze, Christine. "'The Whole Thing You're Doing Is White Man's Ways': *fareWel*'s Northern Tour." *Canadian Theatre Review* 108 (Fall 2001): 48-51.
• Mojica, Monique. "Women's Voices in Native American Theatre." Panel at Miami University, Oxford, Ohio, October 1997.
• Richardson, Troy. Conversation with Monique Mojica, Spring 1996.

ABOUT THE EDITORS

Monique Mojica is a Kuna and Rappahannock actor and playwright based in Toronto. She began training at the age of three and belongs to the second generation spun directly from the web of New York's Spiderwoman Theater. She is a long-time collaborator with Floyd Favel on various research and performance projects investigating Native performance culture. Together with Jani Lauzon and Michelle St. John, she founded Turtle Gals Performance Ensemble. Their first play, *The Scrubbing Project*, explores racism, tradition and memory using vaudeville as a madcap metaphor for navigating identity. It was co-produced by Turtle Gals and Native Earth in association with Factory Theatre in the Fall of 2002.

Ric Knowles is Professor of Drama at the University of Guelph. He is a member of the editorial team of the journal, *Canadian Theatre Review*, and the editor of *Modern Drama*. He edited the collection, *Theatre in Atlantic Canada* (Mount Allison University) and co-edited *Modern Drama: Defining the Field* (University of Toronto Press), and he is the author of *The Theatre of Form and the Production of Meaning* (ECW Press), *Shakespeare and Canada* (PIE International), and *Reading the Material Theatre* (Cambridge University Press). He is currently President of Playwrights Canada Press.

THE INDEPENDENCE
OF EDDIE ROSE

WILLIAM S. YELLOW ROBE JR.

WILLIAM S. YELLOW ROBE JR.

INTRODUCTION TO *THE INDEPENDENCE OF EDDIE ROSE*

Actor, director, playwright, poet and teacher William S. Yellow Robe Jr. is an enrolled member of the Assiniboine/Nakota nation, from the township of Wolf Point in the Fort Peck Reservation in Northeastern Montana. He wrote his first play in sixth grade at the Wold Point Elementary Grade School. He attended Northern Montana College and the University of Montana, has taught theatre and playwriting at the Institute of American Indian Arts in Santa Fe, New Mexico. He is presently a Faculty Affiliate in the English Department at the University of Montana in Missoula. He is the former Artistic Director of Wakiknabe Theater Company in Albuquerque, and the Founding Artistic Director of the No Borders Indigenous Theater Company in Missoula. One of twelve recipients of the Theater Communications Group (TCG)'s National Theater Artist Residency Program, he is now serving as Playwright in Residence at the Trinity Repertory Company in Providence, Rhode Island. The first playwright to receive the First Nations Book Award for Drama from the Returning of the Gift, in Norman, Oklahoma, he has also been awarded a National Endowment for the Arts Playwrights' Fellowship, a Jerome Fellowship, and a Princess Grace-USA award. A member of the Dramatist's Guild and the Native Writers Circle of the Americas, he also serves on the Board of Advisors for the Missoula Writers' Collaborative in Montana and Red Eagle Soaring in Seattle.

William Yellow Robe is the award-winning author of more than thirty plays, which have received readings and productions across the United States at such venues as the Mark Taper Forum in Los Angeles, the American Conservatory Theatre in San Francisco, the Joseph Papp Public Theatre/New York Shakespeare Festival, Honolulu Theatre for Youth, Ensemble Studio Theatre in New York, and the Montana Repertory Theatre in Missoula. Five of his one-act plays—*The Star Quilter*, *The Council*, *The Body Guards*, *Rez Politics*, and *Sneaky*—have been published by the University of Oklahoma Press in a collection entitled *Where the Pavement Ends*.

The Independence of Eddie Rose was first produced in June 1986 as part of the University of Montana's Montana Masquers Playwriting Festival, under the direction of Rolland Meinholtz, and it has received many productions since, including two by the Seattle Group Theatre in 1987 (when it won the Seattle Group Theater's Multi-Cultural Playwriting Festival award) and again in 1990 as part of the Goodwill Arts Festival. It received staged readings at New York's Ensemble Studio Theatre in 1989, directed by Jack Gelbert, and at Yale University's Theater Studies Department in the same year, directed by David Krasner. It was published in an earlier version in 1999 in *Seventh Generation: An Anthology of Native American Plays*, edited by Mimi Gisolfi D'Aponte for Theatre Communications Group, New York. The title and some aspects of the action seem at first to position *Eddie Rose* within a long North American tradition of "leaving home" plays, in which young boys enact an Oedipal narrative by fighting for their independence from an oppressive father/loving mother, eventually breaking free and starting a new life. Thus Eddie's perverse father figure, his mother's abusive boyfriend, Lenny (who, as a rival, is not much older than Eddie), blocks his access to independent subjectivity, while his mother's potentially incestuous love for him is equally oppressive. In this reading, the play ends with Eddie's apparently successful plea to his mother to "give me back my life. I want to leave here alive." "Thank you, Mom," he says, after she has signed the papers that provide him freedom from a prematurely paternal relationship to his younger sister. "You gave me back my life."

Similarly, at first glance at least, the play seems to participate fully in a dramaturgical tradition of brutal realism, depicting as starkly as it does the almost numbing realities of daily life for many First Nations people in North America, and perhaps risking reproducing and reifying the sense of helpless inevitability that is so often the social impact of realist social vignettes. Thus the play presents an apparently transparent, unmediated window on the realities of alcohol and drug dependency, prostitution, and family breakdown – though Yellow Robe is at pains to point out that the play "doesn't try to suggest that all Native people have struggled with alcoholism," which, as Aunt Thelma says in the play, "was not our way" (personal communication with the editors). But the strength of the realist form resides in its honesty, and there is a real and urgent need to acknowledge the lived experience of a portion of the population that is most often excluded from representation. Besides, as the frequently quoted passage from Lyle Longclaws has it, "before the healing can take place the poison must first be exposed."

The real impact and importance of *The Independence of Eddie Rose*, however, incorporates but exceeds its relationship to either of these familiar dramaturgical traditions, and concerns itself neither with plotting Oedipal narratives nor exposing the poison, but with pointing towards the healing. The play incorporates a critique of colonialism's emasculation of Native men – "big kids without diapers," according to Eddie's mother, Katherine. But like so many other Native plays, it also locates "healing" in the realm of the grandmothers – the ancestral/familial line of women that include, of course, Eddie's own "Grandma," frequently invoked, but also his Aunt Thelma who teaches him, in the significant absence of his uncles, to ritually bathe in sage smoke before he enters "that house of death" to rescue his younger sister, Theia (and with her, hope for the future through a pointedly female lineage). In one representative sequence the play moves from the bleak ending of its third scene—the horrific sexual abuse by a prison guard of Eddie's friend Mikey—to a matrilineal scene between Theia and Thelma in which the older woman teaches her niece her grandmother's song and introduces her—in contradistinction to drinking as "something we always do" (explaining that "your grandmother... never drank")—to another ritual, of hair burning, that is performed "when someone dies" as a way of avoiding the onset of evil. The sequence prepares the audience for a final scene in which Eddie's mother, Katherine, reclaims her women's role as she recognizes her sister Thelma's gesture of cutting off her braids as an act of mourning for Katherine's own apparent spiritual death. "My boy," she tells Eddie, taking over the task from her son, who is about to set fire to the braids, "women do this. Just go." The play's final gesture is not Eddie's exit and the familiar dramaturgical closing of the familial door, but his reaching out to steady his mother's trembling hand as she resolutely lights the match.

As William Yellow Robe said recently in an e-mail message to the editors, "*Eddie Rose* shares a voice with all Indigenous peoples who struggle with colonialism in all its aspects. It is a struggle many people face on a day-to-day basis. [The play] has never offered an apology for the issues and how they are presented, but offers hope for those who face this struggle outside the world of theatre."

CHARACTERS

KATHERINE ROSE
Mother of Eddie, she is in her early thirties.
EDDIE ROSE
Son of Katherine, he is around fifteen or sixteen years old.
THELMA ROSE
Sister to Katherine, she is in her mid-thirties.
THEIA ROSE
Sister to Eddie. She is ten or eleven years old, and a daughter to Katherine.
MIKE HORSE
A breed and a friend to Eddie. He is fourteen or fifteen years old.
LENNY SHARB
A breed and a boy friend to Katerine. He is in his early twenties.
SAM JACOBS
He is a breed and is in his late thirties, early forties.

THE INDEPENDENCE OF EDDIE ROSE

WILLIAM S. YELLOW ROBE JR.

PROLOGUE

TIME: Early in the morning. PLACE: KATHERINE Rose's house, living room.

On stage are EDDIE Rose, THEIA Rose, KATHERINE Rose and LENNY Sharb. They are standing in the house area. They are located in the living room area. The furniture in the living room includes metal folding chairs and a table. THEIA sits holding an old gray Snoopy doll. EDDIE is sitting on the floor and has a paper sack in front of him. There is a sound of a door being slammed over and over again.

EDDIE
One it, two it, three it....

As he gets to three, KATHERINE Rose explodes and chases LENNY across the room and out of the house.

KATHERINE
And don't you come back here you son of a bitch! You stay the hell away from me, from my family. We don't allow thieves in this family. I'll get the cops after you. I'll kill you!

THEIA
Eddie... Eddie?

EDDIE
Don't cry Theia... don't. Remember. Don't cry!

KATHERINE
I don't love you. I don't care what you do. I hope you die!

THEIA
Why Eddie?

EDDIE
You'll just get her madder.

KATHERINE
You no good breed son of a bitch!

EDDIE
Come on, come with me Theia. It'll be all right.

THEIA
No.... No, I can't move.

EDDIE
Nothing's going to happen. Go hide. I'll help you. Hide.

KATHERINE
Stop looking at me! Stop looking at me you...you old breed bitch! You're not even enrolled here! At least my kids are enrolled!

EDDIE
I'll help you hide, all right?

EDDIE takes THEIA to his room. Blackout.

SCENE ONE

TIME: A half hour later. Same day. PLACE: Living room of KATHERINE Rose's house.

KATHERINE Rose stands drinking a beer. She crosses to the metal table and sits.

KATHERINE
I... I showed him. Even that old woman, Peterson, damned breed, she's, she's not even enrolled anyway. She, she was standing out on her porch watching. Her old shrivelled arms holding that stink cat of hers. She looks like an old burnt up doll anyway. Now she'll have something to tell her mormon honeys.

EDDIE
Yeah. You did it Mom.

KATHERINE
He won't be doing anything bad around here. My babies.

EDDIE
Yeah. Sure thing.

KATHERINE
(cries) I don't want anybody doing that to my babies.

EDDIE
Real good Mom, real good. I gotta' go...

KATHERINE
Well! What's wrong with you? *(pause)* Huh? Are you ashamed of me?

EDDIE

Mom. I just want to go... go outside.

EDDIE gets up and crosses to the door, but KATHERINE stops him and turns him around to face her.

KATHERINE

Don't lie.... Don't lie to me my boy. Tell me what's wrong? You know I'm not the one sending you off to school. You were the one they caught drinking. You mad at me? Answer me!

EDDIE

Don't get bent out of shape Mom. *(breaks free for a moment)* You.... You'll just get mad at me.

KATHERINE

(mocks EDDIE) "You'll get mad at me." I suppose! Why would I do that? *(grabs EDDIE)*

EDDIE

Because.... Because you're drinkin'.

KATHERINE

Is that all? *(pause)* Maybe I should kick you out too. *(crosses back to table and sits)* What do you think? Huh? I'm not good enough to be your mother?

EDDIE

I didn't say that.

KATHERINE

Eddie? Do you love your old mother?

EDDIE

I... I... I like you... I guess. See you.

KATHERINE

Come here! *(stops EDDIE)* I said come here. Come here Eddie. *(EDDIE slowly gives in to her.)* Good. Come here my boy.

EDDIE crosses to her. She gets up and hugs him.

Ohhh.... My boy... my beautiful boy.... My baby... *(gently caresses his cheeks)* Poor thing. I'm just mean to him. *(kisses his cheeks and then tries to kiss him on the lips)*

EDDIE

Don't Mom. *(He struggles and breaks free.)* Please. God...

KATHERINE
Some man you are.

EDDIE
I'm your son.... God.... I said I... I... like you...

KATHERINE
Don't make me laugh. You're just a boy... a baby. *(She crosses to the couch and lies down.)* You don't love me. You mope around, telling everyone you want to leave. Then go! I won't stop you. It'll be just me and your sister here. We don't need you.

Pause.

I know, I know. Coming back here with silver lips and a nose, from sniffing paint. Trying to act good now. You buy drinks and weed. You and your friends. Stink little shits. Don't try to fool me. You don't fool me at all. *(Her beer can drops.)* Just me and my baby... babies here...

EDDIE waits a moment. Then he walks over to the couch and looks at his mother.

EDDIE
Mom?

He slowly crosses the floor and goes to his room where THELA is hiding. He looks into the room and returns to the couch. He gently sits on the floor. He looks at his mother one more time. He takes a book of matches from his shirt pocket and gently and quietly lights one of the matches. He holds the match in the air and looks at it. Then he eases the match towards the couch. Then his hands stops moving. The flame of the match burns down to his fingers. He lets the match drop. He uses his other hand and muffles his cry. He places his burnt fingers into his mouth and begins to cry.

Mom.... Mom...

Blackout.

SCENE TWO

TIME: Later in the morning. Same day. PLACE: KATHERINE Rose's living room.

EDDIE is in the kitchen area. He has his paper sack from the opening of the show. He is placing some canned food into the sack. There is a knock on the door. EDDIE quickly takes the paper sack and hides it. He goes to the door and it is slowly opening. He takes a frying pan and gets ready to attack.

The door quickly opens and it is EDDIE's aunty, THELMA Rose. THELMA sticks her head into the house.

THELMA
Hello. Hello.

EDDIE
Oh. Uh.... Hello.

Aunty THELMA enters. She is a large woman. She wears a scarf and has an old gray flannel coat on. She carries a small paper sack.

THELMA
Hello my nephew.

Her hair is woven in two braids. She takes off her coat and sets it on one of the chairs. She goes to the table and clears a place for her sack. She removes some groceries and some bread.

How are you? *(no response)* Eddie. *(She turns and looks at him.)* Eddie? *(no response)* Do you hear me, nephew?

EDDIE
Can't you see? You're supposed to know. Ah... just forget it, Auntie.

THELMA
What.... Where's your sister?

EDDIE
Hiding.

THELMA
Where?

EDDIE
I don't know. We won't find her, only if she lets us. She was in a trunk in the basement last time. She almost stopped breathing. So I punched a hole in the trunk and she won't be blue in the face any more. It's a good place for her. Maybe when I go off to school I'll take her with me, we can do one of those magic acts with a saw.

THELMA
Oh dear. Hiding out in your own home. I suppose. *(laughs)* You two kids. *(laughs)* I've come to help you get ready for school. Well, where's your mom?

EDDIE
In her room. *(THELMA heads for KATHERINE's room.)* Aunty Thelma. Wait up. Can I ask you something?

THELMA
Yes. What is it?

EDDIE
While I'm gone, off to school, you know. Uh.... Would you do something for me? If you can? Can you keep Theia? If you need help in taking care of her I can send you some money, okay? I'll get a clothing order for school. It isn't much, but I can cash it, even sell it, and send you some of it. I heard about other kids who do it.

THELMA
Oh? Why?

EDDIE
You see it. She goes downtown and starts drinking and she'll let him back in. What's the use of even having a door anyway.

THELMA
Why do you want your sister to stay with me?

EDDIE
It's not just her. I don't like the way Lenny looks at her. He does it in a funny way.

THELMA
I'll watch him. Don't worry. It'll be all right.

Pause.

School's coming up. You should be happy you're going to school. Not a lot of young people today get a second chance to finish their schooling. Your mother and me didn't have that chance. *(pause)* I know you'll be leaving behind a lot of your friends... and your family, but your family will always be here.

EDDIE
That's not it. It's just as bad at that school as it is here I bet. Maybe I can hitch back home. Even in this I don't have a say.

THELMA
Not all the Indian boarding schools are that bad Eddie. You really don't know.

Pause.

Listen, your momma could find a job. She'll have her own money then. You kids will have money too. She could hire someone to stay here all the time with Theia. Maybe it'll be me. I wish.

EDDIE
Me too.

THELMA begins to clean.

THELMA
Are these from last night?

EDDIE
No. This morning.

THELMA
Ohhh.... My. This early.

She takes the bread and slices a piece of it for EDDIE. She takes a jar of jam and puts some of the jam on the bread and gives the bread to EDDIE.

She must have been very courageous then, enit?

EDDIE
I guess.

THEIA enters from EDDIE's room.

THEIA
Eddie?

THELMA
Oh! There's my girl. Come here pretty one.

THEIA goes to THELMA who has arms out ready for her. She hugs THEIA.

Who's the pretty one? Who's the prettiest one?

THEIA
Aunty Thelma!

THELMA begins to make her a piece of bread with jam.

Eddie? *(no response)* Eddie?

THELMA
Your sister's talking to you.

THEIA
Is it all right to be around here? Has it stopped?

EDDIE
Yeah.

THELMA turns THEIA around and looks at her very closely.

THELMA
Oh-quaw.... My pretty girl. My little pretty girl.

THEIA
We had it out this morning Aunty Thelma, enit Eddie?

EDDIE
Yeah. See. She knows and she can't do anything for herself. What–

THELMA
Stop it Eddie. I'm here now. Everything's going to be all right. He's gone now. You don't have to be afraid. Don't cry. Go and get a rag and wash your face.

THEIA does.

See. She'll be all right.

EDDIE
But it's always the same. You're not here all the time and I won't be either, but he'll be here. He shows up all the time. I'll probably run into him at that school. I'll be of no use to anybody over there in school. Not like here.

THELMA
Oh behave now. You don't know that. *(checks to see if THEIA is near)* Listen to me nephew... my boy. You have a chance to continue your education. After they expelled you from school... I'm afraid you won't go any place. You'll be like one of these so-called basketball stars. Hanging around the streets in town, bumming people for drinks and having a wife with a big belly and kids. No way of supporting yourself, or them. Now my boy, you have a second chance. Don't let it go.

He stands and gets his paper sack.

EDDIE
I don't want to go to school. I've learned enough. I don't know if I want to be in this house. I wish I could leave now. Just do it without any worrying. She'll kick us out anyways.

He exits.

THELMA
Shnu-gah. Crazy. It's just the same thing.

She follows him to the door. EDDIE moves to another part of the stage which is a graveyard. Lights slowly dim in the kitchen area where THELMA begins to pick up beer cans from the floor. She picks up a pair of dirty underwear and throws it on the floor in disgust. Eddie reaches the graveyard and stops near a grave. He kicks an empty can of spray paint. He starts to clean one of the graves. He removes old faded plastic flowers and finds a plastic bag which has fresh paint in and on it.

EDDIE

Didn't even save me a sniff.

THEIA enters the kitchen area. THELMA kneels and wets her handkerchief and begins to wipe THEIA's face.

THEIA

We're the last ones again, huh Aunty Thelma?

THELMA holds her and then motions her to go to the bathroom. THEIA does.

Eddie removes a few cans of food from the sack and hides them near the headstone. He checks around the area for anybody who might be watching.

EDDIE

Grandma? Watch these for me, please? I'll be back for them. Thank you for doing this for me. I hope at least you can hear me. I wish you were here. I know you can help me.

Lights fade out in the graveyard area.

THELMA finds an ashtray filled with cigarette butts. She tries to find a place to dump it. The garbage can is full. She finally opens a paper sack and places the butts into it. THEIA enters with a washcloth, wiping her face.

THEIA

How's this Aunty?

THELMA

Oh, yes, pretty girls should always have a pretty face.

THEIA

Not greasy, like greasy fryebread, huh?

THELMA

It's good you're learning to do these things yourself. You're getting to be a big girl.

THEIA

I can learn more when I live with you.

THELMA
What? Live with me?

THEIA
He said he would ask you if we can live with you. That's what he said.

A noise comes from KATHERINE's room. THEIA starts.

THELMA
Don't be so scared. You'll have an old wrinkled face before you're barely a teenager. You'll look like this. *(makes a face)*

THEIA
Not that bad Aunty.

KATHERINE enters.

KATHERINE
What's going on out here?

THELMA
Hello, my sister. Oh. I suppose? Who else did you think it was, a ghost? Just came by to see how things are going. Came to help get my nephew ready for his trip for school. I hear you and Lenny have split the sheets.

KATHERINE
Had to. I got sick of looking at his chapped lips, old dried up things any way. Who told you this? I know. Come here. *(THEIA does.)* Did you say anything?

THELMA
Eddie said something, but looking at this house, I could guess what happened. I was the one who asked these kids. I'm their aunty, remember? Your sister?

KATHERINE
Eee.... Look at your hair. Go and get a brush. You look like you're from Fraggle Rock, bushy head. Go on. *(THEIA does.)* I just don't want it going all over the place. It's nobody's business.

THELMA
As long as you didn't make a big thing of it, no one will know.

KATHERINE
That old stink thing.... He got me really mad this time. I was saving money so Eddie could get some things on his trip to school, pop, chips, you know. And here, that son of a bitch stole it.

THELMA
Eddie?

KATHERINE
No. Lenny. He took my money. I was saving it for Eddie and he bought beer with it from the bootlegger. Even the money I made from making beaded belt buckles, he took that too. That was early this morning.

THELMA
And you drank with him?

KATHERINE
No. It wasn't that bad. I didn't even know he did it until I went to see for myself. He came into the room with me and started to talk to me about how he loves me. "The light of my eye," I suppose the white blood in him was talking When I found out. I grabbed my knife I keep and put him on the run. He even tried to blame my babies.

THELMA
And he's not going to come back?

KATHERINE
I won't let him. He won't be able to get anything past me. I won't put up with his lies. I'm not going to get weighed down with his lies.

THELMA
Are you sure?

KATHERINE
You're making my head hurt. I just said so, didn't I? Gee, Thelma listen to me.

THELMA
I just want to be sure this is what you really mean and you really want it.

KATHERINE
Yes! What about it!

THELMA
Nothing. I was just asking. Oh say, did you ever hear anything from those people at that place for the job? Did they ever call you back?

KATHERINE
No. Not yet. They did say they would call me by Friday, tomorrow. I gave them Iris' phone number. She said she would tell me when they call. By next week, I'll be making those little dentist tools. It's good money too. I think they pay over four dollars an hour. We sure could use it. I can start

to save money and get the things we need. Do things I want to do. I won't have to be stuck with these stink young guys like Lenny.

THEIA enters with a brush.

THEIA
I found one Momma. See?

KATHERINE
I suppose. I nearly forgot about her. Where did you go?

THEIA
I had to look around. I finally found one in Eddie's room.

KATHERINE
Come here baby girl. Sit down and I'll move the herd. *(THEIA does.)* You have pretty hair, my girl.

THEIA
I know-a!

THELMA
No shame.

The two women laugh.

KATHERINE
(mocking THEIA) "I know...." Oh stink thing.

THEIA
That's what Lenny says too. He thinks I have pretty hair.

KATHERINE
Don't you listen to him any more. He doesn't know anything. You hear?

THEIA
Yeah but... okay.

KATHERINE
Now sit still.

THEIA
You're brushing it too hard.

KATHERINE
I know what I'm doing. I've brushed your hair before.

THEIA
Ow!

KATHERINE
Sit still! You don't take care of your hair. I should cut it.

> *KATHERINE grabs THEIA by her hair and shakes THEIA's head using her hair.*

THEIA
Ow... ow-ow-weee...

THELMA
Don't! You're hurting her! Katherine!

KATHERINE
She's my kid! Sit still, damn you!

THEIA
I will... I will Momma...

KATHERINE
Sit still!

THELMA
Katherine, she said she will.

> *KATHERINE releases THEIA and then slaps THEIA with the brush.*

THEIA
Oww! *(She starts to cry.)*

KATHERINE
Go on! Get away from me. *(pushes THEIA away)*

THEIA
Don't Mom.

THELMA
Gee.... You didn't have to do that Katherine.... You...

KATHERINE
Go to your room. Don't come out until I say so.

THELMA
You don't have to treat her like this Katherine.

KATHERINE
Don't you tell me how to raise my kids Thelma. I've been doing it all by myself up to now. I don't need you to step in now. *(to THEIA)* I said hurry up.

She gets up and hurries THEIA along by pulling her arm.

THEIA
Momma.... Please.... Don't!

KATHERINE
I'll give you "don't." You get your little brown ass to bed!

She pushes THEIA into her room and slams the door.

THEIA
I hate you!

KATHERINE
Good. And don't talk back either.

THEIA
I'm not. Bitch.

KATHERINE pulls on the doorknob.

KATHERINE
You open this door!

THEIA
Nah-bah-nooks.

KATHERINE
You little shit! You open this door! Do you hear me? *(no response)* Now she decides to be quiet. You think you're smart, don't you?

THEIA
I am.

KATHERINE
Baby, open the door...

THELMA
You won't be able to do anything. Come and sit down.

KATHERINE
These kids are growing up too fast... and tough. That's good.

THELMA
I guess.

KATHERINE
I... I don't know if I can have them around me much longer.

THELMA
As long as you're good to them, you'll have them with you. You'll see.

KATHERINE
It doesn't look that way Thelma. Eddie's getting to the point now where he doesn't listen to me. You know, his father didn't want him. That son of a bitch came home drunk and threw him against the wall. Then he stormed out of the house. I walked over and picked Eddie up. I... I couldn't hear anything. His eyes were always shiny when he was young and now they're turning dull, like something inside him was leaving. I felt his heart and like a small drum, it was still beating away. I took off my shirt and held him close. I knew he was a tough kid. They both are.

Pause.

We only have each other. No phone, no car, we live in this box, and if these other things are not supposed to be mine to have, fine. Those two kids are the only things I have in this world I can call mine.

THELMA
Oh! Not that pitiful.... Stop it. We didn't get them from K-Mart, under a blue light special-a! *(laughs)* Listen to me my sister. I do all kinds of things, both good and bad. When they took my boy away from me. I thought I would go insane. I wanted to kill myself. I failed. Mom told me to just give him up, don't say his name. He was dead to us. But, but I know one of these days, I'll be at a celebration and someone will walk up to me and say, "Mom." I know it'll be him. Stop thinking like you are. Besides, nearest K-Mart is over a couple hundred miles from here.

They laugh. Blackout.

SCENE THREE

TIME: An hour has passed since Scene Two. PLACE: The Tribal Detention Centre.

EDDIE is being searched by SAM. SAM is a man in his late forties. He reaches out and steers EDDIE's arms into the air by using a stick. MIKE is wearing a T-shirt, jeans and no shoes, or socks. He has on a headband. There are only a standing metal ashtray and two metal stools in the area. Once SAM has EDDIE's arms in the air, the search gets more detailed.

EDDIE

Hey!

SAM

Shut up! You got ten minutes. That's all.

EDDIE

I know, I know. You told me.

MIKE

Eddie...

SAM

Quiet Mikey. Hey, see, your friend is learning the rules here. He's pretty fast in pickin' up what we do here. In a short time, a couple of days, he'll know what to do to get by. He's not a smart mouth. *(pokes EDDIE's back pocket)* Wait. What's this?

EDDIE

I don't know.

SAM

Let's see kid. *(removes a small candy bar from EDDIE's pocket)* These guys aren't supposed to get anything. I told you that. Christ, don't you got any ears?

EDDIE

Don't get mad. I didn't know until after you just told me. I didn't even know I had it.

SAM

Yeah, right. It climbed into your pocket. Well now you know. What do you think I should do?

EDDIE

(softly) Bend over.

SAM

What did you say? *(no response)* I should give you a rap across your lips. Maybe I should turn your little kiester around and toss it. Would you like it if I go and do that? Huh?

EDDIE

No... I don't know.

MIKE

Let him stay, please.

SAM

(looks at MIKE and mocks him) "Let him stay please." Shit. Shut up Mikey. Your girlfriend can stay. Just for ten minutes and then you'll have to haul your ass out of here. *(unwraps the candy bar and begins to eat it)* Hey. This is pretty good. I haven't had one of these before. I don't eat much candy. Makes my teeth hurt. Not bad, but you still can't beat a Hershey's bar.

EDDIE

(softly) Have you checked your shorts lately?

SAM

You smart mouth.... Remember. Ten... *(checks his watch)* No. Seven minutes. And no smoking Mikey... or kissing.

    SAM exits.

EDDIE

Big stink guy. When you getting out?

MIKE

I don't know. They haven't found my mom yet. As soon as the cops find her she'll come and get me and I can get the fuck out. At least until the trial. After that, I don't know, could be sixty days flat.

EDDIE

What do you suppose happened to her?

MIKE

Probably riding around somewhere, partying someplace, passed out someplace, maybe she left town. I sure the fuck hope they do find her.

EDDIE

Damn.

MIKE

If they don't find her I have about four days flat before my trial.

EDDIE

Don't worry then. Fuck. You'll be out in no time.

MIKE

What would you know hey? You don't know shit about my mom.

EDDIE

Don't start talking like this. Behave.

MIKE

My mom? You want to know something about my mom Eddie? This last summer, when we went to that celebration with your aunty Thelma? We sneaked out of her tent that night to go to the 49. I was with Denise Sky.

EDDIE

Yeah. We both wound up snagging. Better'n any fucking cowboy.

MIKE

Yeah. Then Denise went with you to get that friend of hers for you, and when you guys were gone, I went to the trees to take a piss and all of a sudden there was this blanket that came and wrapped me up.... It was kind of cool at first, but it had that smell, it was stink. Then these hands were touching me. It was kind of nice at first. I heard this voice, it was saying something. The voice said, "You can have me for all the change in your pocket." I tossed off the blanket to check this one out. And damn it... I fucking hate this place Eddie. I really do. I want to get the fuck away from here. Fuck! It was my mom Eddie. It was my own mom. *(pause)* Talk about reaching out and touching someone.

EDDIE

Yeah. Reach out, reach out and fuck someone up. *(pause)* How did they catch you this time?

MIKE

Oh. After you left that night, I was with Nose and his sister, Brenda. Then we were getting stoned in his car. We really got wasted. I guess the cops came right up behind us, red and blue lights blazing away. They made us get out and searched us. Stink fuckers. They really searched Nose's sister. Poor Brenda, after they felt her up the cops let her go.

EDDIE

What did you and Nose do? *(slams his fist into his opened hand)*

MIKE

What could we do hey? No way Jose, we weren't brave enough. Me and Nose just stood there. Those cops would've worked us over. *(pause)* I wish we could both leave and then we could party.

EDDIE

Ah bullshit. That's why I want to leave.

MIKE

Yeah, boarding school. Big thrill there Eddie.

EDDIE

It might not be tomorrow for school, but it sure the hell is going to be soon.

MIKE

You're going to leave! Take me with you!

EDDIE

Behave. I'm not babysitting anymore, this is for real.

MIKE

You know what? I can get out. I can get out if you help me.

EDDIE

Can he hear us?

MIKE

No. Stink fucker anyway. He doesn't even watch us. We were lighting up a number just when he came to tell me you were here. You know what? Two guys got out of here.

EDDIE

Yeah?

MIKE

Shit man, they just walked out the back door, ankle to ankle. The guy here at the time didn't even care. The cops were the ones who noticed they were gone when they came to pick them up for court. *(pause)* Eddie. No court until Monday. The cops won't be around. *(pause)* I have a way of getting out of here. We could be gone, together.

EDDIE

You? You know how to get in, shit. How are you going to get out?

MIKE

You'll see, you'll see, but I'll need your help once I'm out.

EDDIE

You don't even know where I'm going. They'll pick us both up.

MIKE

No they won't. Eddie, listen to me. Listen hey, you and I, we could share a room together. We'll have so many women, we'll wear out a mattress every month.

EDDIE

Shit, wear out your wrist is more like it.

MIKE

It isn't so bad in here.

EDDIE
Yeah. Then stay.

MIKE
No but, but Eddie. If we got a place to ourselves it doesn't have to be around here. Nose has a car... the police took it to his house and gave the car to his parents. Since Brenda didn't get into that much trouble, they let her hold the keys, until he gets out.

EDDIE
Why?

MIKE
I don't know. I guess her mom doesn't trust their dad. But anyway, we could get them from her and we could really book out of here.

EDDIE
Where to?

MIKE
Off the Res. We don't have to stay in any little rinky town. We could go to a city. I have relatives all over the place.

EDDIE
You got money?

MIKE
No, but I have a stash hidden at my house. We could get it and sell some of it.

EDDIE
Why don't you just wait and see if your mother shows up? *(pause)* I mean, that way, I leave by myself, and you, you don't have to worry about being stopped, or picked up.

MIKE
You mean "you." *(pause)* It's just as bad in here. I want out! Take me with you Eddie.

EDDIE
But... you... I thought you said it wasn't so bad in here?

MIKE
Fuck. I lied, okay? This jailor here, he says he's Indin' but he's not. And.... And he gives different ones cigarettes... and let's them smoke in the TV room. Let's them do a whole bunch of stuff. He leaves them alone after, but first they... they have to do something for him. He asks certain ones, one way, or the other is what everyone says... *(pause)*

Stink old fucker. *(pause)* He.... He's always asking me if I like to smoke.

EDDIE

Gives you a good reason to quit.

MIKE

Fuck yeah, but I'm serious as hell hey? I want out of here. Take me with you.

EDDIE

I know you do. Lookit, couldn't you tell the cops? They should be able to do something for you.

MIKE

Who do you think they'll listen to? He's been working here for a long time. They'll listen to me, duh. No way! I heard it from Nose. He's been in here more times then me.

EDDIE

Nose will let us use his car?

MIKE

Yeah.... Yeah! I can get us some money too. We got a car, no real reason for me to stay, you're going.

EDDIE

I don't know.

MIKE

Eddie. I don't want to be here.

EDDIE

Yeah.

MIKE

I got an aunty in Seattle. It would be a long drive to Seattle, but I think I have enough money to get us there. She'll take care of us.

EDDIE

She will?

MIKE

Yeah. It would be a lot better than anything here.

EDDIE

I know.

MIKE

They have concerts and better things in Seattle than we have here. Better looking chicks. Even the white ones are supposed to be good looking.

EDDIE

What if we get caught?

MIKE

It'll be me handcuffed in the back seat of a cop car heading for reform school. You? You'll be eating a Snickers bar on a bus going to boarding school.

EDDIE

You want me to get the car and bring it here?

MIKE

Yeah. And all I need is a pair of shoes and jacket. And my stash. It's damn good weed.

EDDIE

This is a hard one Mike.

MIKE

If you want you can get it now.

EDDIE

Your smoke?

MIKE

Sure, just don't smoke up all my weed.

EDDIE

Okay. Sounds cool. Where do I meet you at?

MIKE

Not far from here. Near the stockyards.

EDDIE

How long?

MIKE

About a couple of hours.

EDDIE

I'll help you. You'll help me? And we book together.

MIKE

Yeah. *(offers his hand to EDDIE)*

EDDIE
How you gonna' do that Mike?

MIKE
You'll see. I promise you Eddie.

EDDIE
Don't fuck around Mike.

MIKE
I'm not. You'll see.

EDDIE
Alright. *(shakes MIKE's hand)* One it.

MIKE
Two it.

    SAM enters.

SAM
Are you girls through? Time's up.

EDDIE
Let go of my hand.

MIKE
Remember. You promised. *(releases EDDIE's hand)*

EDDIE
Yeah, yeah.

SAM
Come on and hurry up why don't you? You can see your little friend tomorrow. He's been a bad little boy. He'll be with us for some time. Don't worry. We'll watch him for you. Better'n his own mom. *(pause)*

EDDIE
Fuck.

SAM
What?

EDDIE
Nothing.

SAM
You better get out of here. Your time's up. Come on! Let's go!

EDDIE
I'll see you Mike.

SAM
You wait here. I'll take you to the television room.

MIKE
Eddie...

EDDIE stops but is pushed along by SAM.

SAM
Keep moving kid, don't drag your ass.

They exit.

MIKE
You have to help me Eddie. Please help me Eddie. Don't want to stay here. Don't want to be here. Ain't going to be here. One-it, two-it, three-it, four-it, five-it, you're-it, I'm not it. Oh fuck... help me please... Mom... I don't want to be it.

SAM enters and MIKE continues to count silently.

SAM
You shouldn't hang around guys like him Mikey. He's a real bad apple. Get you into a lot more trouble than you are in now. *(crosses and sits on a stool)* You're a good boy Mikey. I know. I know the decent ones when I see them. I had to work on it.

MIKE
(softly) One-it, two-it, three-it... *(continues)*

SAM
Nah, hell, you've still got some good in you yet. And I guess it's all right if you want to smoke cigarettes. Hell. Most young guys do that when they're your age. I know because I did. You know what Mikey? I knowed some bad little boys who turned out okay. Even when they did smoke. You know what I mean Mikey?

I was like you in a lot of ways, I learned to make things my own. Had to. People. Shit on them and their pity. *(removes a pack of cigarettes from his shirt pocket)* But you're a good little boy. I know you are. And it's all right if you want to have a smoke. You want to smoke Mikey? You can if you want to. All you have to do is do something for me. *(unzips his pants)* Everyone is in lock-up right now Mikey. No one will hear us. No one knows you're up here. They think I'm cleaning this place. *(starts to rub his leg)* Come on. Don't be afraid. There's nothing to be afraid of. Almost everyone here has done this before. And they don't talk about it. Come on. I'll let you smoke after you're done. It'll be good.

MIKE slowly walks to SAM. SAM readjusts himself on the stool. The next two lines run together.

SAM

Be a good little boy Mike. Come on. That's it... that's it.... Eww...

MIKE

Fourteen-it, fifteen-it, six-teen it... ain't it...

Blackout.

SCENE FOUR

TIME: Later in the day, afternoon. PLACE: KATHERINE Rose's house.

THELMA sits combing THEIA's hair. The house is cleaned. There is a small pile of garbage near the door. THELMA combs very gently and sings a song to THEIA.

THELMA

This is your grandma's song. She used to sit on a chair and slowly brush my hair and she would be singing this song. It was quiet and all I could hear was your grandma singing.

THEIA

Grandma?

THELMA

Yes. She died right after you were born. You don't remember her. Oh. I don't know. You might. She really liked you. She used to hold you and sing to you. She used to call you Pretty One. She used to babysit you and your brother.

THEIA

Eddie too?

THELMA

Even Eddie. She helped raise you two kids. She watched both of you. Even fed you too, but sometimes she had problems holding you and your bottle. You were so tiny, but very big to her hands. She still could hold you though. She didn't want to let go. *(pause)*

My baby boy Paul, and Eddie and you were her only three grandchildren, but you were her favourite.

> *THELMA begins to clean the hair from the brush. She takes the hair and places it into an ashtray, and then takes a match and lights the match, setting the hair on fire.*

THEIA
You're burning up Aunty!

THELMA
No, no. You burn the hair. If you let the hair go without taking care of it, it can bring bad things to you, even ghosts. These are some of the things we did. When your grandmother died, your mom and I, we cut our hair. We women do that when someone dies. When it is someone close to you and you love them, like your grandmother, our mother.

THEIA
Really? *(pause)* Aunty Thelma? Is drinking something we always do? My teacher, Mrs. Johnson, she said it was because we always drink, is why we lost everything we had. It was our own fault.

THELMA
No. This is a lie baby girl. We never used to drink at one time. Your grandma, my mother, as old as she was, never drank, she used to say it was never a part of the Indin' people.

THEIA
Oh. Aunty Thelma? Eddie said I was going to be moving to your house.

THELMA
No. I think he was just saying that. I don't think your mother wants you to leave. She wouldn't want that to happen.

THEIA
Oh.

THELMA
But one day, you might. Who knows. One day you might be living with me. I didn't have a baby girl.

THEIA
All right!

> *EDDIE enters.*

THELMA
There you are. Where have you been?

EDDIE

Where's my mom at?

THELMA

She went out to get some groceries. I told her I would watch Theia. She should be back soon.

EDDIE

Hey, Aunty Thelma, have you thought about letting Theia stay with you?

THELMA

Yes. I told her it might happen one day, but not now. You kids still have your mother.

EDDIE

Yeah, but it would be better if you were our mother. You could take her now before she gets back.

THELMA

Oh. Not that bad.

EDDIE

Yes it is.

THELMA

Theia. Go to your room. *(THEIA does.)* Don't start this now Eddie. I thought you did something crazy like running away. I was worried. Where have you been?

EDDIE

Seen a friend. Mike...

THELMA

Him? I heard he was locked up. How did you talk with him?

EDDIE

With my mouth. Christ, Mike isn't all that bad. If you've heard it from my mom, she's one to talk. Me and Mike are alike in a lot of ways.

THELMA

Like how? What makes you two the same?

EDDIE

We come back to an empty house all the time. We cook for ourselves and whoever's with us. Our mothers are the same. It's not different for him and me. Everyone says we have a mother, but we don't.

THELMA

Oh! I suppose Eddie. Your mother is here in the house for you.

EDDIE

Yeah. Drunk and wasted, but never sober!

THELMA

Don't let me hear you say anything like that about your mother. She's my sister. You remember that. His mother... I feel sorry for him because both he and his mother are pitiful. Your mom and I ain't in the bars selling ourselves for a drink. His mother is always in the bars. She's a whore! Pitiful is all they are. Don't you ever compare your mother to that woman. Your father never wanted you, but she does! That should count for something.

EDDIE

Yes we are! Our own mothers have tried to "have" us.

THELMA

What?

EDDIE

You hear me Aunty Thelma. Our mothers have tried to "have" us.

THELMA

What are you saying? No. Eddie. No. That couldn't have happened. You didn't know what your mother was trying to say to you. It wasn't like you think.

EDDIE

I was there. I'm always here. I try to tell you things but you don't listen. What do I have to do to show you. You want to wait around and see it happen for your own eyes. You see how she treats me and Theia. *(pause)*

This morning, this morning, she tried to kiss me. Not like you do, but she did something in a way... I don't know how to.... Just don't mind Aunty Thelma. *(pause)* When I go, I want you to take care of Theia. If you don't do it. I'll come back and do it. *(pause)*

What do I have to do? I don't know what I'm supposed to do. I can't see anything I used to. I used to be able to know. I didn't know how I did it, but it wasn't hard. I could see what I had to do and when to do it. Now I don't even know because I can't see any more.

THELMA

Eddie. Let me see. Let me see what I can do. You are still young in a lot of ways. It'll change. Things are always changing from one day to the next. You could be wrong. You don't know what your mom was doing this morning. You could have taken it in the wrong way. You...

EDDIE

I know what she did Aunty Thelma! Fuck!

THELMA

Behave Eddie. You don't know...

EDDIE

Shit!

THELMA

Don't start talking like that around me.

EDDIE

All right! All right! I won't talk to you like that, but will you listen to what I'm saying? I have to go. I can't wait until tomorrow. Please take Theia. Take her to your home and before I get ready to leave I'll stop by and see if you've done it.

THELMA

But Eddie, nephew, it isn't something I can do. She's my sister, we aren't like other people. I cannot take Theia as my own. It's not our way. Just stay here and leave tomorrow. If you try to leave you might not make it, you might have some kind of trouble. You're not even ready to leave.

EDDIE

Yes I am. Just do it, please Aunty Thelma. Please do it for me, for both us kids.

THELMA

Eddie.... Eddie! Where are you going? Please Eddie, stay! Don't leave. Come back here nephew. Please come back.

Blackout.

SCENE FIVE

TIME: A few minutes from Scene Four. Same day. Evening. PLACE: The graveyard.

EDDIE enters. He goes to the headstone and sits. He takes out a small plastic bag with pot in it. He takes out some papers that are with the weed. He rolls himself a number. He takes out some matches and when he is done rolling, he lights up. He kicks back and takes a big toke. He coughs a little.

EDDIE

You weren't shitting there Mike. It is good. Thank you Grandson. Hey Grandma, you know what that stink guy said...

He turns to face the headstone and then realizes something has changed. The paper sack he left is gone. The wrappers he used to cover his canned goods are on the ground. He starts to look around the place.

Oh shit. How.... Who...

Someone has taken his stash. He sits down. He puts out the joint and places it back in the bag.

Grandma. I thought you were going to watch this stuff for me. I asked you. You probably didn't hear me like everyone else.

He hears a dog barking in the neighbourhood. He stands and picks up a rock, and throws it at the barking dog.

EDDIE
Damn stink dog.

Blackout.

SCENE SIX

Time: Night, same day. Place: KATHERINE's house.

THELMA is trying to prepare a meal. She is very flustered from her talk with EDDIE. THEIA is hiding.

THELMA
Something fast.

She begins to look for some potatoes and finds them. She starts to look for a clean knife and pot.

Isn't there anything around here that's clean?

She cleans the knife and pot. Slowly the house door opens and a paper sack being held in the air enters the open space between the door and the wall. KATHERINE pops her head into the room and looks around.

KATHERINE
Hello. I'm back. With some fresh deer meat. Not that Indin'-a!

She slowly enters and draws the sack to her.

What are you doing?

THELMA
Cooking something to feed these kids with. Do you need help with that?

KATHERINE
Nope.

> *THELMA has gone to her but stops.*

What's the matter? Are you starving?

THELMA
No.... I'll get the door.

> *She crosses to the door.*

KATHERINE
No! Wait, wait, Thelma.

THELMA
Oh. Why? It's...

> *LENNY enters carrying a case of beer and two bottles of wine.*

LENNY
Hold up! Hold up.... Hello Thelma.

> *THELMA stops at the door and turns away.*

THELMA
Where did you pick this up at?

KATHERINE
Lenny, or the grub?

THELMA
Why is he here? Katherine?

> *THELMA walks over to KATHERINE, takes the sack from her and sets it on the table.*

KATHERINE
Met him at the store. He was standing there just looking pitiful.

> *THELMA removes bags of potato chips, candies, slim-jims, etc., from the sack.*

THELMA
Is this all? Where's the meat you were supposed to buy?

LENNY touches himself.

LENNY
It's right here.

LENNY and KATHERINE laugh.

THELMA
I wasn't talking with you. I was talking with my sister.

LENNY
But you wanted an answer and I gave you one. Katherine and me made up and she's decided to take me back. I don't see where you really have a say in it Thelma.

THELMA
I'm asking my sister, not you.

(to KATHERINE) Why did you bring him back? You know the kids don't like him. He's only going to bring you trouble. If that's what you want, I suppose it's okay, but you should have thought about this. You shouldn't have brought this thing back with you.

LENNY
If you want me to Kathy – I'll leave. I don't want to come between you and your sister.

THELMA
Yes. Leave.

KATHERINE
No. No. He can stay. It's my house. He can stay if he wants to. I'll decide... I'll decide whether it's all right, or not. Set the drinks down over here baby.

LENNY sets the beer and wine down on the table.

THELMA
I don't like it.

KATHERINE
I don't care what you like. Don't be so mean. Lenny gave back the money he took, enit Lenny?

THELMA
What?

KATHERINE
He did.

LENNY
I hocked my ring, my watch, just so I could give back what I took from Katherine. It was a nice watch too. It had a silver band and the ring was gold with a small diamond on it. It was real nice. It was all I had.

THELMA
If it was all that valuable, where's the money at?

KATHERINE
I have it. Christ. Relax. You sound like I don't know what I'm doing. It'll be all right. We can have a party now. Where are my babies? Eddie? Eddie? Theia? Baby girl? Don't be mad Thelma. I know what I'm doing.

THELMA
So do I, and I don't like it.

KATHERINE
Who cares?

LENNY
What am I doing then? Thelma? Tell me what I'm doing then, huh? You tell me? I've given back the money to Katherine.

THELMA
Don't talk like you're so high and mighty because you're not. I know what you're up to. You just want her drunk so you can get all the money. The first time you pass out, he'll be running through your pockets in no time at all. You don't fool me Lenny. I know what you're up to.

LENNY
Settle down. You have no proof of anything. *(to KATHERINE)* She's probably just jealous of you and me.

Blows her a kiss.

THELMA
Bullshit.

KATHERINE
Yeah. You want a beer baby?

Gives him a beer.

Don't get mad Thelma, sister. It'll be all right. You want one?

THELMA
No.

KATHERINE
Oh Christ! Now you'll be mad for the rest of the night.

THELMA
What do you expect Katherine? He stole from you, stole from my nephew. He's the reason why these kids are so upset. And now I'm supposed to make believe everything is all right? No. I don't like this man. He's no good.

LENNY
Ahhh.... Shit! You don't even know me. You never met me. You've always ignored me. Why the fuck, why the fuck are you getting so bent out of shape over it? If you don't like it, why don't you leave? No sense in making a big scene out of it. You're the one who's getting everybody upset, not me. Don't try to blame me for getting people mad.

KATHERINE
Just because you can't keep a man.

THELMA
What? What did you say?

KATHERINE
You heard me. Just what I said. You're just jealous of me because you've never been able to keep a man. And you could never get a young one, like I can.

THELMA
Are you sniffing glue? You know that's not it.

KATHERINE
It has to be. There isn't any other reason why you hate Lenny.

THELMA
Look at him Katherine? If I'm jealous of you for picking this up, I have to be nuts.

KATHERINE
Maybe you are, but I'm fine.

THELMA
And you're going to let this man near your kids?

KATHERINE
Yeah. Sure. He's not getting them upset. He's going to be their dad.... You know how it is when you have a man, or have you forgotten-a! But, hey, sister, Thelma. You know how kids are? Kids, especially my babies, they have a way about this kind of thing. When a new father comes along they...

THELMA
Especially when the father comes along straight out of a bar. Not knowing who, or what they are. And you, you bring them into your home and allow them to smear themselves all over you and your kids.

KATHERINE
To hell with you.

THELMA
Don't get mouthy with me Katherine.

KATHERINE
Ah fuck! See? At least I have my kids. I have them right here with me. Remember?
You, you used to do a lot of partying when you were young. If you didn't, maybe you still would have your boy here with you today. He wouldn't be living with some white family in Utah. Hell, you still might have a man.

THELMA
At least he wouldn't be eyeing my little girl like this no good bastard.

LENNY
Are you gonna' let her say shit like that about me?

KATHERINE
Fuck you Thelma.

THELMA
Don't talk to me like that Katherine. I'm still your sister...

KATHERINE
Ha! You're just an old bitch!

THELMA
Damn you! At least I don't look it. You're supposed to be the baby between us.

> *KATHERINE attacks THELMA, pushes her against the table and they fall onto the floor. LENNY starts to laugh. He jumps up on the table to get a better look, making cat sounds. He howls. THELMA rolls KATHERINE on her back.*

KATHERINE
Oh fuck! Help me Lenny.

LENNY
Here! Stop that you girls.

THELMA
Now talk smart, huh! Talk smart to me now!

LENNY
Leave her alone Thelma. You smash her, she'll fart and we'll have to air this place out.

THELMA
I'm going to sober you up, one way or another.

KATHERINE
You old bitch. Leave me alone!

LENNY hands KATHERINE a sack of potato chips.

LENNY
Here! Use this baby.

THELMA intercepts the bag and uses it on KATHERINE.

KATHERINE
Get off me!

LENNY
Goddamn it! Leave her alone!

THELMA grabs a handful of KATHERINE's hair.

KATHERINE
Ow! Lenny...

LENNY
Let go of her!

THELMA
See. You can't even take care of yourself. Your kids... you little...

LENNY frees THELMA's hand from KATHERINE's hair, but as soon as he gets one hand free, THELMA's other hand grabs a fistful of hair. Finally, LENNY slaps THELMA.

LENNY
Damn bitch! Leave-her-alone! Knock it off!

He grabs THELMA by the braids, lifts her off from KATHERINE and then hits THELMA, knocking THELMA to the floor.

THELMA

I'll get you for this!

LENNY

Go on! Get your fat nosey ass out of here.

KATHERINE grabs onto LENNY's side and buries her head into him. She doesn't look at THELMA.

KATHERINE

Thank you baby, thank you... I need you baby...

THELMA

I guess you do.

KATHERINE

You're just jealous of me.

THELMA smiles and waits a moment.

THELMA

Who would be jealous of a drunken woman who's tearing apart her home, her family? No. Not me.

She walks to the table and picks up a paring knife.

Pitiful. You are just pitiful. Nothing else. Watch me sister. Watch what I do.

KATHERINE doesn't respond until LENNY does.

I didn't listen, but you watch Katherine. See? See this? And you remember this.

Holds the knife.

Every day my sister. Sometimes, late at night too, when we were told as little girls by Mom, not to be out when it's late, you never see who is there, but somehow, I make it over here.
No matter what. I come so see how your... our kids are. And I come here, really, to see how you are. How you are making it through the day. I try to do things for you and our kids. Food, clothing, even water, when they shut if off, I bring these things, even if I do without.
And our boy, my boy, Eddie, he asked me to keep Theia. I've tried to keep these two kids alive in this house. I can't even keep the little one from being afraid... I've failed. And it hurts me real bad. If I try too hard, it will finish me off for good. And I won't do that, not for your, for them.

If I walk out that door Katherine, my sister, that's the last time you will ever hear me say, "sister" to you. Because we never speak the name of those who have died.

No response from KATHERINE.

I'll pray for you... I'll pray for them. Because from now on...

She cuts her braids.

You are dead for me.

Blackout.

ACT TWO

SCENE ONE

TIME: Later in the night. PLACE: In the graveyard.

EDDIE is sitting near the grave, smoking a cigarette. THELMA quietly enters. She stops and watches EDDIE.

THELMA
Nephew?

EDDIE turns quickly to see who is calling him.

EDDIE
Damn. I...

THELMA
Nephew. Nephew what are you doing here?

EDDIE
I had a stash here and somebody already beat me to it.

THELMA
Get away from there. You shouldn't be here.

EDDIE
That's why I'm leaving.

THELMA
Come here my boy. Come to me.

EDDIE
I thought you would be at your house, or ours. I wanted to make sure I saw you and Theia before I left.

THELMA goes to him and hugs him.

THELMA
Please wait, Eddie. My boy. Wait. I have something for you. Please forgive me Eddie. I'm so *ew-shi-ga*. I couldn't do what you wanted. Please forgive me son.

EDDIE hugs her and notices her braids are gone.

EDDIE
What? Damn! Did he do this to you?

EDDIE breaks the hug. His hand reaches for the braids that aren't there.

THELMA
You, your mother, Lenny, none of you had anything to do with this. It was my decision.

EDDIE
Now you know, huh, Aunty Thelma? *(pause)* You know now?

THELMA
Yes. I do.

EDDIE
I come here to talk with Grandma. Some of my friends are here. I come here to talk with them. I tell them too, but they don't hear me. I'm all alone Aunty Thelma. I have no one. Sometimes, certain days, I wish I was with them. I just want to be like them.

THELMA
Don't talk that way. Don't you let me hear you talk that way. I know it's hard, but don't think that way. There are a lot of people here, in this world, who will listen to you. They know you are going through this and they know because they have gone through it.

> *She steps a few feet from the grave.*

I'm going to show you something. Something you can do so that you will always have someone with you. You will be able to make it through the days. It isn't hard. And when you get older, you will learn more about it. It will help you. Because from now on you will always have your people in your heart. I want you to go back to your house and get your sister.

> *She touches him.*

I don't want you to go into the house weak because they will get stronger from your anger and weaken you. That is how they have been living. *(pause)*

Shhh... now be quiet. You have to do this thing before you can go in there. That house is dead. If you go in there now, they'll win, and you'll be dead like them. I won't let this happen. So you must do what I ask you, for you, for your sister. Do you understand me?

EDDIE
I guess, yeah?

THELMA
Good. Now come over here.

She takes his hand and leads him a few feet from the graves. She removes a small bowl from the pocket of her jacket. She sets the bowl down. Then from her other pocket she removes a small paper sack. From the sack she takes out a small amount of sage. She places the sage into the bowl. She lifts the bowl up into the air and prays. She sets the bowl down and removes a book of matches from her coat pocket, lights one of the matches and uses it to light the sage. The flame goes out and then there is the smoke of the sage. THELMA fans the sage.

Here. I want you here. *(points to a place near the bowl)* Now, wash yourself in the smoke.

EDDIE
What?

THELMA
Wash up.

She rubs her arm as if she is bathing herself. EDDIE dips his hands into the smoke and begins to bathe himself.

THELMA
Pray nephew. My boy, pray. *(EDDIE does.)* Now you are ready my... my son. This will help you. Your uncles should have shown you this, you are a man. Now I want you to go into that house of death and bring Theia to me if you can. Don't let them get you mad, they'll try everything to get you angry. When you have Theia, come to my house, I'll make something for you kids to eat and a place to sleep. Go now.

She gathers her bowl and sage and exits. EDDIE watches her. Blackout.

SCENE TWO

TIME: Later in the night. Same day. PLACE: The living room area of KATHERINE Rose's house.

KATHERINE and LENNY are on the couch. They are slowly kissing one another. THEIA sits on the side of the couch. She has taken the blanket that covered the couch and is now hanging over the edge. She has made a small tent for herself. The door opens and EDDIE enters. LENNY is first in seeing EDDIE and grabs KATHERINE by her bottom and gives her a hungry kiss.

EDDIE
Theia?

THEIA comes out from underneath her tent.

THEIA
Eddie? Eddie!

KATHERINE pushes LENNY off.

KATHERINE
Knock it off! Where the hell have you been?

KATHERINE struggles and crosses to EDDIE. THEIA waits to make her move.

EDDIE
Come here Theia. Come to me.

KATHERINE
What have you been smoking, dope?

EDDIE
Don't be afraid Theia. I'm here to take you.

KATHERINE
Hey. I'm talking to you. Answer me!

EDDIE
Mom. Stay out of my way! I'm going to take Theia out of here.

KATHERINE
You aren't taking shit from this house.

EDDIE
I don't want to fight with you.

KATHERINE
Fight? Shit! You don't talk to me like that. You get your ass out of here.

EDDIE
Mom. You can't hold her. I'm going to walk out of here tonight with Theia.

KATHERINE
Bullshit!

EDDIE
Give her to me!

KATHERINE
No!

THEIA tries to go to EDDIE but she is cut off by LENNY.

If you were a man I would give her to you. You're nothing but a baby.
I know. Now get your ass out of my house.

EDDIE is ready to move out of her way, but stops.

KATHERINE
Go ahead! Go ahead and try it you little baby. I'll beat the hell out of you.

EDDIE
No. Not this way, I won't hit you, or that guy. I won't give you that. I'll get
the goddamn cops Mom.

LENNY and KATHERINE laugh.

LENNY
Ewww! I'm real scared Eddie. Hey, you scare me.

KATHERINE
Shut up Lenny. You. Good. Go ahead and do it! Get the cops. You think
they'll break their ass for you? Hah!

THEIA
Eddie. Help me.

LENNY grabs THEIA and holds her tightly.

LENNY
No. Nope, bad little girly. You stay with us. He's crazy.

EDDIE
Take your hands off of her you fucker!

LENNY
Fuck you, you punk!

*THEIA throws her elbow into LENNY's groin and he releases her and she runs
into EDDIE's bedroom. EDDIE cheers.*

Ow! Ow... little shit.

KATHERINE
You dumb shit.

EDDIE
Hide Theia! Hide!

LENNY
Fuck Katherine, don't talk like that to me.

EDDIE laughs.

Fuck you!

EDDIE
Theia! Stay hid and I'll come back for you. Just wait and I'll be here.

KATHERINE
No you won't.

She slaps EDDIE. He is ready to return the slap, but stops.

Get out! See! You can't even defend yourself. I would've hit back.

EDDIE
I know.

KATHERINE
Goddamn it! You smart mouth little shit. Get out of my house.

EDDIE turns and begins to leave. KATHERINE follows him to the door.

You no good little bastard. And don't you come back here. You can stay there with that old bag Thelma. Your new girlfriend, huh Eddie?

Blackout.

SCENE THREE

TIME: Later in the night. Same day. PLACE: At the playground, near the housing projects.

MIKE is hiding. EDDIE comes running. MIKE jumps out and nearly tackles EDDIE, but misses.

MIKE
Eddie! Eddie!

EDDIE stops.

EDDIE
Oh fuck! Mike. I forgot.

MIKE
No shit you forgot. I was waiting for you. Where the fuck were you hey?

EDDIE
> I got to go to the police Mike. I gotta' book.

MIKE
> Wait. Wait Eddie. You and I are supposed to leave. Remember? You promised me! You gotta' take me hey!

EDDIE
> No, listen Mike. A lot of shit has happened since then.

MIKE
> Where's the car?

EDDIE
> Didn't get it.

MIKE
> Well, we don't really need it. Where's the shoes and the coat?

> *EDDIE starts to take off his jacket.*

> Not that desperate Eddie. *(He starts to laugh. EDDIE goes to remove his shoes.)* No. Don't do that fucker. Keep them on. When we go we can pick up a pair for me on the way to Seattle. Havre has as K-Mart. Don't sweat it.

EDDIE
> I said, "No."

MIKE
> What do you mean no? Man. You said we were going.

EDDIE
> You haven't heard me. I'm going to get the cops.

MIKE
> What the fuck for? Are you going to tell on me?

EDDIE
> No, no, that's not it. Lenny's back and...

MIKE
> Fuck them! When we go we won't have to worry about that shit. Let's go now.

> *He grabs EDDIE's arm and tries to pull him. EDDIE breaks away.*

EDDIE
> No fucker.

MIKE

I can't stay here Eddie. I got to go this time. No shit. If we fuck around I'll get caught by the cops. Now let's go!

EDDIE

You go to Seattle. Take my fucking shoes, my jacket. I got to go and get the cops.

MIKE

You fucker! What kind of shit is this? Man, oh man, Eddie, you stood there in that fucking place and told me, promised me, you would go to Seattle. Now let's fucking go!

EDDIE

I can't. Why don't you just stay here? If the cops pick you up, it won't be no fucking big deal. It'll mean you'll have three, or four more days to stay. That's all. You knew what was going on with me. And you try to tag on to me! Fuck Mike, you shouldn't even be out here!

MIKE

If I go back there, that old shit-faced guard will kill me! I'm in deep shit Eddie. Please go with me.... Just before you left, the fucker came back and he started to tell me how he thought I wasn't a bad little boy.

EDDIE

What... what happened?

MIKE

He, he wanted to know if I smoke. He offered me a whole pack of cigarettes. Zips his pants open...

EDDIE

Oh fuck! Mike... I didn't...

MIKE

He eased down his shorts and I seen his dick. It was just there. Small, stink and with all this hair. He wanted me to come closer. I wanted to fucking throw up. I wanted to throw up and all I can hear is this voice. I reached out my hand and he grabbed it and put it on his dick, he used my hand to stroke his cock... I touched it... it felt soft.... He closed his eyes and put his head back like he was going to sleep.... And... I... I YANKED THAT FUCKER HARD! He fell off the stool and rolled on the floor groaning. I used that stick he has and bashed him in the head! Then I picked up the stool and rammed that fucker on him. I rammed him good. I started running down the hall. I took those stink metal ashtrays and used them to bash in the windows. Glass flew in front of my face. I pushed on those metal fucking doors so hard they sounded like gun shots!

EDDIE

Holy shit Mike! I thought you were lying about that guy.

MIKE

And you want to stay here and help your mother Eddie? You're fucking dumb, man. You want to stay here and live off people like her... like me and my mom? And you know what? That's good. You'll be like your mom, living off people, letting people fuck you!

EDDIE

You should have told me Mike, because, really, I thought you were lying. I guess I should've listened.

EDDIE goes over and touches MIKE's shoulder.

MIKE

Get away from me!

EDDIE

I don't know Mike. I don't know what's going on. It happens every time. It doesn't change around here. For you, or me.

MIKE

And you still want to stay?

EDDIE

I have something now. I couldn't run from this, and now I know I don't have to live with it. You too, I guess.

MIKE

Oh well, I'll see you around.

EDDIE

Mike. Come here and stand with me for just a bit, huh? I want to give you something before we go our different ways.

MIKE stops.

MIKE

All right.

Goes to EDDIE and stands beside him.

EDDIE

One it.

MIKE

Fuck you.

EDDIE
One it, come on and do it, One it.

MIKE
Two it.

EDDIE
Three it,

MIKE
Four it,

EDDIE
Five it,

MIKE
Sic... I mean...

>   *EDDIE punches MIKE in the shoulder.*

Ow, you fucker.

EDDIE
You flinched. Again?

MIKE
One it,

EDDIE
Two it,

MIKE
Three it,

EDDIE
Four it,

MIKE
Five it,

EDDIE
Seven... oh shit...

>   *MIKE hits him. They both laugh. EDDIE reaches over and hugs MIKE.*

MIKE
Eddie?

EDDIE
Yeah?

MIKE
Did I hurt you?

EDDIE
No.

MIKE
Oh. *(pause)* Eddie. *(breaks the hug)* I'll see you, huh?

EDDIE
I'll pray for you Mike.

MIKE
You gonna give me one of those medal guys? Saint something.

EDDIE
No. I'll pray for you like Indins do. It's different. Okay?

MIKE
I don't know how to do that. We'll get lost for sure.

EDDIE
I'll find you. It'll be different. We'll always be brothers.

MIKE
Yeah. *(begins to exit)*

EDDIE
Mike.

    MIKE stops. EDDIE removes his shoes and gives them to MIKE.

Take-em. You'll go longer.

MIKE
Yeah. Beats the fuck out of having blisters.

    Blackout.

SCENE FOUR

TIME: Late in the night. New day. PLACE: KATHERINE Rose's house.

KATHERINE is wearing a shirt only. LENNY is wearing just pants. KATHERINE is looking for THEIA.

KATHERINE
She's around here somewhere. Lenny. Go and check Eddie's room again.

LENNY
Shit. I don't wanna be doing this hide-and-go-seek shit all night long.

KATHERINE
You should've kept an eye on her. Where the hell is she?

LENNY
Just when it's getting good. Shit. Let's just leave her and let her crash wherever the hell she's at. You and me can get back to what we were doing.

KATHERINE goes behind the couch. She finds a pile of clothes and starts to sort through it.

KATHERINE
No. I want to make sure she's.... Oh.

LENNY
You remember how good it is, huh?

KATHERINE
Dream on. Look. *(points to THEIA, removes more items to get her)* Baby girl.... Little baby girl.... Get up my baby girl. *(no response)* Come on baby girl, you have to go to bed now.

LENNY crosses behind the couch.

LENNY
Damn. If we're not going to do anything until you've done your good mother shit, I might as well do it and get it done. *(He picks up THEIA's arm.)* Get up girly. Time to get your ass to bed. *(begins to lift THEIA, she awakens)*

THEIA
Momma? Mom.... Let me go!

LENNY
Whoa.... Settle down! Christ! Bad girl!

KATHERINE
Just put her down. Put her down Lenny!

LENNY
I can carry her if she would stop fighting me. Ow!

KATHERINE
Hey! Put her down! Christ!

> *He does and nearly drops THEIA. She races to her mother and grabs KATHERINE's leg. KATHERINE falls.*

There, there baby girl, don't.... Shit.

THEIA
He touched me!

LENNY
Oh! Big fucking lie! I didn't either.

KATHERINE
I know baby, I know baby.

LENNY
I didn't fucking touch her. All I did was pick her up. You seen it.

KATHERINE
All right! I heard you. Christ. Come on baby girl. I'll put you to bed. Follow momma.

> *Gets up and leads THEIA to the bedroom. THEIA watches LENNY. He slowly follows them.*

LENNY
Hurry it up, huh?

KATHERINE
Yeah, yeah.

> *They go to the bedroom. LENNY stands at the door and watches.*

THEIA
If you keep drinking tonight Momma, will I have to go to school tomorrow?

KATHERINE
Yes. Now get your brown ass to bed. Take your clothes off. I don't want you to sleep with your clothes on anymore. Where are those pajamas you have?

THEIA is undressing.

Hurry. I want to get ready for bed too.

LENNY touches himself.

You won't leave your mother because you love her, don't you baby girl?

THEIA
I guess so. *(pause)* Momma?

KATHERINE
What?

THEIA
Why is he watching me?

LENNY walks away from the door.

KATHERINE
Who?

THEIA
Him. Lenny.

KATHERINE
Where?

She turns to see. LENNY is by the table lighting a cigarette.

THEIA
He was right there watching me.

LENNY
No I wasn't. *(crosses to the door)* You better get used to the idea of having me around. I'm not going to hide every time you're around. Daddy says so.

THEIA
Is that true Mom?

KATHERINE
We'll see. Now get in bed.

KATHERINE enters the living room. LENNY crosses to the couch and sits.

LENNY
Well?

KATHERINE

What the hell were you doing? That's my little girl. You remember that. Nothing better not happen to her, or I'll cut your shit-eating eye out.

LENNY

What? I'm going to be her daddy. You're just upset with all those fucking lies they've told you about me. I love you Kathy baby. I wouldn't do anything. Trust me.

KATHERINE takes a drink from one of the wine bottles.

KATHERINE

You damn right you haven't done anything. Nothing is going to happen. Especially to my baby girl. You're supposed to be so fucking tough. You won't know what tough is until I cut your boney ass.

LENNY

Behave Kathy. *(tries to force a laugh)* Fuck. Give me a break, huh?

KATHERINE

Don't try to fool me. You sure in the hell can't fool me. I know you.

LENNY

Okay, okay, you know. I could've helped you with her if you wanted me to. All you had to do was ask.

KATHERINE

I can do it myself. I don't see why I would ask you for your help now.

LENNY

Can I have a drink?

She tosses him the bottle. He drinks.

Here. *(offers her the bottle)* You're not going to drink any more?

KATHERINE

No. Why?

LENNY

I thought now would be a good time to visit on the chair, or the couch. She's in bed. I think now's a good time to do it. You know?

KATHERINE

You shit!

LENNY

That's why I came back. I wouldn't have come back here. I'm not used to being treated like this. You were the one who told me to come back here. After you threatened to slice the shit out of my ass.... And... I can come and go whenever I damned well please.

KATHERINE

Well, then go! *(She walks away from the couch.)* I didn't force you to come back. I have my ways too. You're not the last one for me. I'll have others. Some of them will be better then you.

LENNY

Uh-huh.

KATHERINE

I mean it. *(She walks back to the couch and sits down.)* You shouldn't worry. You're free.

LENNY

I know I am. *(He sits closer to her. She moves away.)* I don't having anything tying me down.

KATHERINE

Men never do anyway.

LENNY

I can stay if I want, too.

KATHERINE

So.... You are going to stay, huh?

LENNY

Yeah... I mean... there's nothing here for me. I don't have any family here... no relations... can't find work, but I might stay here, for the sake of staying.

KATHERINE

I might go. Yeah. I might be able to get work off the Res. I'll take my little girl with me. Soon. You'll see.

LENNY

When in the hell is this supposed to happen?

KATHERINE

When Eddie leaves. I won't have to worry about him riding my ass all the time. I can think better.

LENNY

Oh shit! I thought you had a job waiting for you. *(laughs)* You'll have a big surprise for you when you do leave.

KATHERINE

Well I am. Don't laugh at me. *(slaps LENNY a couple of times on the head)* Stop-making-fun-of-me!

LENNY

Ow, ow, but why wait? You should do it now, big shot.

KATHERINE

I will. It'll make it easier for me with Theia in school and Eddie gone.

LENNY

For what? Partying?

KATHERINE

Piss on you!

LENNY

Hey... don't get mad hey. Kathy-baby, but it's the truth.

KATHERINE

I know I can do it. I just haven't found the right man. Maybe if I can find one who's strong enough...

LENNY

Oh Christ! *(He pulls away from her.)*

KATHERINE

One who's strong and smart enough, I won't be in the place I'm at. Their fathers weren't much of anything. Couldn't depend on them to do anything right. I had to raise them and their fathers. Big kids without diapers, is what their fathers were like. I don't have time to be doing that. There are things I want to be doing too.

LENNY

(chuckles) Like what?

KATHERINE

I want to do things without having to worry about anybody else but me. I want to go places and see things. Meet different people and things.

LENNY

Then join the fucking army! *(He laughs.)* Or the marines.

She moves closer to make eye contact with him. He doesn't look at her. She slaps him.

Ow! Fuck!

She moves further down the couch from him.

Why the fuck did you do that for? Huh? *(tries to grab her and misses)* Damn. I was just teasing you. You didn't have to hit me.

KATHERINE
You're making fun of me. You aren't listening to me.

LENNY
Yes I am. I heard you. Goddamn you're crazy. But I didn't hear you that good is all.

KATHERINE
Oh Christ, at least Eddie can listen to me. The only thing you want to do is grab my tits and try to get me to go to bed with you. You don't know me.

LENNY
Sure I do.

KATHERINE
Ahh! Get me a drink. *(no response)* Please.

LENNY gets up, grabs the bottle and gives it to her.

LENNY
I've been listening to you. You want a life of your own. See. I know what you're talking about. I've been through the same thing.

KATHERINE
What? What have you been into? You had kids? You just like making them and leaving.

LENNY
No. When I was in this rehab centre in Seattle. *(He sits.)* I couldn't wait to party.

KATHERINE
What? What were you doing in there?

LENNY
I was being treated... for drugs.

KATHERINE

Oh. Big change, huh?

LENNY

Yeah. They had an AA program at the rehab centre I was in. Learned a lot from Bill W.

Pause.

There were a bunch of us in there. Most of them were these Black guys and some Mexicans, a few Orientals. Poor man's UN, that's what we used to say. The rest were white and just a few of us Skins. My brothers.

KATHERINE

What?

LENNY

There was this AIM guy who said we should unite while we were in there. That way we could have a voice.

KATHERINE

He told you that? Christ. You're barely Indin'.

LENNY

I know. Fuck.

Pause.

Anyway, they had these little cots, well, beds, and we had these gray wool blankets. It was pretty warm. It didn't snow much in Seattle, but it was still cold. They had a place for us to wash our clothes. Had a TV, colour and everything. They even had showers and baths, whirlpools – big metal fuckers, with hot water all the time. It was a pretty decent place.

KATHERINE

That's what you should do now. You could use a wash. *(tries to get to her feet)* Holy-lee.

LENNY tries to stop her, but she gets away from him.

LENNY

Come here.

KATHERINE

No. Err...

LENNY

I have something sweet for you. *(touches himself)*

KATHERINE
When did all this happen anyway?

LENNY
What?

KATHERINE
Your bath... no.... When you went to this halfway house?

LENNY
Just last year. *(gets up and crosses to her)* What do you feel like doing?

KATHERINE
Finish drinking this.

LENNY
Then what? Get our clothes off? Hey Kathy baby, baby Kathy girl, well... you know, the kid's asleep.

KATHERINE
Christ. If this is all you think about, you must've went crazy in that place in Seattle. Or hey, did they have women in there too?

LENNY
No.

KATHERINE
No? Then what did you do? Play with yourself?

LENNY
Nothing. I don't have to do that. I can still get it when I want it.

KATHERINE
Don't lie. Huh, Lenny? What did you do? Play with yourself?

LENNY
I didn't do any of that shit. Nothing didn't...

    Pause.

I was only in there for a few weeks, and then, I got out. It wasn't like I was in jail, or anything like that. We took care of each other so nothing like that would happen. We watched and made sure something like that didn't happen.

KATHERINE
Like what Lenny?

LENNY
You know... so... so no one would fuck us. Rape us.

She laughs.

It's not funny! Fuck!

She watches him.

It didn't happen... but, but there was this young kid. He was a pain in the ass to everyone. He just wouldn't shut his fucking mouth and one night, one night, they decided to throw him a blanket party. *(pause)* Everything echoes in the halls, but, but no one heard him that night. He was always talking and then one night. No one heard him. There was this guard. He had to hear.... But he didn't even bother to check. *(pause)* It never happened.

KATHERINE crosses to him and touches his shoulder.

No one heard it.... No one listened to me when I tried.... No one.

KATHERINE
Lenny... Lenny... Lenny? I'm sorry what happened to you. You can stay here if you want, but I have to go to bed. And please, don't get mad, because, I don't want you with me. I just don't want you.... Don't ask me to come with you. All right Lenny? You can sleep as late as you want.

LENNY
Where are you going?

KATHERINE
To my room. I want to sleep.

She steps back and starts to ease herself towards her room. LENNY reaches for her.

LENNY
Just like in AA, after I shared that... you're not going to go to bed with me?

KATHERINE
I don't want to.

LENNY
Fuck!

KATHERINE goes to the knife under the couch. LENNY slowly follows her.

Kathy.

He goes to the other end of the couch and removes the knife.

KATHERINE
No... no... Len...

LENNY
This is mine now. Just like you are.

She goes for the door. He races after her and gets her in a strangle hold.

No... no.... Can't let you do that.

KATHERINE
Please.... Ow! Don't Lenny!

LENNY
Fuck you then!

He hits her in the back and knocks her down.

KATHERINE
Please don't hurt me Lenny.... Help!

He hits her again.

LENNY
Shut up you damn old cow!

He kicks her.

KATHERINE
Help! Help me! Eddie!

LENNY
You fuckin bitch. I'll show you. You think I'm a smelly breed who's not good enough! I'll get what I want.

He stands for a moment and then goes to her bedroom.

KATHERINE
No! No! Stay away from her Lenny, please! Leave her alone! She didn't do anything to you.

He goes into the bedroom. She gets up and stumbles to the bedroom door. The door is locked. We hear some things being tossed.

My baby! My baby!

THEIA
Mommy? Eddie? Is that.... No!

THEIA screams. We hear a police siren. Police lights. Blackout.

SCENE FIVE

TIME: Early morning. PLACE: KATHERINE Rose's house, living room.

EDDIE stands near the door. THELMA is in his bedroom and enters the living room. She is carrying a suitcase. She walks over to EDDIE.

THELMA
Let me do it my son. It would be better if I do it.

EDDIE
No. I have to do it.

THELMA
You must not forget, she is still your mother. She's kept you alive... till now.

EDDIE nods, "yes." KATHERINE enters from bedroom and sits on the couch. She looks straight out and doesn't say a word. Her face is bruised, her arms are scratched and bruised. Then she looks for an ashtray. She sees one on the other side of the couch and reaches for it. THELMA sees her struggling to reach the ashtray. She goes to KATHERINE, but before she gets near, she stops, and then places her hands over her mouth. She goes to the table and looks for her braids. She finds them and walks back to EDDIE and gives the braids to him. EDDIE looks down. THELMA holds him and he looks up. She releases him. From her coat pocket she removes three papers and hands them to him. Then she picks up the suitcase and exits.

EDDIE walks over to the door of his bedroom. He stands for a moment, sneaks a look at his mother, and then goes into the bedroom. KATHERINE looks over her shoulder. She blows a cloud of smoke in the direction of EDDIE. The bedroom door opens and KATHERINE turns back to her position quickly. EDDIE carries a paper sack. He shuts the bedroom door. Then he goes to the house door. He sets the sack down and then goes to the couch and stands behind it.

EDDIE
Mom? *(softly)* Mom?

He takes out the papers.

I'm going to see Theia at the hospital. They told Aunty Thelma she'll be in there for a few days. The doctors want to watch her. I have something for you. The cops told me and Aunty Thelma that you're going to have to sign these. They told me you said, "no."

Holds out the papers.

Here they are. *(no response)* They told me and Aunty Thelma what they are. You have to sign them right away. I'll give them to Aunty Thelma and she'll take them to the agency. *(no response)* Ma?

KATHERINE
What... what are these? *(She slowly reaches up and takes the papers.)*

EDDIE
That first one there.... That's a complaint against Lenny. They have him and will hold him, but you have to sign so they can get him to court. You have to sign there, on the...

KATHERINE
Papers. Those dumb son of a bitches. They think these mean something. Like this is going to change anything. Oh God.

She looks up at EDDIE.

Why... why the hell did they give me all these damn papers?

Waves them like a fan.

See. Eddie. See. You see. This is what I go through when I try to get help for us. They give me all these damn papers. What good are they?

EDDIE
Just, just sign them.

KATHERINE
What is it I'm signing again? I forgot. Come here and help me my boy. Read these papers for your mother.

EDDIE
It's a complaint Mom. The cops say you have to sign it and they'll get Lenny to court and put him in jail.

KATHERINE
That's a big damn joke. *(crumples the papers)* He's going to be out in a few months anyway.

EDDIE
We have to do something.

KATHERINE
No.

EDDIE
At least do that. Sign the damn papers.

KATHERINE
It wasn't my fault what happened. I couldn't do anything. I was here by myself. I had no one to help me. You're supposed to protect me and your baby sister from things like this.

EDDIE
I was kicked out.

KATHERINE
You left me!

EDDIE
You kicked me out! Putting on a big show for him.

KATHERINE
You're trying to be smart. That's all you're trying to do. *(picks up the papers)* You better shut up, or I'm not going to sign these.

EDDIE
Yes you will. *(crosses to KATHERINE)* Don't say that. If you don't, Aunty Thelma will.

KATHERINE
She will, huh?

EDDIE
Why are you fighting for Lenny? When it's time for you to take up for us.

KATHERINE crosses to EDDIE and slaps him.

KATHERINE
Don't say that! Damn you! *(hits EDDIE again)* You little no good... *(EDDIE runs from her.)*

EDDIE
Yes. That's what we want!

KATHERINE crosses to the couch. He follows.

KATHERINE
If Thelma wants you. She's going to have to fight me first. I'm not going to give up my baby girl to that old bitch.

EDDIE

Mom. Do it!

KATHERINE

I'm not going to give up my kids for a bunch of papers. It happened to Thelma, but it's not going to happen to me. I won't let it. They don't think I can take care of my baby. That's all it will mean. Just like Thelma. Everyone was talking about how she couldn't take care of her little boy. It's not going to happen to me.

EDDIE

Don't do this Mom.

KATHERINE

Have your Aunty Thelma sign. *(picks up the papers and tosses them to EDDIE)* She'll get what she always wanted.

EDDIE

Momma, please.

KATHERINE

Please my ass.

EDDIE

I've never said no to you.

KATHERINE

You shouldn't. I'm your mother. You, you don't know what you're talking about. And here, you, you were going to try and lead this family. And see, you can't do it.

EDDIE

That's not it Mom.

KATHERINE

Yes it is! Don't lie Eddie.

EDDIE

All the times you asked if you were doing the right things. What I should have said was, "no." It was the truth. And I said, "yes." I don't know why, but I just did. And now, I'm sorry as hell I ever did.

KATHERINE

And all this time you were telling me you loved me, you were lying to me? *(stands up)* You always hated me?

EDDIE

I always hid it. And now I don't even try.

KATHERINE

Don't say that Eddie.

Pause.

After all I've been through with you? It doesn't mean anything to you. When your dad threw you out of this life, it was me. Me, Eddie. I picked you up, wiped your bloody nose, wrapped your busted arm. I healed you and gave you life. I loved you. *(looks at EDDIE)* You don't care anymore?

EDDIE

I don't know what to do. Every fucking time! At first I said, yes, just so I could get away from you. And now, after what happened, it happened to me too Mom.

Pause.

My mother is Aunty Thelma. She helped me stay here with you. I thought you would change. And they didn't. They may never change. You may never change.

Looks at her and she turns away, he waits and she looks at him.

I feel sorry for Lenny, and for everybody who was in this house, but I don't feel it. So I think it. That's what I do. And I would sit here and look, and then nothing changed. Nothing moved. Just us, and soon, we were moving around and around, always on the same path, never really going anywhere.

Pause.

I cry, but I cry because I can't tell you. I hide my tears because they don't mean anything to you. And I don't cry any more because the tears don't mean anything to me. I can't cry at our own funeral Mom. My tears are nothing but water, laughing, or crying, they taste the same.

Pause.

It'll probably start up all over again, but I don't want to be a part of it. I don't know if you'll have a Lenny with you, or who'll take his place, but it isn't going to be me.

He begins to gather up the scattered papers.

I want out.

Hands her the papers. She sits motionless.

KATHERINE

No Eddie. It isn't true. You know it isn't...

She hugs him and doesn't let go.

You're just mad is all. You know I can take care of you kids. You know I can. Say yes...

EDDIE slowly takes his mother's hands off him. He eases her back down on the couch.

EDDIE

No Mom. No. You can't. Give me back my life. I want to leave here, alive. *(gives her the papers)* Here.

Reaches into his pocket and gets a pen.

Here. Use this.

KATHERINE takes the papers and looks at them.

The first one is the complaint. *(KATHERINE signs it.)* And the next two are the custody papers.

KATHERINE looks at EDDIE. She signs the papers. She slowly hands them to him.

Thank you. *(pause)* Thank you Mom. You gave me life again.

EDDIE takes the papers and places them in his sack. He takes out the two braids and holds them up. He crosses over to KATHERINE. He gets an ashtray.

Mom. Mom. Here. *(holds the braids out)* These were Aunty Thelma's.

He takes a book of matches.

I'm going to burn mine. I want you to have the other and please burn it Mom. *(EDDIE hands her a braid.)* And later... I'm going to pray for you... and Theia. Aunty Thelma says she knows some people who can help Theia. They'll help you too if you want them to. I don't want any more bad things happening to you, her, or me.

Pause.

At least try and heal one of our cuts.

He begins to light a match. Starts to touch the match to the braid. KATHERINE stops him.

KATHERINE
My boy, women do this. Just go.

EDDIE gives her the braid and the matches. She holds the book of matches. She lights one and holds it near the braid. She holds it as the flame burns to the end and touches her hand.

KATHERINE
Ow...

She lights another and her hand is trembling. She holds it in the air. Optional: EDDIE reaches his hand out to her and helps steady her hand.

Blackout.

The end.

ARIA
A ONE-WOMAN PLAY
IN ONE ACT

TOMSON HIGHWAY

TOMSON HIGHWAY

photo by Michael Cooper

INTRODUCTION TO *ARIA*

Cree playwright, novelist, and pianist Tomson Highway, from Manitoba's Brochet Reserve is generally identified with the "naissance" of Native theatre in Canada in the mid-1980s because of his having served as Artistic Director of Native Earth Performing Arts during that period, and because of the wide popular and critical success of two plays: *The Rez Sisters* in 1986 and its 1989 companion piece and sequel, *Dry Lips Oughta Move to Kapuskasing*. *The Rez Sisters* toured widely within Canada and had the distinction of being selected for the mainstage of the prestigious Edinburgh Festival in 1988; *Dry Lips* was selected in 1990 by David Mirvish for the subscription season of the most eminent (and historically most colonialist) of Toronto's commercial theatres, the Royal Alexandria Theatre. Although this identification may in fact represent the moment when the mainstream white audience and critical establishment in central Canada noticed what had been happening for several years prior to Highway's success, it nevertheless registers the emergence of a remarkable talent together with a remarkable increase in both the level of First Nations theatrical activity and the public profile of First Nations theatre artists that coincided with and followed the reception of Highway's plays.

Tomson Highway, the 11th of 12 children, was born on his father's trap-line on an island in Maria Lake in Northern Manitoba, near the borders of Saskatchewan and the Northwest Territories. His first six years were spent with his family fishing and trapping in northwestern Manitoba. He spoke Cree exclusively until he was sent to a Roman Catholic residential school in The Pas, and later to Churchill High School in Winnipeg (and a series of foster homes), where he was forced to learn English and was separated from his family and culture for ten months of the year. After high school he studied as a classical concert pianist at the Universities of Manitoba and Western Ontario, including a year in London, England, in the early 1970s. He graduated from Western with an Honours degree in Music in 1975, and completed a second BA degree in 1976, working and studying with playwright and poet James Reaney. Highway's training with Reaney and his training in classical piano were both major influences on his later dramatic work – classical music serving as a basic structural and organizational principle for many of his plays, including, of course, *Aria*, which Highway describes in notes to the play housed at the University of Guelph Theatre Archives as the extended prelude to the singing of an operatic aria by its central, "mythical Native diva." Highway's account of the play in the theatre is worth quoting at length, if only to set the scene:

The actual staging of this piece centres around this fabulous Turandot-type diva's gown built on a frame, a floor-length dress made of what looks like a rich red velvet, with a train that trails behind the dress forever until it covers the entire upstage area, climbs the back wall of the theatre and becomes, in effect, the curtain of the opera house in which the singer sings her "aria." A black concert grand piano sits on this train immediately behind the body of the gown with an Indian male pianist dressed in full concert attire—tails and all—but with elements of Indian pow-wow dance regalia. Scattered randomly around the centrepiece of this gown are the various props and bits of costume the actress will use as she assumes the various characters – slipping in and out of the frame of the gown, seemingly at will: a cane for the grandmother, an apron for the wife, veil for the bride, crown for the Queen, etc.

The whole piece unfolds in the style of the *recitativo accompagnato* of Italian grand opera, those extended half-sung, half-spoken segments of narrative that connect one aria to the next. The poetry itself is almost of an expressionist character, not entirely unlike the method of presentation utilized in German composer Arnold Schoenberg's legendary "Pierrot Lunaire," only this would be expressionism with a distinctly Cree twist.

The diva, however, never actually gets to sing. Neither does the pianist get to play—or, in fact, move at all—for he remains still as a statue for almost the entire hour-and-a-half length of the show. It is only towards the last ten minutes, when we enter the fabulous dream world of Cree mythology, that the pianist finally springs to life playing music of an atonal, *avant-garde* nature, which becomes increasingly cacophonous and frenzied, the keyboardist, simultaneously, reciting snippets of Cree poetry at certain key points. At the very end, when the diva is finally ready to sing, the piano music releases itself into this gorgeous, romantic "*bel canto*" introductory passage and, as the diva—back, once more, inside the body of her gown—opens her mouth to form the first vowel of her song, the lights fade into blackout. It remains for audience members themselves to sing, in their minds, the aria, the "song of woman."

The play is a little-known, one-woman gem that we are proud to publish here for the first time. It was first performed in a Native Earth Performing Arts Production by the remarkable and mercurial Makka Kleist at Toronto's Annex Theatre in March 1987 under the direction of Larry Lewis. The show was nominated for a Dora Mavor Moore Award and invited a festival of Inuit culture in Kleist's native Greenland as well as to represent Canada at the 1987 Asia-Pacific Festival, held that year in Vancouver.

Aria is linked to Highway's better known plays *The Rez Sisters* (as a portrait and celebration of Native women) and *Dry Lips Oughta Move to Kapuskasing* (through its inclusion of the character of Hera Keechigeesik, and an early sketch of the frame story of the later play). But although this short, one-act, one woman show is smaller in scale than either of those plays, its scope and ambition are at least as great. Here, in a *tour de force* for a solo performer who is called upon to play across an outrageous range of ages, classes, styles, sites, voices, and roles of women, Highway seems to set for himself the goal articulated by his "Executive" character: "to move these incredible motionless men, waken them to the voices of these many thousand women in their blood... make them understand this energy, my spirit... that clings to the pores of my skin like the mouths of a million frightened children." As bride, wife, earth mother, executive, Virgin Mary, drunk, white woman, Woman of the Rolling Head, and even, in one version of the script,

Queen of England (not published here), the diva takes the audience on a raucous, reverential, and riveting tour of Native womanhood ending, appropriately, with Mother Earth herself, "Nuna," "Us-ki," the source of creative, "alive."

CHARACTERS

All played by one woman:
THE KO-KUM
THE MOTHER
THE LITTLE GIRL
THE LOVER OF MEN
THE LOVER OF WOMEN
THE BRIDE
THE WIFE
THE INDIAN WOMAN
THE WHITE WOMAN
THE SECRETARY
THE EXECUTIVE SECRETARY
THE EXECUTIVE
THE DIVA
THE WOMAN OF THE ROLLING HEAD
MARILYN
THE PROSTITUTE
THE EARTH

ARIA
A ONE-WOMAN PLAY IN ONE ACT

TOMSON HIGHWAY

THE KO-KUM

There was a time I could make my way through these stands of trees, endless forever stands of green trees... white spruce and pale green tamarack... green needles quiver in these many, many northern summers of my life. Time was, yes, when my feet were sure and certain in their grip upon this reindeer moss, this grey rock. And yet I flew, like a spray of twelve fluttering songbirds... my spirit... like a mist... floating through tall trees and the bark, the veins of the trunk, nursing like a babe on the very sap. The taste was sweeter than anything this old life or mine has ever known.

I taught these twelve children of mine... to walk through this muskeg... to spring quick and light. Taught these seven daughters to tell the many moods of wind, rain of tomorrow, my five sons to hold conversation with fire and the northern lights. I spent a hundred years and more in the teaching of these things. Yes, time was when I could swim through this sea of green with the ease and toughness of young trout.

I sit here now in this ramshackle house.... The colour TV sits four feet in front of me. There's the smell of unclean babies; small children run crazy in this house—they're all mine, they say, these swarms... little boys... little girls—and they stink. This thing they call a telephone is a living thing. There's the smell of liquor and...

I sit here waiting to die. I sit here all my dark nights, looking into myself and seeing the spirit of other times and better times... I'll never, never see again.

I'm blind. I'm deaf now and my feet are motionless. Sitting here, I wrap my hand around the curve of this cane and search deep into myself, all the nights of my long life, and gaze at boughs of spruce and tamarack... even the singing of the bird I can see now... my spirit... like a mist....

THE MOTHER

There was a gift came down to me. The seed was planted deep. And deep in me began a breathing, taking shape of little arms, little legs, the spine, little liver.

I drink the water and the water seeps into the belly of the child. My liquid is electric... I breathe the breath of self.

-THE BIRTH-

Blood sprays out like sunlight.
Gurgle, my folding flesh, a whisper all in one.
The salty liquid from my eyes is hers.

Hey! The child. My child.
Her veins held up against the light
Are filigree and webs of wonder to behold.
I was mother
I am mother now.

My child flies out the window of my dream and climbs aboard the Earth,
straddles it and makes its loamy texture part of her. Her arm, her little
shoulder blade, her pumping heart covers the surface of my breast...
ihhhh...

There was a gift came down to me.

THE LITTLE GIRL
Mother, Mama, Mom, *ni-mama*!
(sings) Kees-pin ki-sa-gee-hin
See-mak ka-wee-chee-win.
(speaks) Hello.
Wonderful fun kind
Of wonderful wonderful sunbeam
Fancy in the air there
And down upon the ground there
And here
And around and through the sun–
Beam and poked by magic stick.
Choing!
Oh-oh... *(sunbeam out)*
Ma! *(sunbeam back on)*
The wall by my bed
Is the wave on the lake
On top of the wave there's me and my mom
The wave is big
Inside the wave there's me and my mom
The wave is ten, weeny, weeny, weeny
I'm half-way into sleep
The wave.
Sparkle spray
Sunbeam and songbird
Fancy that....
(sings) Sitting in the tall grass
Wave in the white breeze.

(speaks) My magic stick legs like "Y"
Ohhhh, I feel good....
The magic stick prickle and poke
Skin
Nice.... Nice... *(touches "herself")*
Oh-oh...
Mother, mama, mom where are you?
You, *ni-mama*, gave me
These bones and skin
Hair, teeth, lips and eyes that see
See fancy fly among sunbeam and
My magic stick...

I was playing
Lovely games with sun–
Beam and the little stick...
Lovely.

THE LOVER OF MEN

(sings) Hail Mary Mary Mary
Full of grace grace
Full of grace
The Lord is with thee
Hail Mary Mary
Blessed art, blessed art thou amongst women women
(speaks) And blessed is the fruit of thy womb, Jesus.
Pssst!
I'm alive.
I'm for real.
I tell you, I ain't a statue
But the real thing for sure.
You've all seen me before.
Remember me?
On picture postcards.
Standing still as death in church corners
Beside those crucifixes... *(pose)*
Crucifixes plentiful as Coca-Cola.

I was pretending to be Virgin Mary. It's the costume Saladia Big Bush is
wearing for the Christmas concert, Sister. Sister Mary Joseph only asked me
to be the cow in the manger... beside the manger. Saladia Big Bush is too
fat to play the Virgin Mary, Sister, she should be the cow and I should be
the Virgin Mary. Because she was beautiful and holy and... the mother of
Jesus. Because if I think of her more often and pray more to her, I can
forget Cree faster and not have to be punished for speaking it in this
residential school. Because she will help us become more like you, Sister.
That's why. I wasn't laughing at her, I was laughing with her. Cuz where
I come from, Sister, we're allowed to laugh and I think this poor woman,

mother of us all, including you, Sister Mary Alexander, should be allowed to have fun just once in a while. I mean, even the Blessed Virgin Mary herself had to take a shit at least once a day, didn't she? *N'pug-wa-teen oo-ta, ni-mama.*

Holy Mary, mother of God
Pray for us sinners
Now and at the hour of our...

There's this fascination with my body, the sudden appearance of hair in certain corners. Strange and mysterious goings-on. All of a sudden: *je suis la femme d'amour!* I'm aware of the bodies of boys and young men, the way their asses look in skin-tight faded blue jeans, the way the muscles of their arms flex under those T-shirts, the way their... thighs... move... the sweat! I like standing close to them, the way they smell, the way they run, sway, swagger.... So many boys! To be held... held fast... by the arms of my men... on hot musky nights... on nights when the mist has risen...

THE LOVER OF WOMEN
(Lying on floor, she groans with pain.)
I sound like a moose...

The rising and the falling
Of a sea...
The moon is silent but not still
My body in her time of fullness
...we have a centre here
And here...
And here is the flame
And pain becomes power, beauty...

There the moon,
Time
Of my moon;
Moon
Lover
Of
Woman.

THE BRIDE
Here is the aisle before me now
The pews lined row on row
Flowers all in place, organ
Music colours air and I in white
The veil behind me falls in folds
Brushing stone floor with pale whisper.

This man,
He of the long stem and the brazen,
brazen flower I clasp in
Hand as my bouquet
Forever
To the day we die, one or the other.

Given to this man as gem
Cherished and admired for the year.
As food
To be eaten and digested
As receptacle
To children.
Or am I given to this man
As pleasure trove
To be indulged in.

How do I hold his limbs as he makes love
to me.

By my heart he is present
His body close to mine
His hand, his skin that touches mine
The hair...

My white dress is like the dove
That flutters, hovers and descends
The last breath of airborne freedom, I feel.
Pinned by male fuse to the soil
Will I be forever bound
to house
and bound
to giving of my body night and day
and evening time... and teeming
life should sprout out from my flesh?
WHO IS THIS MAN?!

Here is the aisle before me now
And the pews lined row on row
The man in priestly vestments beckons
with his sacred smile
The blood-red carpet awash with holy water
This is the river down which I float
to join him.
He shall fashion from my body, my soul,
the complete being, the complete...

Here is the aisle...

Oh, my God...

> THE WIFE *stands on the porch landing of her house on the reserve. A rickety old washing machine is before her; she is doing laundry. She "talks" a lot with her hands.*

THE WIFE
My husband's socks, my husband's pants, my husband's shirt, my husband's underwear. My shirt, my socks, my pants, my underpants. Hey, the way this life of mine has gone, loving him and him loving me and me and him go fishing in the lake. You throw the net. And the water sticks in the *(hand motions making the shape of the webbing in the net)* catching the sun. Handfuls of light come "phht-phht" in your face. "*Hera Keechigeesik*, don't rock the boat too much. Scare the fish away," he say to me. Me and him. Hey, *ta-p'wee-sa pee-sim*[1]...

The years me and Zachary were fishing and trapping up north, summertime we live in tents. The lake is there, the island, the island hanging from the sky. Our men were all gone hunting. So it was just us women. And the children. Alone.

All of a sudden "haw-woomp." This "phhhrrroommm." Very black. First I thought it was a moose. But no. "Haw-woomp, haw-woomp," the water went, "haw-woomp, haw-woomp, haw-woomp." It was terrible. There was this... *pee-s'tew*[2]... this... foam... foaming in the water. It reached the shore. It was huge. Bigger than any man. Covered with hair. No lips. Eyes flames of ice. It was. The Weetigo! Ohhh, the breath of the Weetigo can freeze you till you're stiff as a statue. Then the Weetigo enters you. Right into your soul. And you become. The Weetigo! And you eat people. Brrrr.

So anyway. There. The Weetigo. On the shore. Right before our very eyes. So us women. We grab our children and take to the hills. And we waited. And I watched.

The Weetigo went into my tent! Rowwwowwwwooorrrr! *(roars and bangs the sides of the washing machine)* It roared and raged. The tents were in shreds. The dogs? All dead. He was so big he tripped on the stove and burned our camp to the ground. Everything was in flames.

Then. And only then. "Haw-woomp, haw-woomp, haw-woomp, haw-woomp, haw-woomp," it swam back to the island. Brrrr! The Weetigo is a terrible, terrible thing to see.

---

[1] This phrase is used at various times in this monologue, in various permutations. Its approximate meaning, in Cree, is "Hey this sunshine sure feels good...."
[2] "Pee-s'tew" means "foam" in Cree.

(*Abruptly, she begins to sing, happy as a lark.*) La-la-la-la-la-la-la the mouth of high July, hey! (*speaks*) The life of wives sings in the summer the furniture needs dusting, hey! *Ta-p'wee-sa pee-sim nee-ta-cha-ga-soo.* "*Hera Keechigeesik,* that yellow sunshine sure looking good on that brown belly of yours," he say to me. Zachary. My Zachary.

My husband's socks, my husband's pants, my husband's shirt, my husband's under.... The time that Nataways woman brought his underwear home to me. In a box, all nice washed and folded.

She stands there. Curlers. Blouse wrinkled and dirty tits stink of ashtrays and men. One step down on my rickety porch, paint is gone long ago, wood rotten sand blow through the cracks. Jacket, Zachary's pup, the ugly one, dropped his shit by the step again.

That Giselle Nataways. She took a shit on Liza Jane Manitowabi's lawn. She opened her legs to seventeen-year-old Dickie Bird Halked right in front of Black Lady Halked's face. She made two babies by Raggedy Annie Cook's husband without missing one single goddamn bingo game. But no woman come near Zachary Keechigeesik.

I, Zachary Keechigeesik's wife, never let her children go hungry, never missed a payment at Andy Manitowabi's store. I, Zachary Keechigeesik's wife, walked 40 miles to the Anchor Inn in January through that blizzard to sober up Rosie Kakapetum the medicine woman to save this woman's own mother from the blood from that accident, the gun in that drunken brawl this woman's own father was the one that pulled the trigger and just about shot her foot off. I walked that 40 miles.

She stands there. Her lips smile. But her eyes? *Ee-pa-pee-it a-wa k's'ka-na-goos. Ku-nu-wa-pa-ta oos-kee-si-g'wa.*[3] I freeze. I hear rushing water in my head. (*screams uncontrollably*) I kick with my knee. I kick and I kick and I kick and I kick and I kick. (*Pause. Calm again, she whimpers.*) Blood got all over my hands. Blood and clumps of sticky bloody hair. I kicked her in her pregnant belly. Her shitty brown bum spread naked in the dirt by my broken steps, squeaking like a sick mink.

I was ever alone. Three days. I sit in my living room. Curtains shut. Don't eat. Don't wash. Nothing. Three days. Stare straight ahead. Three days.

He come home, shy as a puppy dog, this... suitcase full of dream visions under his arm – the very first TV on the reserve. So. So now me and him and him and me. We lie on this couch at midnight. (*pause*) Can't see the TV too good cuz his knobby old knee's in the way, hey. *Ta-p'wee-sa ma-na a-wa pee-sim.*

---

3 Cree: "She's laughing at me, this female dog. Look at her eyes."

THE INDIAN WOMAN

Oo-oo n'si see-tuk
Hey, ta-p'wee sa mi-thoo ki-noh-s'koo-si-wuk
Oom-see-si ka-ga-noh-pi-ma-g'wow ma-na see-tuk
Hey, tas-kootch ma-na oo-tee pee-cha-eek
Ee-moo-see-thi-muk a-wi-nuk
U-wi-nuk ee-nee-pa-wit
U-wi-nuk ee-pa-gi-ta-ta-moot
U-wi-nuk ee-p'mat-sit
Oo-oo n'si see-tuk
Hey, ta-p'wee sa mi-thoo us-ki-tu-goo-si-wuk
I-thi-gook ma-na een-tay-thee-ta-man
Ta-na-ta-g'wow; ta-na-ta-g'wow
I-goo-see-si nee-s'ta tay-si-pa-gi-ta-ta-moo-yan
Tay-si-moo-see-ta-an pee-cha-eek
Oo-oo n'si see-tuk these trees...4

THE WHITE WOMAN

The taxis.
The taxis are yellow this afternoon
And seem to float just centimetres
Above the grey cement, the two
the taxis and cement–
Are separate and apart.

The traffic.
The traffic is heavy, this afternoon
And seems to float just centimetres
Above the grey cement, the two
The traffic and cement–
Are separate and apart...
makes horrible racket,
This traffic.

4 *(Translation for production personnel only, not for audiences.)*
These trees
So tall, straight
I look at trees like this
Inside of me—here—
I feel someonew, a being
Someone standing there
Someone breathing there
Spirit alive and living
These trees
Green so rich
I want
To talk to them
Walk in them
Breathe in them
Live inside their breathing
These trees

The stores.
The stores are numerous this afternoon
So are the windows in these stores
You can see your own reflection in them
As you pass. There are also many
Restaurants in which to have lunch
And talk business and sometimes
Of things that touch the heart.

The spirits.
I see no spirits whatsoever
On this cement, I don't know
What this other woman is talking about.
I walk on this cement, and the two
This cement and I–
Are distinctly separate and apart.

THE SECRETARY
What the well-dressed girl will wear:

Wash'n'wear polyester chalk-stripe wrap-around in slimming come-again navy blue. Sixteen ridiculous dollars. Designed to please the man who calls her "secretary girl."

Cute little navy blue pumps with heels high enough to entice, low enough to run. *Armé de Salvation*. $4. But only her best friend needs to know.

This snappy ensemble is completed by a fin-blue cotton T-shirt with slit-neck and droopy loopy sleeves by Alfred Sung. $125. She was depressed and she... simply had to go shopping.

Nevertheless.
She stands.
A veritable soldierette.
On the brink of pay equity.
Success will be hers before you can say:
"Phew-phew!"

THE EXECUTIVE SECRETARY
(in the rhythm of a slow samba)
Today:
I live in closer proximity
To the man in the pin-striped suit
My vocabulary has increased
The first time I heard the word
"Proximity" I thought it was some new
Disease or at least some obscure Brazilian
Dance not unlike the bossa nova, the cha-cha

Or the samba. Hey!
Living in closer proximity
To the man in the pin-striped suit
I'm aware of the greater power
I've acquired over my own fate
My destiny, my life
My will and I appreciate
That power I embrace that power
And that power looks attractive
And beguiling on my sleeve
On the shank of the old left leg.
I'm no longer some lowly minion
A servant girl, a lackey
A gofer or an ornamental exercise
I'm Executive Secretary now and
I live in more intense proximity
To the man, the man in the pin-striped suit
More intense proximity to
The man in the pin-striped suit
Is a state of being I much
Appreciate I get to stand
Behind the man and place my
Hands upon his back so that
He doesn't fall when he finds
He doesn't have the time or
Finds he is incapable or
Finds he doesn't have the answer
Like right now, he'll ask me and
I'll go: "Yes, this is the way"
Or "No, that's not the way"
Or "Yes, I'd do it this way"
Or "No, the prices are extravagant"
          horses are an asset"
     begonias will not do"
Or "It's more than once I've
Climbed into your shoes and
Steered you through the darkness
Of your pin-striped mind, my man
That's my job"
Living in such intimate proximity
To the man in the pin-striped suit
I began to feel that the pin-striped
Suit is sticking to my skin.
In little bits and pieces this morning
I got up and there before me
In the glass two pins and a stripe
Were sunk into the
Outer layer of my forehead not an inch

From my brain at noon I'm
Eating lunch with my soup spoon
Raised with three pins and two stripes
Announce themselves on the palm
Of my right hand so it seems
That if I choose persistence
In this close proximity to the man
In the pin-striped suit! Oh... but...
Well, it's like a tool, a hammer
Or a sickle or a sword that I
Wield and I flash and I order
Secretaries hither and secretaries thither
Flocks, gangs, hordes of secretaries
At my bidding and they part
Like the deep Red Sea before
My gliding, whispering
Sleek and sinuous Executive
Secretary form young girls
Sprouting shards of fire-painted
Fingernails in love within electrified
By their IBM Selectrics and I
Glide past them like an elegant fish
To the side of the man
The man in the pin-striped suit.

My vocabulary has expanded
"Proximity" is a concept
That I appreciate
So
Much.

THE EXECUTIVE
Good morning, gentlemen.

Gentlemen, in October of 1986, the Executive Committee of the Ontario
League of Native Brotherhood Centres hired me as Executive Director to
operate and monitor the costs of programmes province-wide. It must have
become evident to the Executive Committee and every member of the
Board that the status of the organization is tenuous and unstable at best.

With reference to the Ontario Native Courtworker programme, first put
into place in 1961 to reduce the percentage of Natives incarcerated in the
Canadian penal system, the success quotient has stabilized at 40%. It was
your goal to train and equitably distribute Native courtworkers to
Brotherhood Centres across this fair province. It was to be incumbent
upon the Courtworkers to interpret legalese to Native offenders, access
lawyers and interpret to the courts the cultural perspective of Natives
standing trial.

Time and money for the implementation of this essential service has been eaten away by the bickering, by the jockeying for position and by the ridiculous political posturings within the Executive Committee itself. It is my contention that in becoming abscessed with the might of its own power, this Executive Committee has forgotten what it was first put in place to do.

As a result of mismanagement, misdirection, and what amounts to near criminal negligence, our Courtworkers are facing impossible working conditions and are inadequately paid for responsibilities too numerous for them to negotiate.

I can walk into the Premier's office tomorrow and get that additional $200,000. You've tried. You've failed. I'm telling you, I can do it. I have the interest, the personality, the speaking ability, the power, the vision, the determination, and the drive.

We could put that $200,000 into a comprehensive training package and put at least eight more Courtworkers into the system. However, in the interest of maximum efficiency with respect to the delivery of programmes to our Native community, I can offer each member of the Executive Committee: $100 a week for in-town travel; a Tilden rent-a-car credit card; dental, medical, optical, family, and other benefits. And a darned good business lunch. In return for which, the Executive Committee will grant me tenure. And complete unlimited... control.

So this is what it's like. This is what I came to do. To change this fabulous masculine world. Succeed? Of course. I'm a success. I sit on top of the world, men scattered at my feet like roses at a shrine. And here I thought I would move these incredible motionless men, waken them to the voices of these many thousand women in their blood... make them understand this energy, my spirit... that clings to the pores of my skin like the mouths of a million frightened children. So...

Thank you, gentlemen.

THE DIVA

Woman... alone... forest
Hunter
Marry... her lodge
Two sons... good wife
Grown careless... work
He spies on her
Naked
Hissing snakes
Penetrating... every orifice
Hunter kills... snakes
Soup... blood...

Feeding... wife.
"You have eaten blood of your lovers."
She runs... see... dead lovers
Sons... flee
Hunter gives... medicine... for protection.
"If sky red tonight," he tells sons, "I have died."
Wife returns
Hunter axes... her head
Slashes her body
Throws it to the sky
Woman's skull attacks... devours
Fleeing sons see red sky... know...
Coldness...
Mother's rolling skull cries
"Come to mother."
Sons throw medicine...
Thorn patch... entangles skull
Boys escape
Beaver helps her
Chase
Mother's skull again cries
"Come to mother."
Sons throw second medicine
Huge cliff stops skull
Boys escape
May-may-quay-sik helps her
Chase
Skull cries
"Come to mother."
Sons throw third medicine
Flames surround skull.
But still... skull chases
Boys throw fourth medicine
Poplar stumps entangle skull
Skull frees itself
Chase...
"Come to mother."
Boys throw last medicine.
Water gushes
Water bird helps skull
But falls in water
"My sons. Save me."
Boys throw rocks.
Split skull
Skull sinks
Boys free...

THE DIVA/THE WOMAN OF THE ROLLING HEAD
I loved my husband once.

Then in my soul one night
Crept the dark spirit silently
And in the forest I made love
To ten thousand snakes
Night after night.

Crying, writhing,
Singing at the moon,
One night he saw me there
My husband saw me then
And cut my head off with an axe.

My body falls
But I refuse.
I will not die.
I will not die.

My head leaps.
My mouth leaps.
I tear his throat.
Feast on his flesh.

My sons
I tear their throats.
Feast on their flesh.
And my sons, sons
And on and on and on

    "Babies. My babies. Come to your loving mother."
    I am the Woman of the Rolling Head
    I loved ten thousand snakes
    I loved ten thousand snakes
    I loved ten thousand snakes
    "Children. Come. Come to me. Your mother..."

(speaks) I can't. I can't. This is wrong. This is all wrong. The wrong way.
Wrong way. Wrong way to tell the stories. We've forgotten how to tell the
old stories. They're fading. Fading. No. No. They can't. Can't. What am
I doing here. What am I doing here.

MARILYN
Ooooh!
How long
Are you going to
Love me
For?

THE PROSTITUTE

Hey, mister. Gotta cigarette?

Hey, mister. Got the time?

Hey, mister...

Hey...

Starlight, starry night, bright light and I'm alright...

Hey, mister. Wanna buy me a drink?

Hey, mister...

He sits there in his brand-new sky-blue/chrome Chevrolet Impala. Drives by in the starry night and doesn't even see the goddamn stars...

Chevrolet Impala, eh? Hey, where's that guy in the great big BMW who came to me last week, whimpering between my legs like a puppy dog in need of a home?

Hey, mister. Wanna give me a ride?

Street life gets to one sometimes and after a while... what the hell and damn it all anyway, a girl's gotta make a living and a girl's gotta be able to buy a drink.

Starlight, moonlight, I'm alright...

Car lights glide past me. Glide past. These men, these anonymous men, these lonely men, they cast their hungry eyes at me and peer real deep into this little old red heart of mine. What the fuck do they wanna see? The reflection of themselves and their lolling tongues?

Hey, mister. Wanna see me? The real me?

Wanna see the me beneath all this lipstick, rouge, eye-liner shit I've slapped on my face to make myself look just a little more white?

Hey, mister. I promise you, mister, it'll make you feel so good you'll come for days. And it'll cost you only sixty bucks. Sixty bucks. That's all.... What do you expect, pork chops at the IGA down the street is going for $3.95 a kilo this week and they don't even come anywhere near...

Hey, mister. Hey, wait a minute. I was just.... Oh shit.

Gettin, a little chilly. Gotta buy me more pantyhose tomorrow. My ass is gettin, a little loose around the edges gotta do something about it, maybe take up judo or Tae-kwon-do or something... that way maybe I can protect myself against any man who may come along and abuse me with his... his fists, like beat me up, like pulverize me, like beat the shit out of me. This way I could just give him a judo chop right across the neck like this, "ha!" and he'd fall dead right on top of my two tits...

Yes, pantyhose...

Well, now, there's starlight and car light and there's nightlight and city light, neon light and street light and starlight and I'm alright and starlight and shit car light's glaring at me like they've never seen a woman before, what's a matter, your wife won't give ya...

Hey.

THE EARTH
And the songbird paused.
My spirit... like a mist.
There was a gift came down to me.
(sings) Kees-pin ki-sa-gee-hin.
(speaks) Strange and mysterious goings-on.
And pain becomes power.
Here is the aisle.
Me and him and him and me.
U-wi-nuk ee-pa-gi-ta-ta-moot.
Are separate and apart.
Like ahmmm... so, anyway.
I touch you and you speak.
Closer proximity to.
I can offer each member.
Ten thousand snakes.
Oooh, how long?
Starlight, moonlight and I'm alright! Hey!

I knew she was alive.
I know Earth is alive.
I can feel through the soles of
My moving feet...
Earth.
Nuna.
Us-ki!

    Blackout.

    The end.

REVERB-BER-BER-RATIONS

SPIDERWOMAN THEATER
(LISA MAYO, GLORIA MIGUEL
AND MURIEL MIGUEL)

SPIDERWOMAN THEATER
(LISA MAYO, GLORIA MIGUEL
AND MURIEL MIGUEL)

photo by Jonathan Slaff

INTRODUCTION TO *REVERB-BER-BER-RATIONS*

Spiderwoman Theater is the artistic creation of three sisters, writer-performers Lisa Mayo, Gloria Miguel, and Muriel Miguel, who are Kuna/Rappahannock. Founded in 1976, it is the oldest continually running women's theatre company in North America. Their productions, which evolve and develop as they remain in repertory over many years, have been performed across North America and around the world from Amsterdam to Berlin, Brussells, Nancy, Florence, and Stockholm, and from Australia and New Zealand to Beijing, China. They include *Women and Violence; Cabaret: An Evening of Pukey Songs & Disgusting Images*; *Lysistrata Numbah*; *The Fittin' Room*; *Sun, Moon, Feather*; *The Three Sisters from Here to There*; *I'll be Right Back*; *3 Up, 3 Down*; *Winnetou's Snake Oil Show from Wigwam City*; *Reverb-ber-ber-rations*; *Power Pipes*; and *Persistence of Memory*. Lisa Mayo, Gloria Miguel, and Muriel Miguel each received an honourary Doctorate of Fine Arts in 1996 from Miami University in Oxford Ohio, where Spiderwoman's papers are deposited as a major part of the Native American Women Playwrights Archives. In addition to their work together each of the women have also created and produced solo shows for Spiderwoman Theater.

Lisa Mayo is a founding member of Off the Beaten Path as well as Spiderwoman, a performing member of Masterworks Laboratory Theater of New York, and a classically trained mezzo-soprano. She studied at the New York College of Music, studied theatre with Uta Hagen, Robert Lewis, Walt Witcover, and Charles Nelson Riley, and performed and studied with Tina Packer and Kristen Linklater. She has taught theatre crafts and acting as part of the Minnesota Native American AIDS Task Force, and has directed the Native American Actor's Showcase at the American Indian Community House, where she serves on the board of directors.

Gloria Miguel studied drama at Oberlin College in Oberlin, Ohio. In addition to her work with Spiderwoman she has worked extensively in film and television, toured the United States in *Grandma*, a one-woman show by Hanay Geiogamah, and Canada as Peliajia Patchnose in the original Native Earth production of Tomson Highway's *The Rez Sisters*. She performed as Coyote/Vitaline in the Northern Lights production of Maria Campbell and Linda Griffiths' *Jessica* in Edmonton, and as Maria in a Chicago dramatic adaptation of Louise Erdrich's book, *Love Medicine*. She was drama consultant for the Minnesota American Indian Youth AIDS Task Force, teaches drama at the Eastern Disctrict YMCA in Brooklyn, and has been visiting professor and drama consultant at Brandon University in Manitoba.

Muriel Miguel is the artistic director of Spiderwoman Theater, and is also a founding member of Open Theatre, Off the Beaten Path, Thunderbird American Indian Dancers, and Native American Theater Ensemble. She originated the role of Philomela Moosetail in Tomson Highway's *The Rez Sisters* and of Lulu in a dramatic adaptation in Chicago of Louise Erdrich's book, *Love Medicine*, and she directed the premiere productions in Toronto of Monique Mojica's *Princess Pocahontas and the Blue Spots* in 1990 and The Turtle Gals' (Jani Lauzon, Monique Mojica, and Michelle St. John) *The Scrubbing Project*. She developed and directed a project for the Minnesota Native American AIDS Task Force in 1991, and co-directed *Indian Givers* with the Native American Youth Council of New York City. She has taught theatre at Bard College in New York and at the Centre for Indigenous Theatre in Toronto.

Spiderwoman uses storytelling as a basis for their productions, and they understand storytelling as "the way you feel and know where you are with your family, your clan, your tribal affiliations, and from there in to the history of how you fit into the world":

> Storytelling starts at the kitchen table, on your parent's lap, on your aunt's and uncle's laps. Storytelling begins there, about who you are.... Then it continues from there about who you are in the family, of where you are as a tribal member, as part of that particular nation; then where that nation is in the community; and where that community belongs in the world. (Muriel Miguel, in Haugo 228)

They call their working technique "storyweaving." They interconnect and weave stories and fragments of stories with words, song, music, film, dance, and movement, to create a complex emotional, cultural, and political tapestry in an overlay of interlaced designs. Their work is often difficult to follow on the page, but when performed it comes fully to life as physical, embodied, and emotional connections are woven together seamlessly and with considerable theatrical nuance. The company takes its name from the Hopi goddess Spiderwoman, who taught the people to weave and said "There must be a flaw in every tapestry so' that my spirit may come and go at will." Spiderwoman locates contemporary topics in historical context and examines them through the techniques of Native storytelling and contemporary theatrical conventions, aiming to empower Native people, particularly women, and to enlighten, educate, and entertain a wide and diverse general public.

Reverb-ber-ber-rations was first produced in New York City in March 1990 at Theater for a New City, written and performed by Lisa Mayo, Gloria Miguel, and Muriel Miguel, directed by Muriel Miguel, with set design by Tom Moore and lighting design by Zdenek Kriz. An early version of the script was published in *Women and Performance: A Journal of Feminist Theory* 5.2 (1992): 184-212. According to the playwrights:

> *Reverb-ber-ber-rations* began when we were in performance with our previous show, *Winnetou's Snake Oil Show from Wigwam City*. Since *Winnetou's Snake Oil Show* was such a broad farce, we wanted to squeeze in some real moments. We kept trying to find those moments and discovered that we were not able to do it without making it look forced. We promised ourselves that in our next production, somewhere we

would use "Mama's Caul," a story that is in *Winnetou's Snake Oil Show from Wigwam City*. This story would be a springboard for the show. After all it all began with our mother, the psychic. The show would be about the rejection of the spirituality of our mother and then the realization that not only was that spirituality in us, but in our children and grand-children. The stories of *Reverb-ber-ber-rations* are about our search for and acceptance of our own spirituality.

Reverb-ber-ber-rations is an echo within an echo within an echo, a circle within a circle within a circle. Events are repeated over and over again and each time, like it was the first time because everything old is new again. *Reverb-ber-ber-rations* is a tribute to our mother.

It is a fitting tribute, dealing as it does with (as the title of a subsequent show has it) the persistence of memory across generations: memory, culture, and spirituality embodied and perpetuated through mothers, grandmothers, daughters and granddaughters. The sisters stake their claim, and they do so powerfully – most explicitly in the "statements" that close the play. But they also do so with outrageous (and disarming) humour, and without sentimentality or specious appeals to easily appropriated "Indian authenticity." As Rebecca Schneider has argued, "[m]uch of Spiderwoman's work is related to the issue of 'Indian-ness,' adroitly played in the painful space between the need to claim an authentic Native identity and their awareness of the historical commodification of the signs of that authenticity." (237). In *Reverb-ber-ber-rations* they negotiate that space through their own powerful, disruptive, and undeniable bodily, autobiographical, and genealogical presence as they "drum memories and countermemories onto the stage, layered and folded over upon one another, repetitive, hysterical, rich" (227).

Works Cited:

Ann Haugo. "Circles Upon Circles Upon Circles: Native Women in Theater and Performance." *American Indian Theater in Performance: A Reader*. Ed. Hanay Geiogamah and Jaye T. Darby. Los Angeles: UCLA American Indian Studies Center, 2000. 228-55.

Schneider, Rebecca. "See the Big Show: Spiderwoman Theater Doubling Back." *Acting Out: Feminist Performances*. Ed. Lynda Hart and Peggy Phelan. Ann Arbor: U of Michigan P, 1993. 227-55. Rept. with revisions as "Seeing the Big Show" in Rebecca Schneider, *The Explicit Body in Performance*. London: Routledge, 1997. 153-75.

CHARACTERS

GLORIA
LISA
MURIEL

THE SET

Spiderwoman's vision was to have a space out in the ether, a place where time was diffused, a place where long distances were short, short distances shorter or longer, somewhat like the light of a star flickering through the eons. There is a large backdrop which curves down to the floor. It is a sky blue with an infinite spiral painted on it which becomes a road. There are three legs cut out in the shape of abstract trees which are also painted with gold spirals. USC there is a hammock because the Kuna people use them and also to create that suspension in space. A chime is attached to the hammock to create incidental sound. We were always told that clicks, breezes and sounds were the spirits talking to you. DSL, there is a round tea table with 3 chairs with the Spiderwoman drop, a large drop made of quilts, surrounding it. There is a large Cochiti drum USL with three stools around it. Our drum is treated with great respect. Every night, before we perform, we bless the drum. It is placed on a special blanket, never on the bare floor. The women of Spiderwoman are at an age where we feel we can sit at the drum. Spiderwoman is at an age where it is important to listen to the heartbeat of all our communities and the drum is our heartbeat.

NOTE

Thank you: Paul Ortega for Trail Song.

REVERB-BER-BER-RATIONS

SPIDERWOMAN THEATER
LISA MAYO, GLORIA MIGUEL AND MURIEL MIGUEL

The pre-show music is Pow Wow music, Grand Entry. As the lights and music go down, we hear "Kakik Bali" Balinese music. The Balinese music is interrupted by the Noise Band #1 in the dark. LISA is "playing" an aluminum garbage can, GLORIA, a toy violin and MURIEL, a heavy chain. First, MURIEL throws the heavy chain and yells a continuous sound, the others join in. Out of the sound comes the first words.

GLORIA
Elizabeth!

LISA
What?

GLORIA
What was that?

LISA
Where's Muriel?

MURIEL
I have to pee!

LISA
Not now, not now!

GLORIA
It's under the bed.

LISA
Gloria, help me.

GLORIA
Oh, shut up you old fool!

MURIEL
I have to pee!

LISA
Can't you hold it?

The lights bump on, brightly revealing them. They are surprised and embarrassed to be uncovered in such a private moment. To cover her surprise, LISA taps her garbage can and starts to sing Cole Porter's "Night and Day."

LISA

Like the beat, beat, beat... *(etc.)*

After a couple of lines, MURIEL and GLORIA join in.

TUTTI

Like the tick, tick, tock... *(etc.)*

Just before the chorus, MURIEL begins to exit SL and GLORIA begins to exit USR. LISA begins to cross SR, singing the "Night and Day" chorus.

LISA

Night and Day... *(etc.)*

LISA places her garbage can in front of the DSR wing and continues singing. MURIEL and GLORIA have exited.

Day and night... *(etc.)*

When LISA sings the line about "the roaring traffic's boom," MURIEL and GLORIA echo the "boom" from off-stage. LISA continues to sing "In the silence of my lonely room" etc. Before the last line of the song, there is a scream offstage.

Night and day.

MURIEL enters USL. It is the end of the clowning, time to get back to work. She puts up her guardians. A word about guardians. Each of us choose someone who will keep us safe. These are our protectors. The guardians make the stage a safe place to tell our stories. They are all placed to the four directions. This happens at the same time that LISA speaks.

ELIZABETH INTRO

LISA

Everything old is new again
We all have the gift
Every person has the gift
But we don't always listen to the messages
Don't let your lights go out

MURIEL has finished putting up her last guardian. She crosses to the drum and begins to beat.

I am an elder in my community
Some of the things that I will be saying here tonight are very serious.
We will be at the drum
I work to keep in touch with the six directions
The four directions and up and down

> *LISA points to each direction. As she points, the drum beats for each direction, honour beats.*

I skate on the rim
We are on the rim of limitless dimensions
Good intent attracts psychic protection

> *LISA begins to put up her guardians. GLORIA enters from USR.*

GLORIA INTRO

> *GLORIA crosses SL into wings as if she is running away from something, crosses SR as if she is a macho Indian man, crosses SL as a sexy woman rolling her hips, crosses SR as a grandma then crosses to CS.*

GLORIA
I have many walks
I am here
I have been here for a long time
Planted on earth
I am mother
I am grandmother
I am lover
I am sister
I am daughter
I am granddaughter
I am aunt, grand aunt
I am cousin
I am sister-in-law
I am mother-in-law
I am friend
My heartbeat and blood carry messages
From the past, through me
Into the future

> *GLORIA begins to put up her guardians. MURIEL gets up and crosses to DSC as GLORIA is turning to SL. When LISA has finished putting up her guardians, she sits at the drum and begins to beat.*

MURIEL INTRO

MURIEL

> I never said that
>> I would never say anything like that
>> In fact, I should not even be here
>> Point of fact, I was born into the wrong family
>> If I was born into the right family
>> I would have a name like Leota Lone Dog,
>> Dawn Smoke, Beverly Little Thunder
>> Not Muriel
>> My mother's a witch
>> I didn't say that
>> How embarrassing
> My mother's a witch
>> I didn't say that
>> How embarrassing
>> I knew I should not have come
>> Damn it!

> *LISA stops drumming.*

> Oh, go away
> I do not have any powers

> *GLORIA stops drumming. MURIEL stands SR looking at LISA and GLORIA.*

MAMA'S CAUL

LISA

> She came into the world
> With an extra piece of skin
> Covering her head
> It was a caul

GLORIA

> C-A-U-L. Caul
> And Grandma said that she saved the caul
> And that one day
> She was going to give it back to Mama

> *MURIEL goes to the drum and sits.*

MURIEL

> Grandma kept the caul
> All wrapped up on tissue paper
> In a special box

LISA stands and crosses DSR as she is talking.

LISA
One day she showed it to me

MURIEL and GLORIA start to beat drum.

It looked like a piece of wrinkled brown paper bag
Then she wrapped it up again
And put it away

GLORIA stands and crosses DSL while she is talking.

GLORIA
Grandma said
    Your mother was born with a caul
    So she has strong psychic powers

MURIEL stands and crosses DSC while she is talking.

MURIEL
She can tell the future
She can see through anybody
She can tell the meaning of the symbols
Left by coffee grounds and tea leaves
In the bottom of cups

LISA
When Mama went into a trance
Mama said everything changed in the world

They all turn upstage, touching the air as if they feel the spirits.

TUTTI
Mama said, Mama said, Mama said *(They freeze.)*

GLORIA
(turning downstage) All sound stopped

MURIEL
(turning downstage) It became very quiet

LISA
(turning downstage) So quiet that she could hear the sounds
That had been in the room

TUTTI
Long ago

GLORIA

And she could see the people who had been there too

MURIEL

She could actually see them
Then thoughts would come into her body
(She backs up, gesturing thoughts coming into her body.)

LISA

Then she would tell you what she had received
(GLORIA, then LISA, each repeat the gesture.)

GLORIA

(crossing DSR) All her friends came to her for advice

MURIEL

(crossing SR of GLORIA) And those friends told other friends

LISA

(crossing SL of GLORIA) And so it continued
And Mama became

TUTTI

A wise woman

MURIEL

Grandma said you should be thankful

GLORIA

You have a gifted Mother

LISA

Grandma had the gift too
And all of my mother's children have the gift

> *All begin to give the names of people in the family who have the gift, then walk
> in a large circle. As MURIEL gets to centre stage there is a loud howl. LISA
> and MURIEL look around for the sound. "Trail Song" begins and continues to
> grow louder during GLORIA's monologue and then fades away.*

TRAIL SONG

GLORIA

Do you hear it?

> *MURIEL and LISA nod yes, look at GLORIA, GLORIA bows. MURIEL
> and LISA cross SL to the tea table which is draped with a quilt. A teapot, cups
> and saucers, bread with a knife.*

The coyote is near. The birds they hear. The trees whisper. Do you hear? I feel it. Smell it.

Don't see anything. *(GLORIA steps upstage.)*

I hear. Do you? It's coming! It's coming! Oooh!! *(GLORIA spins in a circle.)*

I don't know what to do. I'm not going to look.

Yes, look. It's here.

I'm not ready yet.

> *During the remainder of the speech, at the tea table in low light, LISA pours hot water into the teapot.*

I don't see anything. Nothing's there. I feel it. Hear it.

I don't see anything

It's leaving and I didn't see it. Coyote saw it. The birds, they heard, the trees whispered.

I felt it. I heard it. It was here. I didn't see it

Do you?

> *MURIEL howls. Lights come up on the tea table.*

TEA PARTY I

> *A mad tea party, apropos of nothing. LISA prepares tea.*

LISA

> Patter, patter briny drops
> On my kerchief drying

GLORIA

> Tea parties, I love tea parties *(GLORIA crosses to the tea table)*

LISA

> Spatter, spatter salty streams
> Down my poor cheeks flying
> Brine enough to 'merse a ham
> Salt enough to build a dam

> *LISA pours a cup for GLORIA and MURIEL and takes MURIEL's for herself.*

MURIEL

> I don't have a cup
> *(to GLORIA)* You took my cup

GLORIA

> No. I didn't

MURIEL
> Yes, you did.

> *MURIEL grabs GLORIA's cup. LISA pours another cup for GLORIA.*

I was blue just as blue as I could be
Say something

GLORIA
> Flowers are dead

LISA
> They are withered

GLORIA
> Dead

LISA
> Withered

GLORIA
Dead

LISA
> Withered

GLORIA & MURIEL
Dead

LISA
Every day was a cloudy day for me. Then good luck came a knocking at my door. Which show should we take?

MURIEL
The other one

LISA
Pourquoi?

MURIEL
Pourquoi, pourquoi, pourquoi?

GLORIA
I should care if the wind blows east or west, we should do the one we do the best.

LISA
We could send the props from our base

MURIEL

Send! Base! Never! I wouldn't trust our props with those people

GLORIA

I should mind if they say it can't be true. Then we should present our lecture demonstration.

LISA

I should smile, that's exactly what I'll do. That would be graceful.

MURIEL

It would not.

GLORIA & LISA

Why?

MURIEL

I would have to think

GLORIA

(laughing) What do you mean?

MURIEL

I should fret if the worst looks like the best. It would be easier to continue the other show.

GLORIA

We could present the same lecture demonstration.

MURIEL

The one where you forgot to come out on stage

LISA

You were between the layers when you were in that place. Skies were gray but they're not gray anymore.

GLORIA

Oh, that day. That was the day I was walking backwards. I was blue, just as blue as I could be.

LISA

Contrary

MURIEL

(to LISA) Just, what did you tell those people?

GLORIA

(to LISA) Say something

LISA moves tea kettle to stove, blows her nose and crosses to centre stage and then to the drum.

LISA
Blew !!

MURIEL
Oh, blew

GLORIA
Blew?

MURIEL
You know as in Blue Moon, Blue Danube, blue note, blue as in wind

GLORIA moves to the drum.

LISA
Brilliant!

MURIEL crosses to SL side of hammock, humming the song "Where or When."

BACKYARDS

MURIEL
I had this tiny, tiny apartment
In the kitchen, the window looked out
Over one yard, another yard and then the third yard was my family's
house and their yard. *(hums "Where or When")*

I would look over this yard and that yard and my family's yard
Sometimes I would see one of my family; my mother, Aunt Ida, Uncle
George, Uncle Frank
Sitting in this garden chair, next to the shed
Staring out over the yard.

MURIEL starts to move DS.

What do you see?
What do you see in the yard?
Grandma, Grandpa, Uncle Davy
Someday you are not going to be there
I will look out my window and I will see you sitting there in that garden
chair, by the shed
Looking out over the yard and you will not be there
What do you see when you look at the yard?

MURIEL crosses DSL.

Sitting in this chair
Pussy willows
Daffodils
A string of coloured lights
When you are not there
What will I see?

MURIEL crosses to stand in front of DSR tree.

I sit in the yard
My daughter looks down at me
Ma, what do you see?
Someday you are not going to be there
I will look out my window
I will see you sitting there
In that garden chair
By the shed
Looking out at the garden and you will not
be there anymore

LISA beats four honour beats. Continues to beat. GLORIA stands and crosses to CS.

SUNDANCE

GLORIA

I'm not dancing in the sundance
I'm dancing in my other world
I'm not dancing in the sundance
I'm dancing in my other world
I'm not part of the ceremony

MURIEL crosses to the drum and joins LISA.

I'm outside watching
My sister, my daughter dance
Feeling the power of the dancers
The eagles, three of them
Swoop down, dip and fly off
The dancers honour them

Four honour beats then they change to a round dance beat. MURIEL stands crosses CS passing GLORIA as she returns to the drum.

MURIEL
>At the sundance
>>I danced for four days
>On the third day, early in the morning
>I looked down and I saw ants
>crawling around my feet
>They crawled up my feet
>Ran up my skirt
>And on my mola
>Were these two ants
>They said I was going to be alright
>They would comfort me and give me strength

>*MURIEL goes back to drum, continues drumming. GLORIA gets up from the drum and crosses DSC.*

GLORIA
>I'm not dancing in the sundance
>>I'm here to touch this ancient earth
>>I'm not dancing in the sundance
>>I'm here to touch this ancient earth
>>I drive off in a van, stop
>I leave the group, walk for a while
>Stand alone, quiet

>*LISA crosses to behind the SR side of the hammock.*

LISA
>>I was on vacation in my polyester pantsuit
>>At the corn dance in Taos, New Mexico
>>Standing behind the rope
>>With the tourists
>Beautiful sunshine day
>Cloudless sky
>I became aware of my heartbeat
>And I could hear my blood
>Surging through my veins

GLORIA
>The black hills sparkle
>>Slate gray, sand coloured
>>Pink, blue, quiet

>*GLORIA crosses DSL.*

MURIEL
>In the sky there was this cloud
>>I looked up into the cloud

and the formation of the cloud
Became my father's face
My father said
It was right I was dancing
He would give me strength
Would watch over me
Take care of me

LISA

I heard a singer from high atop the *pueblo*
And another singer from the opposite direction
Sounds mingled with the echoes all around.

GLORIA

Softly I feel a breeze pass by me
The breeze becomes stronger
I feel them, bodies passing by me
I hear singing way behind one hill
Voices coming from the hills
I feel them passing by me
Bodies passing by me
Wind from their bodies passing by me
And around me

GLORIA crosses to drum.

LISA

Everything changed

LISA crosses DS of hammock.

I was in a house
In the midst of a raging storm
I ran to the back door
I saw the water surging down the hill
Coming toward the house
I had to get out
I ran toward the front
Yelling get out, get out
Get to the rooftops to be rescued

LISA crosses DSC and crosses to the drum. MURIEL crosses DSR.

MURIEL

I started to sway
The medicine man came and hit me on the
Back with his eagle fan
I could feel all the spirits go up

> I heard the wings flapping
> From me, from my body
> From the eagle fan
> I could hear them fluttering around me
> I stopped swaying

MURIEL dances in place to the four directions.

GLORIA

> *(at drum)* The singers came from long ago
> > The dancers came from long ago
> > They greet me, welcome me
> > It's good you're here
> > You belong
> > They understood

LISA crosses to behind hammock with her beater.

LISA

> I got out before the surging water of the flood reached me
> Vibrations from the drums
> Entered my body from the earth on which I stood
> In my purple polyester pantsuit
> Behind the rope with the tourists
> At the corn dance

MURIEL

> What held me up was those two ants
> > on my blouse
> > What held me up
> > Was that cloud father
> > That cloud father held me up

GLORIA

> They sang, they danced

MURIEL

> The men were dancing
> > The men were piercing
> > They were running away from the tree
> > And pulling the thongs out of their chests

LISA

> Hot tears on my cheeks
> > Deafening roar of blood in my ears

GLORIA

> *(singing)* They sang, they danced

> They sang, they danced
> They sang, they danced

MURIEL walks downstage.

MURIEL

A man was piercing from the back
> He was dragging a white buffalo skull
> And he couldn't pierce
> The buffalo skull would not leave him
> He went around and around the circle

GLORIA

I felt uplifted and happy
> I was greeted by the ancestors
> They welcomed me
> I returned to Oberlin

LISA

> The message was clear
As I stood
In my purple polyester pantsuit
Behind the rope with the tourists
At the corn dance
In Taos, New Mexico

MURIEL

He pulled and he pulled and he pulled
> Then they took a little girl
> And put her on the skull
> And he pulled and he pulled that little girl
> That was on the buffalo skull
> And he pulled and he pulled and he pulled
> Around and around the circle
> Until he was set free
> And I said to myself
> I'm really Indian

GLORIA: 3 honour beats.

LISA

The message was clear

GLORIA

Now I knew what I had to do

As they are repeating these last lines, LISA is exiting DSR, GLORIA USR, MURIEL SL.

NOISE BAND #2

They enter with their instruments from the first noise band, they play them accompanied by vocals. It is pure nonsense like the running noise inside one's head.

TEA PARTY II

MURIEL crosses to tea table.

MURIEL
I was blue just as blue as I could be
Say something

GLORIA
Flowers are dead

LISA
They are withered

GLORIA exits USR with her violin and the crosses to tea table.

GLORIA
Dead

LISA places her garbage can SR in front of SR tree and crosses to tea table.

LISA
Withered

GLORIA
Dead
MURIEL & LISA
Withered

GLORIA
Dead

LISA
Withered...
Every day was a cloudy day for me. Then good luck came a knocking at my door. Which show should we take?

MURIEL
The other one

LISA
Why?

GLORIA
I should care if the wind blows east or west, we should do the one we do the best.

LISA
We could send our props from our base

MURIEL
Send! Base! Never! I wouldn't trust our props with those people

GLORIA
I should mind if they say it can't be true. Then we should present our lecture demonstration.

LISA
I should smile, that's exactly what I'll do. That would be graceful.

MURIEL
It would not.

GLORIA & LISA
Why?

MURIEL
I would have to think

GLORIA
(laughing) What do you mean?

MURIEL
I should fret if the worse looks like the best. It would be easier to continue the other show.

GLORIA
We could present the same lecture demonstration.

MURIEL
The one where you forgot to come out on stage

LISA
You were between the layers when you were in that place. Skies were gray but they're not gray anymore.

GLORIA
Oh, that day. That was the day I was walking backwards. I was blue, just as blue as I could be.

LISA
Contrary

MURIEL
Exactly, what did you tell those people?

LISA stands, blows her nose and crosses to CS.

GLORIA
Say something, say something, say something

MURIEL and GLORIA cross to the hammock. GLORIA sits in hammock, MURIEL stands SR of hammock.

AROUND MY NOSE

LISA
What I have to say is not sad or heavy
But it is serious
I have not seen my mother since she left her body
but I feel her presence all the time
She comes to me as a breeze
around my nose and on my hands when I'm working
She is here in this room right now
I feel her
I received a message from her recently
She said that she likes my work,
she likes my husband
And she is happy for my recognition

LISA crosses to tea table.

BUTTERFLY

MURIEL
After the sundance
I was sitting on the bank of a river

GLORIA begins to hum under MURIEL.

It was really quiet
I was sitting by myself
I put my hand out
A butterfly came and sat there
That butterfly talked to me
I talked to the butterfly

That butterfly looked at me
I looked at that butterfly
We stayed this way for about five minutes
Looking at each other
And talking to each other
Then the butterfly flew away

> *MURIEL crosses to tea table. The light focuses on GLORIA who is swinging in the hammock, singing in Kuna.*

GLORIA
After my father's death
I knew I had to return to Nargana
My father's blood, my blood, our blood
He wanted to return to heal open wounds
Rectify his guilt
He died, I returned for him
(singing) Tague *(MURIEL and LISA echo it.)*
The first time in Panama City
Uncle Joe said
You want to find brother
Yes, we walked through the *barrio*
We asked many Kunas
You know Francisco Mojica?
No
Are you from Nargana?
No
You know Francisco Mojica?
No
You know Francisco Mojica?
Yes, he works on the docks
Esmerelda knows where he lives
We met Esmerelda in a café
She gives me an address
We take a cab to the other side of the city
He is working, his wife and small children
are home, my nieces and nephews
Next day, on my way to San Blas
My brother is waiting for me at the airport
(singing) Tague *(MURIEL and LISA echo it.)*
We spend time, we make plans, we talk
Why, why didn't my father send for me
I waited, he never came
When I returned to New York
We lost contact again
My father's blood, my blood, our blood
Twenty years later
I travel again to Panama City

I asked every Kuna I met
At the hotel
Are you from Nargana?
At the palace
Are you from Nargana?
Do you know Francisco Mojica?
At the conference
Are you from Nargana?
Do you know Francisco Mojica?
At the airport
Do you know Francisco Mojica?
Yes, I am married to his daughter
(singing) Tague (MURIEL and LISA echo it.)
When I arrived at the hotel
After I returned from San Blas
A message was left for me from my nieces
The next morning, my family was waiting for me at the airport
They were all there, nieces, nephews, grand nieces, great grand nephew and
my sister-in-law
I spent the last day and evening in Panama City
at the home of my brother with my family.
Through me my brother was connected with his father
My father's blood, my blood, our blood
(singing) Tague (MURIEL and LISA echo it.)

SÉANCE (A STORY OF GREAT DENIAL)

Crossing to GLORIA, MURIEL helps her out of hammock.

MURIEL
Hey, Gloria, remember Rita?

GLORIA
Rita?

LISA
(from the tea table) Rita?

GLORIA
Oh, yeah. Elizabeth's friend

LISA
Muriel, don't tell that story.

MURIEL
My sister was invited to Rita's house

LISA
(*crossing to CS*) Muriel, I don't want you to tell that story.

MURIEL
Rita had a friend who was in trouble. Rita asked this man to do a ceremony.

GLORIA puts her hand over LISA's mouth to keep her from speaking.

GLORIA
We met Elizabeth in the street and she invited us too

MURIEL replaces GLORIA's hand with her hand over LISA's mouth.

MURIEL
We got to Rita's house. There were people sitting on the floor, holding hands

MURIEL & GLORIA
(*to LISA*) Talk, talk. Tell the story

LISA
The man conducting the ceremony began to hyperventilate. (*MURIEL and GLORIA make hyperventilating noises.*) I'd never seen anything like that before. I didn't know what to do.

LISA crosses SR away from MURIEL and GLORIA covering her ears.

GLORIA
A flash of energy went around the circle, entered my body and started to occupy my soul and I went zzgrzzgr... and I pushed it out.

MURIEL
(*crossing SL*) And then it entered me, I calmed it down and pushed it out of my body.

GLORIA
And this fool fell over onto the floor

LISA
(*in a whisper*) I never fell on the floor

MURIEL
(*pulling LISA to the centre*) Everyone got excited. This man who was grunting and hyperventilating (*She hyperventilates.*) didn't know what to do

LISA crosses US, her back to the audience.

GLORIA

Our sister fell over and into the circle. Then she started to talk like Aunt Ida

GLORIA imitates Aunt Ida. MURIEL and GLORIA turn and look at LISA.

LISA

(looking at them) I did?

MURIEL

It occurred to me that I did not trust this man who was grunting and hyperventilating, so I said "Do not touch her!"

MURIEL and GLORIA cross upstage to get LISA and bring her downstage centre.

GLORIA

And we took over the circle. We had no idea what we were doing. Elizabeth was going " eeh, neeh, eeh." *(MURIEL and GLORIA shake her.)* Come back, come back, you old fool!

MURIEL

Then Uncle George came through. Don't ask me how, I knew it was Uncle George, I knew. I said "Uncle George, I'm sorry I can't talk to you right now, we're busy. Come back another time."

GLORIA

Then a newborn baby came through, her voice completely changed and she started to cry. Wahhh, wahhh.

LISA

Oh, this is spooky, I can't stand it. *(She crosses SR.)*

MURIEL

Then she came out of her trance. This man was very upset with us for taking over his ceremony.

MURIEL and GLORIA cross to LISA who is SR.

GLORIA

We picked our sister up off the floor, dusted her off and left.

They cross to tea table, DSL.

LISA

We were never invited back.

TEA PARTY III

Lights come up on tea table, they sit and giggle, repeating words from the previous scene.

GRANDMA

MURIEL stands and crosses to CS with her bullroar. She kneels and swings the bullroar in a circle above her head until it begins to hum. She stops. A bullroar is an instrument of wood or paper suspended on a string. It is swung in the air, creating a humming sound. Bullroars call spirits.

MURIEL
My eyes started to go
Unfocus
I blinked
Somebody came inside
A door opened
This person came in from the back
I was still seeing out of my eyes as Muriel but there was another person inside.
My head split open and fell to the floor
My head split open and fell to the floor
That soft spot
That soft spot opened up
That soft spot separated
My head split open and fell to the floor
My head split open and fell to the floor
My skull separated from the top of my head
All the way to the bottom of my head
And my skull split open
My head split open and fell to the floor
And my grandmother stepped into my head.
My head split open and fell to the floor
My head split open and fell to the floor
Behind my eyes
Behind my eyes my grandmother was stepping into my head
I was still Muriel
The sound of wind whistling through gauze
The sound of my heart
My heart
My heart thumping
The sound of blood whistling through my ears
My head split open and fell to the floor
My head split open and fell to the floor
My grandmother stepped into my head and behind my eyes
The voice

I was still Muriel
The contour of my face changed
Behind my eyes were my grandmother
I was still Muriel
The voice, the voice, the voice
The voice that went through the gauze and the blood and the heart
thumping
The sound of my heart through the gauze
The voice, the voice, the voice I heard from behind my eyes changed
This voice changed
My head split open and fell to the floor
My head split open and fell to the floor
My whole face became another face
My voice became different
I changed
My head split open and fell to the floor
My head split open and fell to the floor
And that was the day
My head split open and fell to the floor and my grandmother came inside.

TEA PARTY IV

GLORIA
(out of the darkness) Flowers are dead!

    The lights come on at the tea table.

LISA
    Withered

GLORIA
    Dead

LISA
    Withered

GLORIA
    Dead

LISA & MURIEL
    Withered

LISA
    Every day was a cloudy day for me. Then good luck came a knocking at my
    door

GLORIA
I should care if the wind blows East or West.

LISA
I should smile. That is exactly what I'll do. That would be graceful.

MURIEL
It would not.

GLORIA & LISA
Why?

MURIEL
I would have to think

GLORIA and LISA laugh.

GLORIA
What do you mean?

GLORIA, then MURIEL then LISA shiver. Then their heads fall to the table.

BLUE SKIES (TRANCE)

LISA
(finding harmony) Blue... ue... ue

TUTTI
Blue... ue... ue. *(They begin to sing Irving Berlin's "Blue Skies."*

After a line, GLORIA goes to levitate out of her chair, MURIEL pulls her back down.

"nothin' but blue skies..." *(etc.)*

GLORIA goes to levitate out of her chair, MURIEL pulls her back down.

"bluebirds singin'..." *(etc.)*

GLORIA goes to levitate out of her chair, MURIEL pulls her back down.

"nothin' but bluebirds..." *(etc.)*

GLORIA
(crosses to CS) "Never saw..." *(etc.)*

LISA and MURIEL follow GLORIA to CS.

TUTTI
"never saw..." *(etc.)*

> *They do a dance. All turn to SL. They put their hands on each others' waists and paw the ground with their right feet (slew foot). They continue to sing.*

"my how they fly..." *(etc.)*

> *Two quick steps with their right feet and they put their arms out and fly in a circle. They finish the song. MURIEL's right hand joins LISA's then GLORIA's hand. They pivot counterclockwise to face US, holding hands. GLORIA backs up to SR, playing an imaginary trombone and LISA and MURIEL dance off SL. Indigo-coloured light comes up, then lights CS. GLORIA is at CS.*

PANAMA CITY

GLORIA
Two thousand people killed in Panama City. November 1989, 110 degrees

> *She crosses US to hammock, MURIEL begins to drum.*

I'm in Panama City with the First International Conference against Aggression in Central America.
I'm standing on a grandstand, viewing a parade; a show of strength.
The people are preparing to fight and die for their land and Kuna Yalla.

> *She crosses DS.*

The first wave, a military band, soldiers dressed in camouflage.
Then more soldiers with banners, sailors carrying bayonets; young men and woman wearing straw hats and red bandanas carrying guns.
Boys and girls with bamboo sticks, old men and woman carrying bamboo barricades.
They were prepared to fight the US Army Southern Command invasion.

> *She covers her mouth.*

Three AM the next morning
I step out on the balcony of my hotel room
Panama is steaming hot, the city is still

> *She walks US backwards.*

I have a vision
Toward the horizon, I see red flames leaping up,
Slowly rising, rising until it engulfs the entire sky.
Dec 1989
Two thousand people killed in Panama City.

There is a silent scream, the lights go to indigo, then a blackout as GLORIA exits.

VINCENT

LISA enters SR, singing.

LISA
Hey, hey, dootenday, dootenday, dootenday
Hey, hey, dootenday, dootenday, dootenday

MURIEL and GLORIA echo the song. LISA sings the opening "Starry, starry night" line of the chorus of the Don McLean song, "Vincent."

(speaking) The world of the five senses is the world of illusion *(She bangs on the garbage can and the SR tree with her beater.)* Hey, hey, dootenday, dootenday, dootenday
Reality cannot be seen with the physical eye.

She sings from the chorus of "Vincent."

The responsibility of creators; people who make things, build, mould and shape things is to
Interpenetrate the layers
Bring information between the layers

She sings a bit of the chorus from "Vincent."

Going back into the before to use for the future.

She crosses to the hammock, with only indigo light on her, she sits in the hammock facing US and she swings, singing.

Hey, hey, dootenday, dootenday, dootenday
Hey, hey, dootenday, dootenday, dootenday

She sings from the last verse and the chorus of "Vincent." The lights fade to black.

NOISE BAND #3

GLORIA
Elizabeth!

LISA
What?

GLORIA
What was that?

LISA
Where's Muriel?

MURIEL
I gotta pee

LISA
Not now

MURIEL
I gotta go to the bathroom

GLORIA
It's under the bed

MURIEL
What was that?

LISA
It was the cat

TUTTI
Ooohhhh!

> *The lights come up and they are caught with their instruments in their hands.
> LISA puts her garbage can SR and crosses to drum. GLORIA hangs up her hat
> on the USR tree and crosses to drum. MURIEL drags her chain SL and crosses
> to drum and kneels. They begin to drum, MURIEL stands, they send for the
> first time from the drum. (This is another occurrence where our mother talked
> about good energy and thoughts in a way of prevention. She called it "sending.")
> LISA and GLORIA continue to drum.*

MURIEL
(singing) This is a song for my mother
This is a song for my mothers
This is a song to release the pain, the shame, the secrets

> *LISA and GLORIA stop drumming.*

BOWL DANCE ZUNIGA

> *These represent large bold women with huge hands and feet. Hands and feet that
> can take care of anything. They cross to CS, facing DS they rock side to side.
> They turn to the four directions, they face DS and send #2. They create the*

bowl, grind corn, have a baby, rock the baby, eagles. LISA and GLORIA circle in clockwise motion, GLORIA leading. MURIEL sings DSL same song under scene.

LISA

My mother is my sister
My aunt is my mother
My mother is my mother
My sister is my sister
My sister is my mother

LISA and GLORIA reverse direction, LISA leading.

GLORIA

I care. When you were born, every inch of my body pulsated with joy.
As you grew, I nourished you
We shared our wisdom
I wept when you wept
Went crazy helping you to solve problems
many times, I forgot about myself. My heart hurts, why do you hate me?

GLORIA exits USR and enters wearing a Kuna shawl on her head. She crosses to the hammock. MURIEL and LISA remove their hats, hang them on the trees and cross up to the hammock.

STATEMENTS

LISA

I am a communicator
I have taken the responsibility to interpenetrate the layers
To bring messages between the layers to heal.
We heal with our hands
We heal with our hearts
We make each other laugh
We are the universe

GLORIA

We are born, we die
We are each in possession of great power
in one lifetime
Some we use, some we abuse
Some has given us wisdom

MURIEL

I am an Indian woman
I am proud of the woman that came before me
I am claiming the wisdom of the woman in my family

I am a woman with two daughters, a granddaughter
I am a woman with a woman lover
I am here now
I am saying this now because to deny these events about me and my life
Would be to deny my children

Blackout.

The end.

PRINCESS POCAHONTAS AND THE BLUE SPOTS

MONIQUE MOJICA

MONIQUE MOJICA

INTRODUCTION TO *PRINCESS POCAHONTAS* AND THE BLUE SPOTS

Monique Mojica is a Kuna and Rappahannock actor and playwright based in Toronto. She began training at the age of three and belongs to the second generation spun directly from the web of New York's Spiderwoman Theater. Her theatre credits include acting in the premiere productions of Florence Gibson's *Home is My Road*, Djanet Sears' *The Adventures of a Black Girl in Search of God*, Drew Hayden Taylor's *Sucker Falls*, Tomson Highway's *The Rez Sisters* and Daniel David Moses and Jim Millan's *Red River*. She also played Ariel in Skylight Theatre's *The Tempest*, the title role in the Theatre Passe Muraille production of *Jessica*, by Maria Campbell and Linda Griffiths, and the solo role in the National Arts Centre/Globe Theatre co-production of Floyd Favel's one-woman play, *Governor of the Dew*. Her film and television credits include appearances in "The Outer Limits," "Nikita," "Traders," "The Third Miracle," "The Rez," and "Conspiracy of Silence," and she received a Best Supporting Actress nomination from the First Americans in the Arts for her role as Grandma Builds-the-Fire in Sherman Alexie's "Smoke Signals." Together with Jani Lauzon and Michelle St. John she is a founding member of Turtle Gals Performance Ensemble, a Native women's company which produced its first full-length play, *The Scrubbing Project*, in the Fall of 2002, co-produced by Native Earth Performing Arts in association with Factory Theatre.

Monique has also worked and written on Native and other issues across the Americas, publishing in the *Aboriginal Voices Magazine, Toronto Pow Wow Newspaper, The Runner, Gatherings III*, and *Beyond the Pale: Dramatic Writing from First Nations Writers and Writers of Colour*. She was guest editor of *Canadian Theatre Review*'s special Native Theatre issue (Fall 1991). Her writings include the television script, "Positively Native" (1990); the radio play *Birdwoman and the Suffragettes* (1991) a revisiting of the widespread honouring by suffragettes and others of Sacajawea, the trusty little Indian Guide to the 1804-6 Lewis and Clarke expedition across America, the one-act play *A Fast Growing Mold Bitter as Shame* (1995); and the play published here, also adapted for CBC Radio, *Princess Pocahontas and the Blue Spots* (1990), an examination of the histories, myths, and stereotypes of First Nations and mixed-blood women across the Americas, from Virginia's Pocahontas to Mexico's La Malinche, from Peru's Woman of the Puna to the Métis women in the Canadian west, from Princess Buttered-on-Both-Sides to the Cigar Store Squaw.

The first full production of *Princess Pocahontas* was in 1990 at the Theatre Passe Muraille Backspace in a co-production with Nightwood Theatre under the direction of Muriel Miguel, with dramaturgy by Djanet Sears and Kate Lushington, featuring Monique Mojica with Alejandra Nuñez as musician/composer. Weaving together past and present, north and south, history, documentary, and myth, the play's transformational dramaturgy constitutes at once a scathing satirical critique of "Captain Whiteman" and colonization, a celebration of Native women as "the hoop of the nation," and a rousing intertextual call for solidarity, a call to arms to all women "word warriors" (quoting Paula Gunn Allen) to claim (with Gloria Anzaldúa), "the freedom to carve and chisel my own face, to staunch the bleeding with ashes, to fashion my own gods out of my entrails." The play begins with dislocation—"no map, no trail, no footprint, no way home"—with "nowhere to set my feet, no place to stand." But "throwing a lifeline across the generations" it moves steadily through memory towards remembering, and ultimately to reawakening. "Wake up! There's work to be done!/We're here."

CHARACTERS

ACTOR 1

PRINCESS BUTTERED-ON-BOTH-SIDES: One of the many faces of the Trickster, Coyote. She is a contestant in the Miss North American Indian Beauty Pageant and she is stuck in the talent segment.

CONTEMPORARY WOMAN #1: A modern, Native woman on a journey to recover the history of her grandmothers as a tool towards her own healing.

MALINCHE: A Nahuatl woman who was the interpreter and strategist for the Spanish conquistador, Hernán Cortez. She was also his mistress and bore him one son. Throughout Mexico and much of Latin America, she is referred to as "La Chingada" – the fucked one, and her name is synonymous with traitor. In some legends, Malinche turns into a volcano when Cortez leaves Mexico.

STORYBOOK POCAHONTAS: The little Indian Princess from the picture books, friend of the settlers, in love with the Captain, comes complete with her savage-Indian-Chief father.

POCAHONTAS/LADY REBECCA/MATOAKA: The three names of Pocahontas, a Powhatan woman whose father was the chief of the Powhatan Confederacy at the time of the Jamestown Colony in Virginia. She is best known for saving the life of Captain John Smith when she was eleven years old, and for saving the colonists from starvation. The legendary Pocahontas of the ballads and romantic poetry has become the archetype of the "good Indian:" one who aids and abets white men. Lady Rebecca was what she was named when she was Christianized and married John Roffe. Matoaka was her name as a child.

DEITY/WOMAN OF THE PUNA/VIRGIN: Written for the female deities who have been usurped by the Catholic church and turned into virgins. Deity's name could be Ñusta Huillac, Tonatzin, Coyolahuaxqui or many others. Woman of the Puna was a Quechua woman who along with others, refused to become Christianized, left the Spanish court of colonial Peru and fled to the high tablelands of the Andes called the puna where they lived without men. This area is still considered woman's territory. In this tradition there were also virgin priestesses who were married to the sun. *La Virgen del Carmen* (*La Tirana*), and *La Virgen de Guadelupe* are only two of the Catholic virgins to whom devotion was built upon already existing reverence to female deities and leaders.

MARIE/MARGARET/MADELAINE: Three faces out of the hordes of Cree and Metis women who portaged across Canada with white men on their backs and were then systemically discarded.

CIGAR STORE SQUAW: Princess Buttered-on-Both-Sides embodies another well-known and accepted icon of Native Women.

SPIRIT-ANIMAL: The one who travels with you; she guides, guards and protects.

ACTOR 2

HOST: The beauty pageant M.C.; a cross between Bert Parks and a sleazy Latin band leader.

THE BLUE SPOTS: The "doo-wop" girls who back up Princess Pocahontas and her band.

CONTEMPORARY WOMAN #2: A modern Chilean-born woman who carries her history of resistance from the survival of the Andean women, to the "Amanda" guerrillas to her own story as a refugee. As a woman of the Americas, she accompanies Contemporary Woman #1 on her journey.

TROUBADOUR: The entertainer in the Elizabethan court upon Pocahontas' arrival in England.

CEREMONY: The personification of the puberty ritual. She is the instructions of the grandmothers, she is the fast, she is the songs, she is the dance, she is the paint, she is the sacred blood, she is the initiation.

THE MAN: The husband, the lover, the friend, the "brother" in the struggle whose oppression is fully understood but whom the women end up carrying anyway.

SPIRIT-SISTER: A helper, a guide, an equal on the other side.

MUSICIAN: Plays sampofias, guitar, tiple, drums, pennywhistle, ocarinas, and birimbao as well as a variety of small percussion instruments and vocals.

NOTE ON STRUCTURE, TRANSFORMATIONS AND TRANSFIGURATIONS

There are 13 transformations, one for each moon in the lunar year. These transformations can sometimes be very sudden or they can linger and evolve gradually.

There are 4 sections where there is a transfiguration of three women or entities who are one.

This is the inherent structure of the play, it is not a structure that was imposed on the story, but rather, a structure that was informed by the characters. This means that I didn't realize that I had a "structure" until I went through the process of preparing the manuscript for publication. I learned a lot about trusting my own way of working.

13 moons, 4 directions; it is not a linear structure but it is the form and the basis from which these stories must be told.

SET DESCRIPTION

The theme of the set, costumes and props is also transformation; objects and set pieces appear to be one thing but become something else, they can be turned inside-out to reveal another reality. The pile of cloth becomes a garment, a canal, a volcano; the gilded portrait frame is pulled away from the wall where it has been camouflaged in the foliage of the tree and the rainforest, the pyramid becomes the staircase of a Vegas-style show; and the limbs of the tree of life can be a playground or a place from which to hang oneself.

The tree stands upstage right and is draped in layers of fabric in luxurious textures, there is a platform at the crotch of the tree and it is hollow. At the foot of the tree are placed an enamel basin, cup and pitcher of water, a small pot of red paint, a bucket of sand, and a bag of popcorn. There is a pyramid upstage left with stairs facing both downstage and stage right. A pole downstage left is pegged for climbing and decorated with the faces and clothing of the Métis women. At the base of the pole is an enamel basin of water. At the beginning of the show the stage is bare except for these things and the volcano/cloth placed downstage left and draped along the circle which is centre stage and painted to look like a copper disk. At the end of the show the stage is littered with debris from the stories that are told.

NOTE

An earlier version of *Princess Pocahontas and the Blue Spots* was published in *Canadian Theatre Review* 64 (Fall 1990): 66-77.

PRINCESS POCAHONTAS AND THE BLUE SPOTS

MONIQUE MOJICA

TRANSFORMATION 1
500 YEARS OF THE MISS NORTH AMERICAN INDIAN BEAUTY PAGEANT

The stage is empty. As the lights go to black, CONTEMPORARY WOMAN #2 jumps into spotlight as beauty pageant HOST.

HOST
Good evening ladies and gentlemen, and children of all ages and welcome to the 498th annual – count them – that's nearly 500 years of the *Miss North American Indian Beauty Pageant!* This is George Pepe Flaco Columbus Cartier da Gama Smith, but you can call me Bob, coming to you live from the Indian Princess Hall of Fame.

Crosses centre.

Our first contestant in the Miss North American Indian Beauty pageant, from her home in the deep green forest on the other side of the mountain, by the shores of the silver sea – Princess Buttered-on-Both-Sides!!

HOST begins to "oooo" the first line from the "Indian Love Call" which is echoed by PRINCESS BUTTERED-ON-BOTH-SIDES as she enters dressed in a white "buckskin" dress and carrying an oversized ear of corn. As she weaves through audience, she offers them handfuls of cornnuts from the plastic bag she bought them in.

PRINCESS BUTTERED-ON-BOTH-SIDES
Corn... Corn... Corn... Corn...

The music is a mixture of Hollywood tom-toms, the "Indian Love Call," "The Good, the Bad and the Ugly" and the "Mazola" commercial.

(to audience) Excuse me, which way is east? *(after a member of the audience answers)* Many, many thanks.

PRINCESS BUTTERED-ON-BOTH-SIDES tosses cornnuts to the four directions and places her ear to the earth, she rises, arms and face lifted to the heavens in a classic "spiritual" Hollywood Indian pose.

(pointing to the ear of corn) Corn.

(pointing to herself) Maiden. For the talent segment of the Miss North American Indian Beauty Pageant, I shall dance for you, in savage splendour,

the "Dance of the Sacrificial Corn Maiden," and proceed to hurl myself over the precipice, all for the loss of my one true love, CAPTAIN JOHN WHITEMAN. *(swoons)*

> *Music starts up. The production number is from the movie "Rosemarie" – corn celebration – played on pan pipes with vocalized cartoon sound effects. PRINCESS BUTTERED-ON-BOTH-SIDES performs a Hollywood "Injun dance."*

(teetering on the edge of the "precipice" or stage) OH, that's Niagara Falls down there, but I just can't live without him!

> *Teeters but is saved by the music beginning again. PRINCESS BUTTERED-ON-BOTH-SIDES dances again, removes the buckskin dress and runs to the edge of the precipice once more. She jumps.*

GERONIMOOOOOOOOO!!!!!

TRANSFORMATION 2
ON THE PRECIPICE

> *Scuttling around circle, on hands and knees, searching.*

CONTEMPORARY WOMAN #1
No map, no trail, no footprint, no way home
only darkness, a cold wind whistling by my ears.
The only light comes from the stars.
Nowhere to set my feet.
no place to stand. *(rising)*
No map, no trail, no footprint, no way home.

> *Sees basin of water; brings it to centre.*

He said, "It's time for the women to pick up their medicine in order for the people to continue." *(washes hands, arms)*

She asked him, "What is the women's medicine?" The only answer he found was, "The women are the medicine, so we must heal the women."[1]

> *Washes from basin head, arms, legs, feet. Tiple theme begins.*

> *Squatting over basin in a birthing position, she lifts a newborn from between her legs, holding baby in front of her, she rises.*

---

[1] Art Soloman, from a speech at the Native Canadian Centre of Toronto, Fall 1989.

When I was born, the umbilical cord was wrapped around my neck and my face was blue.
When I was born, my mother turned me over to check for the blue spot at the base of the spine – the sign of Indian blood.
When my child was born, after counting the fingers and the toes, I turned it over to check for the blue spot at the base of the spine.
Even among the half-breeds, it's one of the last things to go.

CONTEMPORARY WOMAN #2
Princess, Princess!

CONTEMPORARY WOMAN #1
Princess, Princess!

CONTEMPORARY WOMAN #2
Princess, Princess Amazon Queen.
Show me your royal blood,
Is it blue? Is it green?
Dried and brown five centuries old,
singed and baked and
covered with mould?

Princess, priestess Caribe Queen,
What are you selling today,
Is it corn, tobacco, beans?
Snake oil or a beaver hat.
Horse liniment,
you can't beat that!

Princess, Princess, calendar girl,
Redskin temptress, Indian pearl.
Waiting by the water
for a white man to save.
She's a savage now remember –
Can't behave!

CONTEMPORARY WOMAN #1
(on tape, starts on "singed") Le le le le le
         le le le le le le le le
one little, two little, three little
no sound no flutter
no movement.

(tape, on "liniment", singing)
ee gih beh bah neh boh eh boh bua
dah leh mah leh yeh
"I am a Starboy
I shoot through the night
In a rocket of silver
That sails on light."[2]
(tape, on "she's a savage")
"I am not your Princess...
I am only willing to tell you
how to make fry bread."[3]
(singing) My black jack daisy
weh nenh yah henh yoh
She got mad at me because
I said hello.
(speaking) "...the concept of betraying
one's race through sex and sexual
politics is as common as corn."[4]

[2] Excerpt from *Star Boy* by Robert Priest and Bongo Herbert, G'tel Records & Tapes, 1984.
[3] Chrystos, from *Not Vanishing*, Press Gang, 1988.
[4] Cherríe Moraga, from *Loving in the War Years*, South End Press, 1983.

CONTEMPORARY WOMAN #2
Princess, Princess!

CONTEMPORARY WOMAN #1
Princess, Princess!

CONTEMPORARY WOMAN #1 & #2
Are you a real Indian Princess?

> *CONTEMPORARY WOMAN #1 & #2 stand together downstage centre, extend their hands, arms feeling the shift in air. They breathe energy downstage, upstage, stage left and stage right until the breath becomes sound and they separate into spirals in opposite directions. CONTEMPORARY WOMAN #2 exits.*

TRANSFORMATION 3
INVOCATION

> *As each woman, group of women or spirit is named, she is placed at each of the four directions in the following order: (counterclockwise) East, North, West, South. MALINCHE also arrives from the South and overtakes CONTEMPORARY WOMAN #1. The name becomes MALINCHE's wail as she is cursed.*

CONTEMPORARY WOMAN #1
Pocahontas.
The women who birthed the Métis.
(surprise) Coyote?
The women of the Puna.

> *Ocarina music, on tape.*

Malinche... Malinche? MALINCHE!!

CONTEMPORARY WOMAN #2
Puta! Chingada! Cabrona! India de mierda!
Hija de tu mala madre! Maldita Malinche!

> *She curses and spits at MALINCHE, exits to instruments.*

> *CONTEMPORARY WOMAN #1 receives each curse as a wound, she furiously hurls herself onto the heap of cloth downstage left and speaks as MALINCHE.*

MALINCHE
They say it was me betrayed my people. It was they betrayed me!

MUSICIAN
(singing with tape) Santa Maria, Santa Maria, Santa Malinche.

MALINCHE crawls backwards on her stomach; picks up cloth/volcano and rises to her knees.

MALINCHE
You spit my name. My name is Malinali. Not Doña Marina, not Malinche, *La Chingada!* The fucked one! *(rises with cloth/volcano as a skirt)* What is my curse? *(runs stage right)* My blood cursed you with your broad face? *(whips cloth causing it to billow, volcano now is at waist height)* Eyes set wide apart? Black hair? Your wide square feet? Or the blue spot you wear on your butt when you're born? *(backs up, stamping feet rhythmically)* You are the child planted in me by Hernán Cortez who begins the bastard race, born from *La Chingada!* You deny me? *(whips volcano, throws it over her head, emerges from under it, downstage right)* I wear the face of Malinali Tenepat. I see this face reflected in the mirror. Mirror my eyes reflecting back at me. Reflecting words. It is my words he wants you see... I am the only one can speak to the Maya, to the Mexica. It is my words that are of value. *(moves downstage right, crosses herself, kneeling with head bowed)* I am christened Doña Marina. They call me "Princess." I am a gift, claimed as value by this man in metal. I can change the words. I have power. Now I ride at the side of Cortez, the lady of the conquistador. Smart woman. I am a strategist. Dangerous woman. *(walking backwards swirling volcano/cloth with feet, sits upstage left)*

MUSICIAN
(singing) Santa Maria,
Santa Marina,
Santa Malinche.
Hija de puta, traidora.

MALINCHE
(on "Marina," gathering edges of volcano/cloth)
On this shell I sit, holding the net,
keeping the balance, watching,
hearing everything–

MUSICIAN
(shouts) Traitor! Whore!

MALINCHE
–and they hardly see me. Look at them, The Spaniards all wear armour and clothing that's heavy and dark and they sweat in their heavy clothes and their hairy bodies.

Rises, picks up volcano/cloth, holds it like a dress against her body.

This morning I told those girls who help me dress to braid my hair tightly, and coil it around my head like two snakes. I didn't want any pieces falling in my face, nothing to distract me. I knew I'd have to listen very hard.

Picks up volcano/cloth, holding it by the hoop at chest level, she walks up ramp to pyramid upstage left.

MUSICIAN
(singing, dissonant) Santa Maria, Santa Marina, Santa Malinche...

MALINCHE
(retreats backwards up ramp upstage left, then whips cloth/volcano, so it writhes)
What is that they say about me? That I opened my legs to the whole
conquering Spanish army? They were already here. I was a gift. Passed on.
Handed on. Like so many pounds of gold bullion, dragged out of the earth,
dragged out of the treasure rooms of Moctezuma. Stolen! Bound! Caught!
Trapped!

> *Hands volcano to MUSICIAN who secures it to the side of the set so that it
> cascades down onto the stage. MALINCHE scrambles up pyramid, crawls
> haltingly down other side.*

The night called *La Noche Triste*. We have to leave Tenochtitlan. Moctezuma
and his children are dead. Whose sad night is it? The bridge has to be
carried. Forty men. And the noise.... They've found us out, that we are
leaving. *(running behind tree and down the stage right ramp)* Cortez and I go
over first and then the rest of them. *(rolling underneath the volcano/cloth,
punching and flailing)* And the screaming and the horses falling in the canals
and we have to run. *(emerging through slit in volcano/cloth to standing)* I look
back, I see the canals piled high with bodies – bodies piled so high. *(arching
spine and rolling onto cloth on floor, following sinking gold)* They are crossed by
climbing over the bodies, as the gold sinks to the bottom of the canals. *(as
if wiping blood from her hands)* It didn't matter how brave the warriors nor
how strong the weapons. You say it was me betrayed my people, but it was
they betrayed me!

MUSICIAN
(singing, as MALINCHE climbs the pyramid nearly to the top and takes volcano)
Puta, chingada, cabrona, India de mierda, hija de tu mala madre, maldita Malinche.

MALINCHE
(sits at top of pyramid, whipping volcano into raging flows of lava) I spit, burn
and char the earth. A net of veins binding me to you as I am bound to this
piece of earth. So bound. A volcano, this woman. *(stands, volcano/cloth at
shoulder level)* I turn to tree whose branches drip bleeding flowers. Bleed
into this piece of earth where I grow, mix with volcanic ash and produce
fertile soil. Born from the earth, fed with my blood, anything alive here is
alive because I stayed alive! I turn to wind. You hear my Llorona's wail
screaming across the desert. Lost in the rain forest, you remember –
MALINCHE!!

> *She wails, raising the volcano/cloth up over her head.*

TRANSFORMATION 4
LIVE FROM TEE PEE TOWN

*From underneath volcano/cloth MUSICIAN joins PRINCESS
BUTTERED-ON-BOTH-SIDES as the SACRIFICIAL VIRGIN,
hooking her arms through VIRGIN's from behind. All hand movements are
MUSICIAN's As they rise from within the volcano, only VIRGIN's face is seen
lip-syncing as MUSICIAN's voice transforms the "wail" into Ima Sumac's, "Las
Virgenes del Sol," sung in operatic style. Then becomes the voice of live, bubbling
lava deep within the volcano.*

MUSICIAN
Um woka, woka, woka.... Um woka, woka, woka...

VIRGIN
Oh – oh.

MUSICIAN
Um woka, woka.... Um woka, woka.... JUMP!

VIRGIN
NO!

MUSICIAN
Um woka, woka.... Um woka, woka... *(mimes diving motion)*

VIRGIN
Have you got the wrong virgin!

MUSICIAN
Um woka, woka.... JUMP NOW!

VIRGIN
I think I left something on the stove.

    VIRGIN exits with volcano leaving MUSICIAN crouched and exposed.

MUSICIAN
Um woka, woka, woka... *(realizing she is exposed, begins her 50s style "doo wops")*
Boom ba boom ba – ba boom... ba boom ba – ba boom...

    *Flourishing to an entrance cue for PRINCESS BUTTERED-ON-BOTH-
SIDES, who does not enter.*

PRINCESS BUTTERED-ON-BOTH-SIDES
(loud stage whisper, off-stage) NOT YET!

    MUSICIAN nervously repeats "doo wops" with entrance cue; no entrance.

(loud stage whisper; off-stage) It's the velcro!

MUSICIAN *repeats doo wop intro, confidently now, with entrance cue.*

(show-biz entrance with hand-held mike) Live from Tee Pee Town... it's Princess Pocahontas and the Blue Spots!

BLUE SPOTS
Shoo bee, doo bee, wa!

PRINCESS BUTTERED-ON-BOTH-SIDES
(a la Marilyn Monroe) Way ya hiya!

> *Descends pyramid and they sing with a drawling country and western feel, the BLUE SPOTS doo-wopping for all they are worth.*

Captain Whiteman, I would pledge my life to you
Captain Whiteman, I would defy my father too.
I pledge to aid and to save,
I'll protect you to my grave.
Oh Captain Whiteman, you're the cheese in my fondue.

Captain Whiteman for you, I will convert,
Captain Whiteman, all my pagan gods are dirt.
If I'm savage don't despise me,
'cause I'll let you civilize me.
Oh Captain Whiteman, I'm your buckskin-clad dessert.

Although you may be hairy,
I love you so-oo,
You're the cutest guy I'll ever see.
You smell a little funny,
But don't you worry, honey,
come live with me in my tee pee.

Captain Whiteman, I'm a little Indian maid,
Captain Whiteman, with a long ebony braid.
Please don't let my dark complexion
Inhibit your affection.
Be my muffin, I'll be your marmalade.
Be my muffin, I'll be your marmalade.
Be my muffin, I'll be your marmalade.
Way ya hey yo.

> *During muffin refrain, the BLUE SPOTS run up centre aisle, screaming.*

BLUE SPOTS
¡Capitan! ¡Capitan! ¡No te vayas, Capitan! Don't leave me!

PRINCESS BUTTERED-ON-BOTH-SIDES

May you always walk in beauty, my dear sister.
Now, was that not spiritual? Many, many thanks, you have made my heart
soar like the noble rabbit. My heart, your heart, bunny heart one heart.
Um hmm.
I would like us to be friends, real good friends, you know what I mean?
I mean like blood brothers, and blood sisters.
Um hm.
I have many names. My first name was Matoaka. Some people call me Lady
Rebecca, but everyone knows the little Indian Princess, Pocahontas, who
saved the life of Captain John Smith.

TRANSFORMATION 5
STORYBOOK POCAHONTAS

Four gestures, once through no words, once with sounds, once with text.

STORYBOOK POCAHONTAS

1) NO! (hands overhead, on knees) He's so brave his eyes are so blue, his hair is
so blond and I like the way he walks.
2) DON'T! (arms cradling Captain's head) Mash his brain out! I don't want to
see his brains all running down the side of this stone.
3) STOP! (in the name of love) I think I love him.
4) Oooh (swooning, hands at cheeks) He's so cute.

Removes Princess dress, stands downstage right.

CONTEMPORARY WOMAN #1

(to audience) Where was her mother?

TRANSFORMATION 6
POCAHONTAS/LADY REBECCA/
MATOAKA TRANSFIGURATION

TROUBADOUR

(complete with Robin Hood hat, singing)
In 1607 the English came sailing across the ocean–
In the name of their virgin queen,
they called this land Virginia-O.

STORYBOOK POCAHONTAS joins in.

In the gloom and silence of the dark and impenetrable forest
They might all have died if it had not been for the Indian Princess
Pocahontas-O.

Her father was a stem, old chief, Powhatan was his name-O
Sweet and pretty was Pocahontas

As he was ugly and cruel-O.

Then into her village strode a man with steps so brave and sure
Said he in a deep voice like a God's
"My name is Captain John Smith-O

(chorus)
Heigh-ho wiggle-waggle wigwam wampum,
    roly-poly papoose tom-tom,
        tomahawk squaw.

LADY REBECCA
How camst I here? I know how to walk, I know how to stand, I know how
to incline my head, how to bow. *(grand curtsy)* My heart is on the ground!

STORYBOOK POCAHONTAS & TROUBADOUR
The fiendish red men they did deem that John Smith he must die-O
    They placed his head upon a stone,
        and raised their tomahawks high-O.

Then from the crowd, there rushed a girl, the maiden Pocahontas
    Shielding his head with her own,
        crying save him save the Paleface-O.

(chorus)
Heigh-ho wiggle-waggle wigwam wampum,
    roly-poly papoose tom-tom,
        tomahawk squaw.

> *LADY REBECCA crosses to wall stage right, swings out larger-than-life gilded
> portrait frame which contains her lace ruff, cuffs and velvet hat with an ostrich
> plume.*

LADY REBECCA
How camst I to be caught, stuck, girdled? I'll tell you Captain, John Smith:
"You did promise Powhatan that what was yours should be his, and he the
like to you; you called him father. And fear you here I should call you
father? I tell you then, I will, and you shall call me child, and so I will be
forever and ever your countryman. They did tell us always (that) you were
dead, and I knew no other until I came to Plymouth. Yet Powhatan did
seek to know the truth, because your countrymen will lie much."[5]

TROUBADOUR
(singing) When Pocahontas went to see her friend John Smith in Jamestown
    She'd run and cartwheel with the boys,
        though she be naked underneath it-O.

---

[5] Quote attributed to Pocahontas (we have no way of knowing if these words actually
passed her lips).

John Smith said of the Indian girls "I could have done what I listed"-O
"All these nymphs more tormented me, crying 'Love you not me?
Love you not me?'"[6]

During these verses LADY REBECCA caresses clothing in frame.

LADY REBECCA

Now see you here, I wear the clothes of an Englishwoman and will disturb
you less when I walk. Here, I am Princess and Non Pareil of Virginia. I am
Lady Rebecca. For me the Queen holds audience. Treachery, Captain, I was
kidnapped!

TROUBADOUR

(singing) There chanc'd to be in Jamestown a planter named John Rolfe-O
His heart was touched by Pocahontas he claimed her for his bride-y-O.

LADY REBECCA

John, my husband, is a businessman, a merchant and a tobacco planter.
I know how to grow tobacco, it is our sacred tobacco plant.

TROUBADOUR

(singing and marching with drum; a funeral dirge)
Yo sangro por ti... yo sangro por ti...
sangro... sangro... sangro...

Continues under Apostle's Creed: live voice and drum layered over taped voices.

*LADY REBECCA fitting neck and wrists into collar and cuffs with much
resistance as if being put into stocks and pillory; fanning herself with ostrich
plume fan.*

LADY REBECCA

I believe in God the Father Almighty, maker of Heaven and Earth, and in
Jesus Christ his only son our Lord, who was conceived of the Holy Ghost,
born of the Virgin Mary, suffered under Pontius Pilate, was crucified, dead
and buried. He descended into hell. I believe in the Holy Ghost, the holy
catholic Church, the communion of saints, the forgiveness of sins, the
resurrection of the body and the life everlasting. Amen. *(music out)*
I provided John Rolfe with the seeds to create his hybrid tobacco plants
and I provided him with a son, and created a hybrid people. I have such a
nice fan to hide my face and fan myself in these hot, heavy clothes.
What owe I to my father? Waited I not one year in Jamestown, a prisoner?
One year before, sent he my brothers to seek me. "If my father had loved
me, he would not value me less than old swords, guns or axes: therefore
I shall still dwell with the Englishmen who love me."[7]

---

[6] Found text from John Smith's journals.
[7] Quote attributed to Pocahontas.

Can I still remember how to plant corn? I'll stay. Never, never go back where anyone might know Matoaka. My name is Lady Rebecca forever and always. I am a Christian Englishwoman!

TROUBADOUR
(singing) Alas for our dear lady, English climate did not suit her–
>> She never saw Virginia again,
>> she met her end at Gravesend.

LADY REBECCA
Says John, my husband:
"For the good of God, for the good of the country, for the good of the plantation. It is righteous and it is good."[8]
No mark, no trail, no footprint, no way home. (reaching through frame, throwing a lifeline across the generations) "It is enough that the child liveth!"[9]

TROUBADOUR
(singing, joined by STORYBOOK POCAHONTAS)
And so here ends the legend of the Princess Pocahontas
>> Fa la la la lay, fa la la la la LELF–
>> if you want any more, make it up yourself.

(chorus)
Heigh-ho wiggle-waggle wigwam wampum,
>> roly-poly papoose tom-tom
>> >> tomahawk squaw.

>> MATOAKA runs to the tree upstage right, climbs half-way up, peeks around
>> tree trunk.

MATOAKA
I belong to the deer clan– (climbing onto platform in tree)
That's my family.
We're the only ones can wear deer antlers when we dance our deer clan dance.
We have to dance running as fast as the deer, kick up our feet, sniff the air.
I am the daughter of Wahunsonacawh, the powhatan. He is head chief of Tsenacomammacah, the nations here in the Tidewater. *Attan Akamik.*
We are the *Renape. Renapewa!*
I belong to the deer clan.
We don't know why they come – the English. What do they want? What do they want? Their homes are strange. They don't raise crops, they are not good hunters. Why do they come to starve on our land? They make my father angry. Where are their women? Where are their families? Who are these men that their people don't want them?

---

[8] Quote from John Rolfe from a letter.
[9] Quote attributed to Pocahontas, supposedly her dying words.

They come to ask for food; always they come. What did they eat where they come from? Still they ask for food. Still they ask for corn. Why do they come to starve on our land?

This is the first year I'll dance with the other girls. My first deer dance. My mother says, I have to have my own paint that's only mine. *(climbing down tree)* So I have to find my own colours and mix my own paint. My mother says I have to wait until I know and I'm really sure that that's how I want it to be. Because these tattoos will be mine forever. It's very important. *(sits, upstage centre)*

> *Enter CEREMONY downstage left with birimbao; she plays birimbao and keeps rhythm with her feet, dancing throughout "Nubile Child" whose cadence is chanted to the rhythm of the birimbao. Alternately, this rattle song is sung:*

Kekaten Pocahontasu patiaquah
ni tahnks minutehs
mawokik
(w)rarenoak odaugh, (w)rarenoak odaugh [10]

MATOAKA

Nubile child. Nubile child thigh strong muscle in the sun back to the sun woman/child–
Nubile child work in the corn basket on her back in the sun. Basket on her back.
Nubile child strong rain woman/child fix the roof woman/child.
Nubile child water from the river sun on the water open up look up!
See your face in the water, hand in your hair woman/child – laugh
Wet your auntie's basket!
Nubile child swimming, not working, nubile child.
Strong, fast, free *(jumps up, runs downstage right)* woman/child – digging–

> *Backing up into circle, back to back with CEREMONY.*

–digging with a stick, find the right roots,
Put them in your basket woman/child. (Tuckahoe, tuckahoe, tuckahoe.)
Name of the flower, name of the leaf, which one for headaches, which one for broken bones, which one to pray, which ones never to touch... (never to touch never to touch never to touch). *(to CEREMONY who doesn't look at her)* And I'm the first one of my sisters to be old enough to dance with the others.

My brothers are teasing me. That's because they know it's important. And you can't laugh. *(laughing, runs up tree, climbs around back of tree while speaking)* It means I'll be a woman now. It means I'll have different work.
It means there are some things I won't be able to do like the little girls.
It means that soon I'll be ready to be a wife.

---

[10] This is found text from John Smith's diaries. It is somewhat garbled Powatan that translates roughly as: "Speak [to] Pocahontas to come, I [have] small basket... this place... clam shell to trade." Translation: Dr. Jack Forbes.

Slides down ramp, upstage right; bounces on knees to rhythm then rises to centre stage.

Becoming woman/child – open up/Look!
All around your world, everything's alive!
Everything is growing, *(embraces tree)* everything has spirit, everything is breathing *(kneels, washes hands in basin at tree)* everything needs water, everything needs sunlight, everything needs rest.

Reaches for pot of red paint from base of tree; in four gestures, paints outer arms, and the tops of both feet with red paint, prepared for initiation, she stands and dances toward CEREMONY upstage centre.

MATOAKA
Nubile child,

CEREMONY
(echoes) Nubile child,

MATOAKA
    strong, fast, free woman/child
    strong legs, brown skin, woman/child
Look all the way around you. *(dances downstage centre)*
Look around your world woman/child *(stops dancing; very still)*
Dark skies, the moon is mine
    stars travel
        woman's time.

TRANSFORMATION 7
DEITY/WOMAN OF THE PUNA/VIRGIN TRANSFIGURATION

CONTEMPORARY WOMAN #1 carries basin downstage centre onto ramp. Sits; offers water with her hand; washes feet, stands and starts up ramp with basin, noticing that she is leaving footprints behind her, she stops, and follows them with her eyes.

DEITY
Let me tell you how I became a virgin:
    I was the warrior woman
        rebel woman
    creator/destroyer
womb of the earth
    mother of all
        –married to none
        but the sun himself
            or maybe the Lord of the underworld.
My butterfly wings transform
    are reborn into flight as
        Grandmother Spiderwoman

spins the threads of stories
as I tell them to you.

MUSICIAN

(singing with guitar)   *Quisiera...*
Because... every step you took was to destroy my
world, and as long as I breathe; You'll never find your
way through jungles of thoughts, to see my eyes
again... to see my eyes again...
Quisiera...

DEITY

I wore a serpent skirt
between my breasts skulls dangle
ornamenting   my power and
whetting   your fear.
Of my membranes muscle blood and bone I birthed a continent
–because I thought–
and creation came to be.

Walks up ramp to downstage right.

I was the leader with the iron fist
the renegade.
You never knew if I was abducted or
ran of my own
free will
to the
Spanish miner/Portuguese sailor-man
(or maybe it was the
other way around)?

WOMAN OF THE PUNA turns upstage, offering basin to tree.

WOMAN OF THE PUNA

Defiant, I refused to turn my back on the mother ways.
Betrayed by our own fathers brothers uncles husbands... *(places basin at tree)*
We run to the puna– *(runs up into tree)*
(from platform)
In the high tablelands
my sisters and I
refuse to weep, *(stands with rope noose in hands)*
our eyes, instead, spit fire. *(drum begins; tape)*
We, in secret, herd together, *(sampoñas; live, inside tree)*
honour the mother,
live without men,
demand our purity be
reclaimed.

We, hung ourselves, slit our throats,
        cut the breath of
        our male children.

VIRGIN

Let me tell you then, how I became a virgin.
Separated from myself my balance destroyed, scrubbed clean
    made lighter, non threatening
    chaste   barren.
No longer allied with the darkness of moon tides
    but twisted and misaligned
    with the darkness of evil
    the invaders sinful apple
    in my hand!
Ñusta Huillac! La Tirana! La Virgen del Carmen...
Tonantzin! Coyolahuaxqui! The Dark Virgin of Guadelupe
    Draped in ribbons, lace and flowers we are carried through the streets
        Stripped – of our names
        and our light
Let me tell you how I became a virgin,

    Slowly lowering noose; resisting it.

Sexless, without fire
    without pleasure
    without power
Encased in plaster
    painted white.
But oh, if there is one child
    who sees my nostrils flare
    my eyes spark and
    recognizes the heartbeat
    from the stomping of my feet
        in the rattle of the snare drum.

    Sampoñas fade; snare drum continues under CONTEMPORARY
    WOMAN #2.

CONTEMPORARY WOMAN #2

(upstage centre, standing) And when Amanda would go to visit her man, her
compañero, in jail, she would be strip-searched. In order to smuggle liquor or
alcohol for their wounds, anything that would bring some comfort into the
prison, she would fill little bottles, and hide them in her vagina–
–the perfect hiding place.

    Resumes playing sampoñas.

TRANSFORMATION 8
GRANDFATHERS/STAND UP

CONTEMPORARY WOMAN #1 crosses to ramp stage left wrapping herself luxuriously in volcano/cloth, sampoñas continue under.

CONTEMPORARY WOMAN #1

Sometimes, when you are not with me, I pull long, long strands of black hair, that doesn't belong to me, from between my sheets, from between the pages of my notebooks.

CONTEMPORARY WOMAN #2

From between my sheets... the pages of my notebooks

CONTEMPORARY WOMAN #1

Your profile a silhouette against the mid-day sun, I watch you pluck whiskers with a tweezers.
I remember my grandfather sitting in the sun of a soot-streaked city window, plucking whiskers, grazing his face with scissors, smiling at me from the side of his mouth.
You smile a crooked smile, embarrassed that I see them in you – all my grandfathers; those short, dark men with broad shoulders and heavy muscled calves, with hard working feet that were made for climbing coconut trees and walking in the sand; their pigeon-toed gait out of time on the sidewalks of the city.

> *As sampoñas resume, CONTEMPORARY WOMAN #1 runs stage right, searching for the sound.*

I followed the sound of the drum until I found where it was coming from. What was the sound of pipes doing in this northern market? *(centre stage)* You didn't know who I was, and it was months before I could explain to you that this woman, so exhilarated by the sound of the sikus, the pipes, the camu, was feeling the sound running through her veins!
(downstage centre) I remember my grandfathers sitting in my grandmother's front parlour, Sunday afternoons, playing the camu – blowing across the bamboo pipes. Iieeeeee! Iieeeeee!
One of them would start to cry – a high-pitched wail. The others would tease and laugh, but one by one they'd join his cry: a brotherhood of old, brown men mourning their lost home; a sorrowful sound whose bass note is a conch shell blown far out over the water.
You tilt your face to the sky, arch your back, bring the shell to your lips and blow. From the rumble at the soles of my feet to the insistent vibration at the top of my head, I recognize the sound. *(sampoñas stop)*

> *Moves to pot of paint upstage right and in one deliberate gesture, paints the centre part in her hair; returns downstage centre.*

I recognize my lifeline in your face when you bow your head in respect to hold a single kernel of corn in your hand; and Grandpa planted corn in the backyard. *(sinks to knees)*

THE MAN
(crosses downstage centre to CONTEMPORARY WOMAN #1; *touches shoulder)* Parase Negrita, vamos. Mira toda la gente que vino.

> *CONTEMPORARY WOMAN #1 stands; looks at THE MAN, both look at audience, smile. THE MAN buckles and falls to his knees.*

CONTEMPORARY WOMAN #1
Stand up! Look, you are my man, I am your woman. Stand up.

THE MAN
Right on.

CONTEMPORARY WOMAN #1
We, Native women, are the centre of the hoop of the nation.

> *THE MAN falls.*

Stand up! *(helping him to stand)* Stand up on your own two feet. You have two feet *(points)* one, two. Stand up.

> *THE MAN nods, in agreement.*

We are like the earth, we are the backbone...

> *THE MAN falls sideways, climbs onto CONTEMPORARY WOMAN #1's back.*

...and when our warriors go out to fight, we quietly support them. *(to THE MAN)* Not on my back! The baby's up there! Stand up and walk next to me!

> *THE MAN nods, affirmative.*

Now, there is a war being waged on the cement prairie and...

> *THE MAN, crossing downstage of CONTEMPORARY WOMAN #1, following someone hungrily with eyes.*

Hey, where're you...? Not with that white woman over there! *(grabs THE MAN by both arms and shakes him)* We're supposed to be re-building the nations, RIGHT?

> *THE MAN falls.*

(helping him to stand) Stand up. Please stand up. Pleeaase stand up?

THE MAN stands tall.

There!

Now that he is standing tall, THE MAN exits upstage left.

Hey! Hey where are you going? I don't want to do this without you! Hey! Hey!

TRANSFORMATION 9
MARIE/MARGARET/MADELAINE – MÉTIS WOMEN TRANSFIGURATION

With a short, self-satisfied sigh, MARIE crosses downstage left and puts on a buckskin yoke and a pair of moccasins; pennywhistle music begins.

MARIE
So many moccasins! *(short sigh, lifts packsack to her back, held in place by a tumpline across her forehead; dragging canoe onto stage)*
1 pair of moccasins per day per man
divided by 4 women
times 15 men on a one year expedition
equals 5,475 pairs of moccasins per year.

Lifts canoe overhead as if to portage.

So many moccasins!

Portaging in a counter-clockwise circle.

Une paire de moccasins par jour par homme, divisé entre quatre femmes, ça fait également... so many moccasins! C'est a dire, 5,475 pairs of moccasins per year.

Sets canoe down, begins to unpack moccasins for repair, downstage centre.

(to audience) Among my sisters I am the best moccasin maker. I have three sisters, one older and two younger – but I'm the best moccasin maker. That's why I am here. They came, *mistegoosoowuk*, they came and told my father they had no one to help them.
They had no one to make moccasins, to cook for them to show them where to pick berries, to make canoes... no one to help them. No one to help them.
Among my sisters I am the best moccasin maker, so my father sent me.
(sits, unwraps moccasins)
I'm not the only woman here. There are three other women.

We women,
>   make moccasins/ string snowshoes/teach them to
>   walk in the snow/make canoes.
We,
>   hunt/fish/put food away for the winter/teach them to
>   survive.
We,

In voice of CONTEMPORARY WOMAN #1.

translate/navigate /build alliances with our bodies/
loyalties through our blood,

In voice of MARIE.

We birth the Métis.
The Frenchman who is my husband, he has a big mustache and eyes that
I can look right through.
He calls himself Pierre and he calls me Marie. *(laughs)* My name is
Atchagoos Isquee'oo.
The Frenchman who is my husband he smokes a long pipe of white clay,
and in the evenings sometimes he sings:
>   "*Marlbrough s'en va-t-en guerre*
>   *mi ron-ton, mi ron-ton mi montaine*
>   *Marlbrough s'en va-t-en guerre*
>   *(ne) sais pas quand reviendra.*"
The Frenchman who is my husband, I sew him good moccasins.
The moccasins I sew him, the stitches don't loosen at the end of the day
The moccasins I sew him keep his big feet dry and warm. In the summer
months we pick berries, we dry meat so we can make *pemmigan.*
We women carry *(packing up)*
>   tents/pots/tools/*des couteaux/des fusiles/*hides for moccasins.
We carry,
>   cloth/beads/*des miroirs/des épingles/des aîguilles* for the other people that
>   we meet and we trade them for their pelts; *Amisk/nigik/wachusk/*
>   *sagweesoo/ateek/moosa.*
>   Beaver/otter/muskrat/marten/mink/moose
I speak for them when they have no words.
We portage with the canoes on our backs, *(picks up packsack and canoe,*
continues circle)
we portage, we portage.
We birth the Métis.
Une paire de moccasins par jour par homme, divisé entre quatre femmes. Among my
sisters I'm the best moccasin maker.

> *MARIE puts down canoe and packsack, notices MARGARET's calico*
> *dress hanging on post/ladder downstage left along with her kerchief and*
> *MADELAINE's tartan shawl, she backs up, then reaches for it; as the articles*

of clothing are removed from the post, the mask faces of the hordes of Métis women are revealed.

MUSICIAN, joined by MARGARET, moans, interrupted by ratchet and percussion instruments.

MARGARET

(putting on calico apron-dress, she is stunned, numb, rum-dumb) My husband didn't have a good hunt this season. *(putting on kerchief, ratchet sounds)* I am the third and youngest wife of a captain of the home guard. My husband didn't have a good hunt this season. *(ratchet sounds)*
My husband likes the cloth, the blankets
that come from the Company trading post.
My husband doesn't wear skins and robes to keep him warm.
My husband likes the liquor, the brandy, the whiskey
that come from the Company trading post.
My husband didn't have a good hunt this season.

Ratchet and rattle, turning walks upstage centre.

We didn't have many pelts to cure to scrape to stretch.
Not many beaver – only one moose...
even the rabbits were scarce.
We have no meat.
None to bring to the fort.
None for us to eat; not even for the children.
I am the third and youngest wife of a captain of the home guard.
I have no children of my own. I help care for the children of the other wives.
My husband didn't have a good hunt this season, so he brought me into the fort; and he left with flour, sugar and brandy.

Loud ratchet and percussive sounds; walking downstage centre.

The women, not from my people, but from the other side of the river, they unbraid my hair and wash it with harsh, lye soap. They wash me.
They can't leave any bear grease that protects my skin from the winter and in the summertime from the sun.
They say the company men will not like the way I smell. *(huge, tearing moan; as if being skinned alive)*
They take away my deerskin clothes except for my moccasins. They put on me clothing made of cloth with little flowers – they twist my hair at the nape of my neck. *(moaning; trying to speak, MUSICIAN joins)*
Mm... mm... mmy name is Wapithee'oo! They call me Margaret. *(walking downstage centre to lip of stage)*
So, we scrub the forts and warm their beds... and their beds... and their beds...
We quickly learn to love their alcohol:

Stumbles onto ramp.

the strong smell goes up my nose,
and burns my lips and tongue, it heats my throat.
I feel it travel to my stomach. It warms me from the inside out.

Singing; very drunk.

"Ha, ha, ha you and me
little brown jug
don't I love thee?"
It makes me happy It makes me laugh.
Iminigweeskeetchik! *(laughing)*
And after all it numbs the cold, it blurs their ugly, square houses in the fort.
(stops laughing) It numbs not recognizing the face of one company man from
the next.

Lots of manic sound.

We die from
smallpox, syphilis, tuberculosis, childbirth.
We claw at the gate of the fort or we starve and freeze to death outside.
We birth the Métis.
When there is no more to trade, our men trade us.
Fathers uncles brothers husbands trade us for knives, axes, muskets liquor.
My husband didn't have a good hunt this season.

*Chimes, moan, and ratchet; removes kerchief, adopts MADELAINE's haughty
stance.*

MADELAINE
YES! Yes, I did try to poison the new Mrs. Johnston! Two days confined to
her quarters with a stomach ache.

Puts on tartan shawl with cameo.

And I would do it again! Hang me, hang me, then, I kill her in my dreams.
(sits, downstage right)
I am – I was married to James Johnston for fifteen years. He easily won my
father's favour – my father the chief Factor, hmmn...? James was a suitable
match.
My cameo – I still wear it pinned at my throat.
Two days! They left me only two days to get out.
Fifteen years null and void! Null and void in two days!
It is called "turning off."
"Turned off," he said, *(stands, crosses downstage centre)* "The only way to tell
you, Madelaine, is that you have been turned off. But James has always been
more than generous with you, Madelaine. But Madelaine, the arrangement
has already been made."

Already been made?
"All your belongings can accompany you. There is a house, Madelaine, where you can live with Mr. Campbell, who has been very kind in accepting your husband's offer."
What reason? What reason? WHAT REASON?
    ...a white wife/a British woman...
    ...a white woman/a British wife.
Fifteen years, James Johnston.
In the morning they arrive and I can see her. Pale, weighted down with mountains and mountains of petticoats.
Trailing 14 trunks and a piano! She flounces into my house with my husband! *(strides up ramp downstage right)*
You only get my leavings! *(chimes)* I'll slit you open right through the belly, just like I skin a rabbit!
Ee goo speek ga aee tuk see gwow moonias swee wuk!

> *Stepping out of MADELAINE downstage right, voice of CONTEMPORARY WOMAN #1.*

CONTEMPORARY WOMAN #1
Which means, "When the white women came."
When Madelaine got angry, she would speak Cree, her mother's language.
So, when the white women came, *"Les filles du roi,"* these women, who were the wives and daughters and granddaughters of the founders of this country – were no longer women. And though turning off is no longer practiced, it is still an essential fiber in the fabric of our contemporary lives.

> *Back into MADELAINE's voice and time frame.*

MADELAINE
Saaa!! *(skinning motion)*
My china tea service came directly from England.

> *Begins to circle counter-clockwise and move upstage centre.*

All that way and not one broken! It's a full set;
with gold leaf around the rim of each cup.

> *Sits upstage centre.*

I sit in my grandmother's old rocking chair...
My grandmother made moccasins in this chair and she showed me how.
"You're a good girl with your hands Madelaine. *Oui ma fille, ça-y-est.*"
Now my hands don't move. They lie in my lap like two dead birds, broken at the neck and lifeless.

(on tape) Disposed of, discarded, replaced, after the white women came.
Ee goo speek ga gee tuk see gwow moonias swee wuk.

MUSICIAN is singing with guitar while CONTEMPORARY WOMAN #1 sheds shawl, kerchief, and calico dress and hangs them on the tree. The buckskin yoke remains on.

CONTEMPORARY WOMAN #1
In the middle of my dream I came face to face to face and the copper hand reached to touch my back. I awakened sad, cold, confused, for the journey had been long and far... *avec Marie, Margaret et Madelaine... avec Marie, Margaret et Madelaine... avec Marie, Margaret et Madelaine, Madelaine... avec Marie Margaret et Madelaine.*

CONTEMPORARY WOMAN #2
Princess, Princess!

CONTEMPORARY WOMAN #1
Princess, Princess!

TRANSFORMATION 10
CIGAR STORE SQUAW/"YOU LIGHT UP MY LIFE"

PRINCESS BUTTERED-ON-BOTH-SIDES as the CIGAR STORE SQUAW crosses to centre stage with an oversized bunch of cigars.

PRINCESS BUTTERED-ON-BOTH-SIDES
(offering cigars to audience) UGH! I used to have this job, standing out in front of the tobacco store, but I didn't like the crowd. Besides, do you think anyone would talk to me? Not even chit chat. Do you think anyone would bring me a dozen roses, or an orchid corsage? No. Do you know what they gave me? Cigars. Do you know, the other day, somebody actually lit a match on me. Do you want to know where? *(indicates pelvic area)* So humiliating. But I want it all! I wanna be free to express myself! *(sets cigars down at tree)* I wanna be the girl next door! *(removes buckskin yoke in exasperation)* I wanna have lots and lots of blonde hair – great big blonde hair. I wanna be – Doris Day, Farrah Fawcett, Daryl Hannah – oh, you know the one – Christie Brinkley! *(hums "Uptown Girl" while putting on white buckskin mini-dress)* I wanna be a cover girl, a beauty queen, Miss America, Miss North American Indian! That's it! According to the "Walk In Beauty Seminar" it's very, very important to have the right look. *(notices dress; screams in horror)* Okay for the talent segment, but for the evening gown competition? The Finals? It's a rag! A rag! *(reaches into pouch of buckskin dress, pulls out and reveals a shimmering evening gown of the tackiest sort, and velcros it onto dress.)*

Ahhh! Isn't this a devastating gown? I designed it myself. So, here I am a finalist in the Miss North American Indian Beauty Pageant! Think of it! Little me from in front of the tobacco store, fighting for DEMOCRACY! HELLO WORLD!!

HOST enters upstage left with tablita-style corn "crown" and ear of corn "bouquet."

HOST

And now, the moment you've all been waiting for... the winner of the 498th annual Miss North American Indian Beauty Pageant, from her woodland paradise... Miss Congeniality...
PRINCESS BUTTERED-ON-BOTH-SIDES!!!!

PRINCESS BUTTERED-ON-BOTH-SIDES is screaming; jumping up and down flatfooted as Host presents her with her "bouquet" and "crowns" her with a headdress covered with small ears of corn which light up. She begins her triumphant walk down the runway, weeping and blowing kisses, while HOST throws popcorn at her feet singing "You Light Up My Life," in true lounge lizard tradition. When PRINCESS BUTTERED-ON-BOTH-SIDES reaches upstage centre she strikes the pose of the Statue of Liberty, and the ears of corn on her headdress are illuminated in full. The following lines are spoken throughout her runway march.

PRINCESS BUTTERED-ON-BOTH-SIDES

Thank you, thank you.... Oh! I can't believe it! I love you all...
You have made my heart soar like a rabbit.... I'll never forget this moment!

She unplugs herself, corn lights out. Exits upstage left. HOST winds up cord from headdress, humming bars from "You Light Up My Life," removes jacket, bunches it up in front of her thighs as if it were a skirt; squats; prepares to sit as if on toilet; she continues to attempt to sit on toilet between each speech.

TRANSFORMATION 11
LAS RATAS

CONTEMPORARY WOMAN #2

It's really hard for me to go to a public washroom and when I do, it has to be fast, because if I stay long enough, this hand is going to come out of the water and grab me. Probably pull me in.

CONTEMPORARY WOMAN #1

I never really knew Annie Mae. Though we'd been in the same place at the same time, we never really spoke.

CONTEMPORARY WOMAN #2

"There is a rat in the toilet!" my father shouted. And there it was, dead, floating in the water. It's really hard for me to go to a public washroom.

CONTEMPORARY WOMAN #1

My most vivid memory of her was when we came across each other at the Sundance. She was sitting leaning against a tree. We looked at each other and smiled, acknowledging the dust, the glaring heat, the desperate little breeze under the tree where we sat. The weight of our history on our backs, the tiredness of the struggle we shared.

CONTEMPORARY WOMAN #2
After the coup, I read a testimonial of a 13-year-old girl. She had been tortured. They were looking for her brother.

CONTEMPORARY WOMAN #1
I never really knew Annie Mae, so when I heard about Annie Mae, murdered at the bottom of a cliff, reign of terror they called it – Annie Mae, beaten, raped, shot in the back of the head.

CONTEMPORARY WOMAN #2
It's really hard for me to go to a public washroom.

CONTEMPORARY WOMAN #1
When I think about Annie Mae, I think about her searching for her hands – the FBI lost her hands.

CONTEMPORARY WOMAN #2
They interrogated her by inserting a live rat into her vagina. The tail of the rat was attached to a wire that was connected to the whole electrical system. With every question there would be an electric shock. It's really hard for me to go to a public washroom.

CONTEMPORARY WOMAN #1
When I think about Annie Mae, I see her, a small woman, smiling against a tree. But her hands...

CONTEMPORARY WOMAN #2
Now when I read this I was still a virgin and I didn't have the idea of what size something had to be in order to fit inside a vagina. Especially something as uncomfortable as a rat.

CONTEMPORARY WOMAN #1
Her hands...

CONTEMPORARY WOMAN #2
And the rats are really big in Chile.

TRANSFORMATION 12
CONTEMPORARY WOMAN/SPIRIT-SISTER/SPIRIT-ANIMAL TRANSFIGURATION

MUSICIAN
(*singing*) And when the thunder strikes you in the heart of things,
You will remember thoughts you never had before.

When the thunder strikes you in the heart.
The thunder... the thunder... the thunder.... La la la la la la

> *Singing continues under following action until CONTEMPORARY*
> *WOMAN #1 speaks; she descends pyramid, SPIRIT-SISTER hands her the*
> *pot of red paint which she offers to sky while walking to centre stage, sinking to*
> *knees; in four gestures, she paints palms, inner arms, neck, throat in reverence to*
> *the initiation and full acceptance of mature womanhood; turning upstage left she*
> *offers paint to pyramid; embraces tree upstage right, overwhelmed with awe,*
> *moves downstage right, SPIRIT-SISTER guides and directs the action in the*
> *following sequence which takes place in parallel worlds of time and space.*

CONTEMPORARY WOMAN #1
Stand me in the rain forest—
    my soul whispers, "home...
            home...." Rise me above
      the rain forest—
I know every ray of filtered light
that ripples the living green
(falls; scrambles up ladder downstage left)

(voice of CONTEMPORARY
WOMAN #1 on tape; singing)
Cuando canto en Tulum,
en Tulum canta la luna–
cuando canto en Tulum,
en Tulum canta la luna.

SPIRIT-ANIMAL
slant-eyed and head swinging low
to the ground,
    my muscles ripple
    from shoulder to haunch,
    now running – now stopping
    to sniff the air.

When you tasted of salt and
oranges,
and the moon sang her
happiest songs to us,
–heart offerings
when we remembered her–
When you tasted of salt and
oranges,
and the falling stars took our
breath away,
the waves of the sea
mixed with my own salt tears

CONTEMPORARY WOMAN #1
(hanging from top rung; climbing down)
barefoot and possessionless I
walk resigned, but not broken,
chest thrust forward I memorize
every leaf, every hill, every bird,
every plot of mountain corn—
knowing these are
    the last things I will see.
The bus winds the mountain turns.
It begins to rain, cold drops pelting the
      window in streaks.

Falls downstage centre.

SPIRIT-SISTER
I promise to return.
The light in the doorways,
the hammocks hung in the homes
of the brown mountain-
weathered people looking up
from the side of the road.

CONTEMPORARY WOMAN #1
I promise to return to carry on the light.

Rising.

Swell my heart in my chest full and warm.
    I turn and say, "If I survive this journey,
it is only because
my heart has decided not to
        burst."

SPIRIT-SISTER
... and she sounds like this:

Both singing.

    ah ah ah   ah ah ah
        ah ah ah
   ah   ah   ah!

While singing, CONTEMPORARY WOMAN #1 takes bucket of sand from base of tree; empties it centre stage, makes footprints.

CONTEMPORARY WOMAN #1
I give myself to this land.

Falls; hangs head and shoulders upside-down off the lip of the stage.

My heart pierced my back split open. Impaled.
My blood stains this piece of earth –
a landmark for my soul.
I promise to return to love you always.

SPIRIT-SISTER
Call to me in a language
I don't understand,

CONTEMPORARY WOMAN #1
(rolls downstage right, comes to kneeling)
Curled beside me, you sleep.
Wake up! There's work to be done!
    We're here.

SPIRIT-SISTER
slant-eyed and head swinging
low to the ground,
my spine arches from
neck to tail.

**CONTEMPORARY
WOMAN #1**
(tape; singing)
When you tasted of salt and oranges
I howled at the pulling in my womb,
–your own trembling
not quieted by whispers–
(of no, no, no)
When you tasted of salt and oranges,

SPIRIT-ANIMAL
(downstage centre, ramp)
I crouch at the side
of the mountain
the guardian-watching

(live voice and tape together)
I put down my sorrow in
an ancient
place,
ahh ahh ahh ahh

(tape only)
wordless, I walk into the sea

I wait.

and the moon she will sing.

(add live voices; CONTEMPORARY WOMAN #1 and SPIRIT-SISTER)
ah ah ah ah ah ah
ah ah ah
AH   AH   AH!

TRANSFORMATION 13
UNA NACION

Lights snap to bright – sudden transition to mundane, urban environment.

CONTEMPORARY WOMAN #1
(standing on ramp stage left) It's International Women's Day–

No, I didn't go to the march. *(cross to centre stage, very deliberately making footprints in sand)* So many years of trying to fit into feminist shoes. Okay, I'm trying on the shoes; but they're not the same as the shoes in the display case. The shoes I'm trying on must be crafted to fit these wide, square, brown feet. I must be able to feel the earth through their soles.

So, it's International Women's Day, and here I am. Now, I'd like you to take a good look– *(turns slowly, all the way around)* I don't want to be mistaken for a crowd of Native women. I am one. And I do not represent all Native women. I am one. *(crosses to tree upstage right; brings empty basin and pitcher of water centre stage)* And since it can get kind of lonely here, I've brought some friends, sisters, *guerrilleras*—the women—"Word Warriors,"[11] to help.

Pours water into basin; CONTEMPORARY WOMAN #2 approaches, kneels by basin, they wet each other's faces, hair, and arms; purifying. With a cupped handful of water each, they sprinkle stage in opposite circles.

CONTEMPORARY WOMAN #1
(in front of pyramid, upstage left) Gloria Anzaldúa!

CONTEMPORARY WOMAN #2
(singing softly, under throughout)
Una nación no será conquistada...
hasta que los corazones de sus mujeres
caigan a la tierra.

CONTEMPORARY WOMAN #1
"What I want is the freedom to carve and chisel my own face, to staunch the bleeding with ashes, to fashion my own gods out of my entrails."[12]

Dips hand in basin again, sprinkles water to stage right.

Diane Burns describes that to hold a brown-skinned lover means: *(face to face, they wash each other's chests over heart)* "...we embrace and rub the wounds together."

She also says: "This ain't no stoic look, this is my face."[13]

Dips hand in basin again, sprinkles half circle.

The Kayapo woman, of the Rain Forest, who stands painted, bare to the waist, holding a baby by the hand, and confronts the riot squad in the capital of Brazil *(walks downstage centre)* and says: *(gesturing with arm; punctuating)* "I am here to speak for my brother and my brother-in-law. Where are your sisters to cry out for you? I am enraged with you! You steal our land! I am calling upon you! I throw my words in your faces!!!!"[14]

---

11 Paula Gunn Allen, from *The Sacred Hoop*, Beacon Press, 1986.

12 Gloria Anzaldúa, from *Borderlands/La Frontera*, Spinsters/Aunt Lute Book Company, 1987.

13 Diane Burns, from *Riding the One-Eyed Ford*, Contact II Publications, 1981.

14 Kayapo woman, from transcription of "The Nature of Things" with David Suzuki, Show #19, "Amazonia – The Road to the End of the Forest," CBC, 1989-1990.

Drum kicks in loudly, a "call to arms." Song begins in Spanish to an Andean rhythm and evolves into a round dance—a "49"—contemporary Native song with English words.

CONTEMPORARY WOMAN #2
(singing; full out)
Una nación no sera conquistada hasta que los corazones de sus mujeres caigan a la tierra.

CONTEMPORARY WOMAN #1
(joins)
Una nación no sera conquistada hasta que los corazones de sus mujeres caigan a la tierra.
No importa que los guerreros sean valientes o que sus armas sean poderosas![15]

During the following musical transition, sung once through without English words, the drum's rhythm changes to the heartbeat of the round dance.

A nation is not conquered until the hearts of its women are on the ground.

CONTEMPORARY WOMAN #2
(joins)
Then, it is done, no matter how brave its warriors, nor how strong its weapons.

Blind Faith leaps in the dark.

Blackout.

The end.

[15] Traditional Cheyenne.

ALMIGHTY VOICE
AND HIS WIFE

DANIEL DAVID MOSES

DANIEL DAVID MOSES

INTRODUCTION TO *ALMIGHTY VOICE AND HIS WIFE*

Although he was born and raised on the (Iroquois) Six Nations reserve on the Grand River in Southern Ontario, Daniel David Moses is a registered Delaware. He holds a BA Degree from York University and an MFA in Creative Writing from the University of British Columbia, is an award-winning poet and playwright, a member of the Writers Guild of Canada, the League of Canadian Poets, and the Playwrights Guild of Canada, has been writer in residence at Concordia University in Montreal, and a member of the board and artistic directorate of Native Earth Performing Arts. He is author of three books of poetry, *Delicate Bodies*, *The White Line*, and *Sixteen Jesuses*, and co-editor, with Terry Goldie, of the Oxford University Press *Anthology of Canadian Native Literature in English*.

Moses' diverse body of plays can be loosely divided into three categories. The "city" plays, which include *Coyote City* (1988), *Big Buck City* (1991), *Kyotopolis* (1993), and *City of Shadows* (1995), tell in wildly different genres, from tragedy through farce to filmic or television science fiction, the story of one Native family, centering around a parodic Christian story of the annunciation (*Coyote City*), Christmas birth (*Big Buck City*), and ascension to sci-fi media "heaven" (*Kyotopolis*), of the "Babe" Fisher. The tetralogy concludes with an afterlife play of voices (*City of Shadows*) that reflects poetically on the action of the earlier plays and is strongly reminiscent of Dylan Thomas's *Under Milk Wood*.

The Dreaming Beauty (1988, published in French as *Belle Fille de l'Aurore*) and *The Witch of Niagara* (1998), read together, constitute Moses' "story/dream plays," and combine the First Nations orature with western "story-time" children's theatre (though Moses resists what he sees as the condescending distinction between adult and children's literatures). The first is a simple, lyrical fable about the five-hundred year sleep (implicitly the period since contact) of "Beauty of our People"; the second is a retelling of the story of the maid of the mist at Niagara Falls, in which evil is exorcized and health restored to a suffering community.

The most complex of Moses' plays can loosely be grouped together as "history plays." These include the sprawling and apocalyptic, historically revisionist 1996 epic, *Brébeuf's Ghost* – also about the exorcism of the here explicitly Christian and colonizing evils that cannibalize the community; the searingly poetic and understated 1996 "vanishing Indian" dyptych set in late 19th-century New Mexico, *The Indian Medicine Shows*; and *Almighty Voice and His Wife* (1991), a revisionist account and reclamation of a story frequently retold in plays, short stories, and popular histories by non-Native authors including such luminaries as Lister Sinclair, Rudy Wiebe, and Pierre Berton. Before Oka, Ipperwash, and other standoffs, the 1885-87 story of Kisse-Manitou-Wayou (Almighty Voice), a young Cree man from Sakatchewan who killed a cow and was hunted to his death, used to be called, by non-Natives, the last armed resistance by Native people in Canada.

Almighty Voice and His Wife was first produced in Ottawa at the Great Canadian Theatre Company in the Fall of 1991, under the direction of Lib Spry, featuring Billy Merasty and Jani Lauzon. It was remounted by Native Earth Performing Arts at the Native Canadian Centre in February-March 1992 directed by Marrie Mumford with Larry Lewis, and featuring Jonathan Fisher and Pamela Matthews. Like most of Moses's work, this is a play obsessed with watching, looking, seeing, and being seen. In the first act, the ironically named "White Girl," the wife of Almighty Voice who seems until the very end of the play to have internalized the white man's gaze, is herself obsessed with white men's use of telescopes, "clear beads they look through" to maintain surveillance while remaining themselves invisible. The telescope, the glass god that she learned of in residential school, and the masculinist glare of the sun are set in explicit contrast to an equally pervasive but female and transformational moon – a constant presence in the stage directions to all of Moses' plays.

The most distinctive feature of *Almighty Voice and His Wife*, however, is its structure. Without anticipating and diminishing the reader's experience of the play, suffice it to say that its second-act interest in and indebtedness to the racist 19th-century blackface minstrel show tradition (like Moses' interest in and indebtedness to the same period's Indian medicine shows elsewhere) results in a direct confrontation of the white man's gaze, a gaze explicitly associated with the objectifications of Western history writing, journalism, capitalism, and the entertainment industry. Here, on the auditorium stage of the abandoned industrial school at Duck Lake (a site with rich historical resonances to the Riel resistance), that gaze—here an explicitly theatrical one—is powerfully confronted, returned, ridiculed, and finally rendered irrelevant. The play's last few lines, untranslated in performance, are in Cree.

CHARACTERS

ALMIGHTY VOICE
At first a young Cree man, early twenties, Kisse-Manitou-Wayou, also known as Jean Baptiste, later his own playful GHOST.

WHITE GIRL
At first a young Cree woman, early teens, the daughter of Old Dust and the wife of Almighty Voice, later the INTERLOCUTOR.

NOTE

The action of Act One incorporates historic events and happens between the end of October 1895 and May of 1897 on the Saskatchewan prairie at, and between, the One Arrow and Fort A La Corne reserves. Act Two occurs on the auditorium stage of the abandoned industrial school at Duck Lake.

ALMIGHTY VOICE AND HIS WIFE

DANIEL DAVID MOSES

ACT ONE

A projected title: "Act One: Running with the Moon."

SCENE ONE

The projected title: "Scene One: Her Vision." A drum beats in night's blue darkness. The full moon sweeps down from the sky like a spotlight to show and surround WHITE GIRL asleep, in a fetal position on the ground. The drum begins a sneak-up beat, the moon pulses in a similar rhythm. WHITE GIRL wakes at the quake, gets to her feet, and takes a step. The drum hesitates. A gunshot and a slanting bolt of light stop her and block out the moon. Three more shots and slanting bolts of light come in quick succession, confining her in a spectral tipi. She peers out through its skin of light at ALMIGHTY VOICE, a silhouette against the moon. He collapses to the beats of the drum, echoes of the gunshots. WHITE GIRL falls to her knees as the tipi fades and the moon bleeds.

SCENE TWO

The projected title: "Scene Two: The Proposal." WHITE GIRL is by the fire, stripping meat for drying. ALMIGHTY VOICE loiters at a distance.

ALMIGHTY VOICE
Hiya. Hiya. Hey girl, I said "Hiya."

WHITE GIRL
I heard you the first time. I'm working here.

ALMIGHTY VOICE
Oh ya?

WHITE GIRL
I am. And my dad doesn't like it, you talking to me.

ALMIGHTY VOICE
Old Dust? What's he got to worry about? He's winning over there. I'm just talking.

WHITE GIRL
It's not your talking he's worried about.

ALMIGHTY VOICE
What you talking about?

WHITE GIRL
You never mind.

ALMIGHTY VOICE
What you talking about, girl? Hey White Girl, what you talking about?

WHITE GIRL
My dad says you already got a wife.

ALMIGHTY VOICE
What's that got to do with anything?

WHITE GIRL
I hear you already had two others.

ALMIGHTY VOICE
You don't have to believe everything you hear. White Girl, you know something? I think you got pretty eyes.

WHITE GIRL
I got no time to be told my eyes are pretty.

ALMIGHTY VOICE
You're pretty fierce for a little girl.

WHITE GIRL
You should leave little girls alone, Almighty Voice.

ALMIGHTY VOICE
You're not that little, little girl.

WHITE GIRL
I'm working here.

ALMIGHTY VOICE
You're big enough.

WHITE GIRL
Go away.

ALMIGHTY VOICE
Is that the way they do it at that school? That's not the way my mother does it.

WHITE GIRL
Spotted Calf doesn't know everything.

ALMIGHTY VOICE
She knows how to strip meat. Here let me–

WHITE GIRL
You could get cut.

ALMIGHTY VOICE
You're pretty fierce all right, little girl. You are like Spotted Calf.

WHITE GIRL
What?

ALMIGHTY VOICE
My mother's not as pretty as you.

WHITE GIRL
Go bother my brother for a while.

ALMIGHTY VOICE
But he's not as pretty as you.

WHITE GIRL
Sure he is. He's my brother. You know what?

ALMIGHTY VOICE
What is it, White Girl?

WHITE GIRL
My brother, Young Dust, he likes you.

ALMIGHTY VOICE
He's my friend.

WHITE GIRL
No, Almighty Voice, he likes you. He thinks you are the pretty one. Your wife won't kiss you? Well, my brother will.

ALMIGHTY VOICE
You're a crazy one.

WHITE GIRL
You're right. I am a crazy one. As long as you know. But my brother does want to kiss–

ALMIGHTY VOICE
I don't want to talk about your brother.

WHITE GIRL
Look, he's coming this way.

ALMIGHTY VOICE
What? No he's not.

WHITE GIRL
But Young Dust does like you.

ALMIGHTY VOICE
And I like you.

WHITE GIRL
I'm just a little girl, Almighty Voice.

ALMIGHTY VOICE
A little girl working away.

WHITE GIRL
You could get cut.

ALMIGHTY VOICE
I want to kiss you, White Girl.

WHITE GIRL
My father's looking at you. He sees you talking to me.

ALMIGHTY VOICE
Let him.

WHITE GIRL
You got to talk to him first, you know.

ALMIGHTY VOICE
I don't want to break that hand game up. All right, I'll go talk to him first.

WHITE GIRL
Then we'll talk.

ALMIGHTY VOICE
Just talk? What will we talk about?

WHITE GIRL
The wife you have now.

ALMIGHTY VOICE
What wife?

WHITE GIRL
The Rump's Daughter.

ALMIGHTY VOICE
Oh ya.

WHITE GIRL
You're going to send her home to her father.

ALMIGHTY VOICE
She won't go.

WHITE GIRL
She will go. I'm going to be your wife now. Your only wife. You can't feed us both. Well then, my father's waiting to talk to you. Go on.

ALMIGHTY VOICE
Crazy.

SCENE THREE

A projected title: "Scene Three: The Wedding Night." A second fire in night's blue. A gunshot and a slanting bolt of light. The reverberations become a social dance-beat on a drum and bring up the rest of the tipi of light. WHITE GIRL enters it and sits. Then ALMIGHTY VOICE enters. The drum and tipi fade.

ALMIGHTY VOICE
Hiya, wife. I said "Hiya, wife."

WHITE GIRL
What can I do for my husband?

ALMIGHTY VOICE
Come here. Look at me. Leave that be.

WHITE GIRL
Does my husband want some tea?

ALMIGHTY VOICE
Your husband wants his blanket.

WHITE GIRL
There. Your blanket's ready for you. It's snowing out. Shall I go for wood to build the fire up?

ALMIGHTY VOICE
Can't you be quiet, girl?

WHITE GIRL
Shall I tell your friends to be quiet? Shall I tell them to go away?

ALMIGHTY VOICE
They'll go when they're full.

WHITE GIRL
Do you want more to eat, husband? I'll go get some more.

ALMIGHTY VOICE
Stay here with me. Look at me, White Girl.

WHITE GIRL
That was a wonderful cow you brought for the feast. It was so fat.

ALMIGHTY VOICE
You didn't eat much.

WHITE GIRL
I'm stuffed full. I have never eaten so well before, husband. Now my father will have to admit his daughter is well fed. You are such a hunter.

ALMIGHTY VOICE
It was only a stupid cow. What's wrong, White Girl?

WHITE GIRL
I was thinking about my mother. She would have made him come. And your father. How could the Mounties take him? The day before our wedding.

ALMIGHTY VOICE
They're stupid. Look at me, wife.

WHITE GIRL
I don't want to be a wife. I don't want to be a woman. That school – I don't know how. I'm only thirteen. I'm crazy.

ALMIGHTY VOICE
You're not crazy.

WHITE GIRL
I am. I am.

ALMIGHTY VOICE
Come here. Let me hold you.

WHITE GIRL
No, it's too dangerous.

ALMIGHTY VOICE
It's not dangerous. Hey come on, pretend I'm your brother.

WHITE GIRL
No, you're my husband. I don't want you to die.

ALMIGHTY VOICE
You're not going to kill me. You're going to kiss me.

WHITE GIRL
I have bad medicine in me. I went to that school. The treaty agent took me.

ALMIGHTY VOICE
But you got away, girl.

WHITE GIRL
School's a strange place. All made out of stone. The wind tries to get in, and can't, and cries. It's so hot and dry, your throat gets sore. You cough a lot, too. I used to even cough blood. And they won't let you talk. They try to make you talk like they do. It's like stones in your mouth.

ALMIGHTY VOICE
You're here now.

WHITE GIRL
I liked it there.

ALMIGHTY VOICE
How could you like that?

WHITE GIRL
They said I could live there forever.

ALMIGHTY VOICE
What are you talking about?

WHITE GIRL
They said everybody at home had died of the smallpox. They said I could live forever but I had to marry their God.

ALMIGHTY VOICE
Hey, you're my wife now and I'm alive. Everybody's alive.

WHITE GIRL

He's going to kill you. He's a jealous god.

ALMIGHTY VOICE

He's another one of their lies.

WHITE GIRL

They say he's everywhere. He can see everything.

ALMIGHTY VOICE

He's got nothing better to do than watch us?

WHITE GIRL

They say he's like a ghost.

ALMIGHTY VOICE

Hey little girl, even your dad didn't know for sure about us and he watched you like a hawk.

WHITE GIRL

Or a white bird. They say he's like a white bird.

ALMIGHTY VOICE

A white bird? A white bird in here?

WHITE GIRL

He made the smallpox.

ALMIGHTY VOICE

Let's get that bird out of here! Where is it?

WHITE GIRL

You crazy, he'll kill you.

ALMIGHTY VOICE

Hey, little girl, I found it! *(He mocks flatulence.)*

WHITE GIRL

Stop that. You're crazy.

ALMIGHTY VOICE

Oh ya? Both of us? Made for each other. *(He kisses and caresses her.)* Little girl, my White Girl.

WHITE GIRL

Wait, husband, wait. I'm afraid.

ALMIGHTY VOICE
Don't be. I'm brave now I got you for my wife.

WHITE GIRL
But I'm afraid.

ALMIGHTY VOICE
What is it now, girl?

WHITE GIRL
It's the bad medicine. They gave me another name when I married their god.

ALMIGHTY VOICE
Shut up about their god! I don't want to hear it!

WHITE GIRL
They called me Marrie. It's the name of their god's mother.

ALMIGHTY VOICE
What's wrong with White Girl? White Girl's a good name. They're so stupid. That agent has to call me John Baptist so I can get my treaty money.

WHITE GIRL
John Baptist. That's the name of one of their ghosts.

ALMIGHTY VOICE
I'm no ghost. I'm Almighty Voice. Why can't they say Almighty Voice?

WHITE GIRL
I'll call you John Baptist too.

ALMIGHTY VOICE
You're not the agent! You're my wife.

WHITE GIRL
It's so he'll kill the ghost instead of you, husband. That god won't know it's us if we use their names.

ALMIGHTY VOICE
So I have to call my wife Marrie?

WHITE GIRL
Yes. Their god won't be able to touch us. Just call me Marrie.

ALMIGHTY VOICE
My crazy White Girl.

WHITE GIRL
Call me Marrie, husband.

ALMIGHTY VOICE
Marrie. Marrie, will you kiss me now?

WHITE GIRL
Yes, husband.

They kiss, caress, and begin to undress.

ALMIGHTY VOICE
Crazy Marrie.

WHITE GIRL
John Baptist.

ALMIGHTY VOICE
My little girl.

SCENE FOUR

The Projected Title: "Scene Four: Flight." A drum beats in darkness. WHITE GIRL pretends to sleep by the second fire. ALMIGHTY VOICE enters at a run, drops to his knees. The drum fades.

ALMIGHTY VOICE
White Girl, wake up.

WHITE GIRL
Go away. I'm sleeping here.

ALMIGHTY VOICE
Where's my Winchester?

WHITE GIRL
How should I know?

ALMIGHTY VOICE
Did my mother take it?

WHITE GIRL
Where have you been?

ALMIGHTY VOICE
I'll be right back.

WHITE GIRL
Have you been with the Rump's Daughter?

ALMIGHTY VOICE
I got to get my Winchester.

WHITE GIRL
Have you been with the Rump's Daughter?

ALMIGHTY VOICE
I'll go wake my mother.

WHITE GIRL
Answer me!

ALMIGHTY VOICE
What?

WHITE GIRL
I'm your wife now. Your only wife.

ALMIGHTY VOICE
White Girl, I was with your brother.

WHITE GIRL
You weren't with the Rump's Daughter?

ALMIGHTY VOICE
We were in jail.

WHITE GIRL
Jail?

ALMIGHTY VOICE
That Sergeant over at Duck Lake, he threw us in the guard house.

WHITE GIRL
But you went for treaty money.

ALMIGHTY VOICE
Well the Sergeant has it now. Somebody told them that cow I shot belonged to somebody.

WHITE GIRL
You're all wet. Here. Get warm.

ALMIGHTY VOICE
Hey girl, I been swimming.

WHITE GIRL
You got away.

ALMIGHTY VOICE
In the freezing Saskatchewan.

WHITE GIRL
What about Young Dust?

ALMIGHTY VOICE
He said it was warm there.

WHITE GIRL
You shouldn't have left him there. They threw you in jail for killing that cow.

ALMIGHTY VOICE
That cow belonged to the Great White Mother. This half-breed told me the guard said no way would I rot in jail like my dirty chief of a father. The Guard said I'd hang for killing that cow!

WHITE GIRL
But that's crazy. They don't hang people over meat.

ALMIGHTY VOICE
I'm not going back to that guard house, White Girl.

WHITE GIRL
They can't take you there.

ALMIGHTY VOICE
They always come after you. My dad's in jail at Prince Albert over the pieces of a plough. He hates their stupid farming, this stupid reserve. They even turn the prairie into a jail.

WHITE GIRL
They can't put the wind in prison.

ALMIGHTY VOICE
Sounding Sky used to mean warrior. Now it's hard labour.

WHITE GIRL
Here. Dry yourself. Get warm.

ALMIGHTY VOICE
But I got to go get my Winchester.

WHITE GIRL
You rest while I find you your Winchester. They can't cross the river so quick. And you need to take some of that beef with you.

ALMIGHTY VOICE
They'll catch me with it.

WHITE GIRL
You got to eat. And the Mounties aren't going to catch us.

ALMIGHTY VOICE
But you can't come.

WHITE GIRL
I'm coming with my husband.

ALMIGHTY VOICE
You'll slow me down.

WHITE GIRL
No I won't.

ALMIGHTY VOICE
But there's snow coming.

WHITE GIRL
Better for us. Two can be warmer than one. You know that. Lie down. Lie down, John Baptist. I'll get your Winchester.

ALMIGHTY VOICE
But White Girl, crazy one–

WHITE GIRL
Lie down, John Baptist, rest. I'll be ready soon. No, rest. Listen, John Baptist, I'm a better shot than your mother Spotted Calf. I got better eyes.

ALMIGHTY VOICE
This is crazy, girl.

WHITE GIRL
Both of us. Remember?

SCENE FIVE

The projected title: "Scene Five: The Killing." ALMIGHTY VOICE and WHITE GIRL sit by the third fire. A drifting beat comes and goes on the drum.

WHITE GIRL
It's all gone. The beef's all gone.

ALMIGHTY VOICE
I don't really like beef.

WHITE GIRL
What's wrong? I didn't burn it.

ALMIGHTY VOICE
No. Cattle aren't like real meat. They're stupid.

WHITE GIRL
They're not buffalo.

ALMIGHTY VOICE
That's for sure. They don't taste right.

WHITE GIRL
I like it. It makes me feel full.

ALMIGHTY VOICE
I'll get something else soon. My wife's not going hungry.

WHITE GIRL
It's good to be hungry.

ALMIGHTY VOICE
It's better to be full.

WHITE GIRL
It reminds you you're alive. That's what my mother used to say.

ALMIGHTY VOICE
What's wrong?

WHITE GIRL
Young Dust said the snow was too deep. The treaty agent wouldn't send the supplies out. Last winter. My mother wouldn't eat. She wouldn't eat. While I was away at that school. She used to like the way I cook.

ALMIGHTY VOICE
I do too, White Girl.

WHITE GIRL
I would have cooked for her.

ALMIGHTY VOICE
Cook for me now, White Girl.

WHITE GIRL
I didn't really want to be there. We had to eat this mush made out of grass seeds.

ALMIGHTY VOICE
No meat?

WHITE GIRL
Mush.

ALMIGHTY VOICE
How about some tea then? It's hot enough. It'll make you feel full.

WHITE GIRL
That's all there is.

ALMIGHTY VOICE
Can we go see your father now? He likes his tea. He always has sugar.

WHITE GIRL
The ice was almost too thick this morning. I was afraid we'd have to melt snow.

ALMIGHTY VOICE
We better go soon.

WHITE GIRL
Snow takes too long.

ALMIGHTY VOICE
That Sergeant's not as stupid as he looks. He'll see we doubled back.

WHITE GIRL
Do you know what glass is? Like thin ice?

ALMIGHTY VOICE
What are you talking about, White Girl?

WHITE GIRL
Some of the walls at the school were made out of it.

ALMIGHTY VOICE
Made out of what?

WHITE GIRL

Glass. A wall you can see through. I didn't know it was there at first, the wall. I tried to crawl through. I saw the sky, the grass moving. Out there. I banged my face. The glass broke. Sharp pieces, too. That's what this is from.

ALMIGHTY VOICE

A place to kiss.

WHITE GIRL

You know what, John Baptist? I dreamed about you. I knew you would come.

ALMIGHTY VOICE

What's the matter?

WHITE GIRL

I was looking at you far away. Through a glass wall!

ALMIGHTY VOICE

The soldiers, they have these clear beads they look through. Far away comes real close. All the walking in between seems to disappear.

WHITE GIRL

It was like that. It was. But it was also like I was waiting in my father's tipi. I could see you coming, I saw the moonlight on the barrel of your Winchester.

ALMIGHTY VOICE

I was bringing meat, I bet, buffalo meat for my wife.

WHITE GIRL

No you weren't. No! Let go.

ALMIGHTY VOICE

What's the matter, White Girl?

WHITE GIRL

You shot and the tipi broke. All the sharp pieces fell down on you, worse than hail. I think it hurt you, I think you got hurt.

ALMIGHTY VOICE

Stop it, White Girl, stop it. Don't be afraid. I'm all right.

WHITE GIRL

That god. That god. I'm afraid.

ALMIGHTY VOICE

That stupid god can't hurt me. That god belongs in that place, in the school. You're here now, I'm here now. He's not.

WHITE GIRL

He's everywhere!

ALMIGHTY VOICE

I told you he's a lie.

WHITE GIRL

He's like the glass. He's hard. He cuts you down.

ALMIGHTY VOICE

I'm your husband now. I won't let him hurt you. He doesn't deserve you.

WHITE GIRL

I'm sorry. I'm sorry.

ALMIGHTY VOICE

Listen, crazy one. You married Almighty Voice, who's not afraid to say his name. Let your glass god hear it. Almighty Voice! – who has listened to our fathers and heard what they say. Almighty Voice who remembers our Creator and our people's ways. Almighty Voice knows how to fight for you. Do you hear what I'm saying? Do you?

WHITE GIRL

Yes. Yes, I do.

ALMIGHTY VOICE

Who is saying it?

WHITE GIRL

Almighty Voice.

ALMIGHTY VOICE

Remember who you are. Remember what your mother taught you.

WHITE GIRL

Almighty Voice, the husband of White Girl!

ALMIGHTY VOICE

I'll break your glass god for you.

WHITE GIRL

Keep your bad medicine!

ALMIGHTY VOICE
It's just a bad smell. A stink. Come on. I'll get the horse. Your father has the tea ready for us.

WHITE GIRL
Husband, look!

ALMIGHTY VOICE
Give me my Winchester. My wife'll have rabbit for breakfast.

> *He loads and exits. WHITE GIRL watches him go, then builds up the fire. She hears a noise from another direction and looks and stops. A shot. She runs toward the place where ALMIGHTY VOICE exited. He enters, dead rabbit in hand.*

ALMIGHTY VOICE
(laughing) Look how fat! This'll make you full.

WHITE GIRL
Husband, be quiet.

> *ALMIGHTY VOICE drops the rabbit.*

WHITE GIRL
It's the god. See his glass eye.

ALMIGHTY VOICE
It's the Sergeant, White Girl. Just the stupid Sergeant. What's he say?

WHITE GIRL
I can't understand him.

ALMIGHTY VOICE
That's that stupid half-breed with him. Stay behind me, girl.

WHITE GIRL
He wants to make peace. There's the sign.

ALMIGHTY VOICE
Get down. He's got a gun.

WHITE GIRL
Where's the half-breed going?

ALMIGHTY VOICE
Stay where you are!

WHITE GIRL
What about the horse?

ALMIGHTY VOICE
No time. Stay there! Where's the other one?

WHITE GIRL
I can't see. Over there.

ALMIGHTY VOICE
Circling around. Don't come any closer. *(He reloads his Winchester.)*

WHITE GIRL
Leave us alone! Go away!

ALMIGHTY VOICE
I'm warning you!

WHITE GIRL
Husband–

ALMIGHTY VOICE
This gun's loaded!

WHITE GIRL
–the half-breed's behind us.

ALMIGHTY VOICE
Keep close. I'm warning you! Stop there! Stay there! *(shooting)* You stupid!

WHITE GIRL
One shot. One shot, Almighty Voice!

ALMIGHTY VOICE
The other one?

WHITE GIRL
I told you glass breaks.

ALMIGHTY VOICE
Gone. Scared his horse, too. He'll bring more Mounties. There will be more from now on.

WHITE GIRL
Glass breaks so easily.

ALMIGHTY VOICE
Wife, look at me.

WHITE GIRL
I'm all right, husband.

ALMIGHTY VOICE
Come on.

WHITE GIRL
No. There will be more from now on. I'll slow you down.

ALMIGHTY VOICE
I can't leave you, girl.

WHITE GIRL
They won't hurt me. They'll be afraid to now.

ALMIGHTY VOICE
White Girl, look at me.

WHITE GIRL
They'll have to take me home. I'll tell everyone how it happened, how he
wouldn't listen. They'll just take me home. I'll just slow them down. We can
meet at my mother's – I mean your mother's house. My mother's gone. She
died of hunger last winter. But I'm all right, Almighty Voice. And I know
I have to go talk to your mother soon.

ALMIGHTY VOICE
What about?

WHITE GIRL
I want us to make her a grandchild. She has to tell me how to get ready.
Women's stuff. I know I have to eat. *(She goes and picks up the rabbit.)* You
better go now.

    ALMIGHTY VOICE exits. WHITE GIRL takes the rabbit to the fire.

SCENE SIX

    *The projected title: "Scene Six: Mid-Winter Moon." A martial beat on the drum
    as the bloody moon rises. Then silence. WHITE GIRL sits near the second fire
    while ALMIGHTY VOICE wanders between the fires.*

WHITE GIRL
Mister. Mister! Mister God! I see your glass eye. Eye-eye! Stinky breath. It's
me. Marrie! Marrie, your wife. Wife wife wife! God, look at me like before.
How they taught me at school. How how. Here's my hair. Look. Here's my
skin. How how, husband god, see what a little girl I am. Great White God
of the ghost men, mother is here. Blood blood blood between my thighs.

Yes, gimme, gimme, gimme something sweet. Oh yes, yes, you're rotten, rotten meat, but wifey wife will eat you up. Mister God, god, stupid god, this is what you want! Come on! Come on, don't leave! I'm your little squaw. Eye-eye! See! Eye-eye, Mister God. Eye-eye!

ALMIGHTY VOICE

Don't talk, cousin. You're being stupid. No one would mistake you for a warrior. And your woman, she's so skinny, no one would call you a hunter either. Or a lover. Could your woman do what my woman has? Could she look those white men in the eyes? They took her back to Duck Lake and kept her in that guard house and she gave them lies for their lies. "Run, husband. We will meet later." She said that to me. Is it a surprise I think about her? I believe what she says. If she is crazy, we all should be. Not a word, Little Salteau! Who's the one who killed a Mountie?

WHITE GIRL

I am the wife of Almighty Voice. You don't know my name. You don't even wonder if I have one. I'm only a crazy squaw. You're watching me but you expect to see my husband. His is a name you know. Almighty Voice. John Baptist. You say these names of his over and over again, like the prayers you say to your glass-eyed god for the grace of your Great White Mother Victoria. But your prayers won't make him come. Mister God Mountie, you don't know what his name means.

ALMIGHTY VOICE

Your sister, Young Dust, she makes me remember how my father used to talk about the buffalo. Maybe because she likes meat so much. I'd like to feed her till she's fat. My father said everyone used to be like that. Everyone used to follow the buffalo. He hates farming. A man shouldn't be a bag of bones. My mother says he gets no meat. In Prince Albert. John Sounding Sky is in jail because his son mistook a Mountie for a cow!

WHITE GIRL

You're laughing with that half-breed. "Let the crazy squaw go home. Easy to keep an eye on her there." So he unlocks the door, walks away to the fire where you play with your silver coin, your dollar. That's what you want to trade my husband's blood for. Why? What is its power? A coin is not the moon. Can't you see it's dead, Mister Mountie? Cold as the bullet my husband kills rabbits or enemies with.

ALMIGHTY VOICE

So my mother Spotted Calf is alone still, running things, hating it. She says there are too many women now. I think there aren't enough men. It's like a war but no one will say so, so there's never any peace. How many of our brothers are there still in Stoney Mountain? How many come home in the spring? My mother says it makes her children crazy, living on snow. Maybe she's right. Come on. Let's go make some blood flow tonight!

WHITE GIRL
You've got a bad look on your face, a blindness, a glassy gaze. What are
you staring at? Your silver dollar? The fire? My husband's bullet. You'll stare
'til they all turn to glass. And what will you see through them then? That
forever place you want to live, the one they promised me in school? I turn
here in the wind toward the river and the moon is there, a woman with
better things to do. She slips away from you, going home.

SCENE SEVEN

*The projected title: "Scene Seven: Honeymoon." The drum beats. The full moon
sweeps down from the sky like a spotlight to show and surround the lovers, lying
together on the ground.*

WHITE GIRL
Almighty Voice, come on.

ALMIGHTY VOICE
Not again.

WHITE GIRL
I want to be sure.

ALMIGHTY VOICE
Let me sleep.

WHITE GIRL
This is the time to do it. Your mother said so.

ALMIGHTY VOICE
I don't want to know that. I don't want to do it for my mother.

WHITE GIRL
Do it for me. It's the best time now.

ALMIGHTY VOICE
I don't want to know that stuff.

WHITE GIRL
Young Dust dreamed we had a son.

ALMIGHTY VOICE
This is none of your brother's business.

WHITE GIRL
Come on, John Baptist.

ALMIGHTY VOICE
White Girl, we got to sleep.

WHITE GIRL
Almighty Voice, do you like my hand there?

ALMIGHTY VOICE
Don't. You keep this up, we'll fall asleep on the horse later.

WHITE GIRL
You fall off, you can fall on me.

ALMIGHTY VOICE
White Girl, we got to move on tonight. Little Salteau said those stupid Mounties are just south of here.

WHITE GIRL
They're hunting quail, not us. I like it here. I like how flat it is. Like your belly.

ALMIGHTY VOICE
White Girl, stop it.

WHITE GIRL
Come on, Almighty Voice.

ALMIGHTY VOICE
Do as your husband says. And don't laugh.

WHITE GIRL
The Mounties don't know we're here. Why worry?

ALMIGHTY VOICE
Go to sleep.

WHITE GIRL
They'll forget about you.

ALMIGHTY VOICE
I killed a Mountie. They don't give up.

WHITE GIRL
But he would have killed you.

ALMIGHTY VOICE
I know.

WHITE GIRL

Spring comes, the snow goes. Too many other things to do. Cows running away through the grass. Fresh meat, husband.

ALMIGHTY VOICE

Can't you be quiet, girl?

WHITE GIRL

Isn't this grass moving in the wind here on your flat prairie?

ALMIGHTY VOICE

I'm your husband, White Girl.

WHITE GIRL

Oh your wife likes to run in the grass, Almighty Voice.

ALMIGHTY VOICE

Stop it. Go to sleep.

WHITE GIRL

They can't see you as long as you're with me.

ALMIGHTY VOICE

We can't hide in that grass, little girl.

WHITE GIRL

We can hide. With me you're in the dark of the moon. It's what your mother talks about. When we're together, it's like we're inside a bead of glass made of wind. They can't get at us. It's my medicine, husband. In the dream – you were in the dream. That's all I can tell you.

ALMIGHTY VOICE

You fasted? When?

WHITE GIRL

The last blizzard. Your mother took me out. In that wind.

ALMIGHTY VOICE

The moon was dark then.

WHITE GIRL

She took me down to the river. I built a fire on the ice. She visited me every morning. And she sang to me.

ALMIGHTY VOICE

And she serves tea to the priest!

WHITE GIRL
And laughs at him. He expects her to give you away. That priest wants her to marry his god too.

ALMIGHTY VOICE
That's crazy.

WHITE GIRL
Instead she gets news of your father in Prince Albert.

ALMIGHTY VOICE
I didn't know. What does she say about my father? Is his cough any better? When One Arrow got back from the jail at Stoney Mountain, he was old. He told my father that the visions of warriors have no more power against the soldiers.

WHITE GIRL
He was old, husband. He was tired.

ALMIGHTY VOICE
Not even Riel's vision, and he was part white.

WHITE GIRL
It's the jail, husband. They watch you all the time. You can't move.

ALMIGHTY VOICE
I was there when he said it.

WHITE GIRL
And it's all stone.

ALMIGHTY VOICE
He gave away his rifle.

WHITE GIRL
You can't see anything but stones. You can't see anything, husband. You forget everything.

ALMIGHTY VOICE
How can you forget everything and be a man?

WHITE GIRL
You're not a man then. You're like a ghost. You're lost.

ALMIGHTY VOICE
I want to see my father. I'm going to Prince Albert.

WHITE GIRL
That's crazy.

ALMIGHTY VOICE
The Mounties won't know I'm there. Why worry?

WHITE GIRL
Your mother says someone's always watching him. You don't know that place.

ALMIGHTY VOICE
I'm going to talk to him.

WHITE GIRL
You have to hide. Your mother said so.

ALMIGHTY VOICE
Shut up about my mother! I don't want to hear it.

WHITE GIRL
She won't let you go.

ALMIGHTY VOICE
Am I a child again? Hiding behind women. How can you look at me?

WHITE GIRL
You're my husband.

ALMIGHTY VOICE
My father is a man. John Sounding Sky still means warrior. But Almighty Voice?

WHITE GIRL
He's a warrior.

ALMIGHTY VOICE
Does a warrior run away? Almighty Voice is a stupid old man, a ghost. He's here, there, nowhere.

WHITE GIRL
You can't go.

ALMIGHTY VOICE
I should be in Prince Albert. John Sounding Sky should be at home with Spotted Calf.

WHITE GIRL
They ache to hang Almighty Voice.

ALMIGHTY VOICE
What good am I here?

WHITE GIRL
I need you.

ALMIGHTY VOICE
What good am I to you, White Girl?

WHITE GIRL
I don't want to be alone.

ALMIGHTY VOICE
You can stay with my mother.

WHITE GIRL
Two women old with no men? Your mother will die like my mother did.
You can't leave me too.

ALMIGHTY VOICE
Your father will take you.

WHITE GIRL
You're sending me home?

ALMIGHTY VOICE
He'll get you a better husband.

WHITE GIRL
He'll get me a worse one.

ALMIGHTY VOICE
Who? Who could that be?

WHITE GIRL
Any ghost man will do. You want me to die.

ALMIGHTY VOICE
You won't die!

WHITE GIRL
I will. For years. Kill me now. Be good to me, husband. Kill me now and
then you can go, go and be hanged.

ALMIGHTY VOICE
You're pretty fierce, all right.

WHITE GIRL
Let go of me.

ALMIGHTY VOICE
For a little girl.

WHITE GIRL
I'll get you your Winchester.

ALMIGHTY VOICE
Stay here with me.

WHITE GIRL
You can kill me, husband. We'll both be dead.

ALMIGHTY VOICE
That's stupid. White Girl who has visions, stay here with me.

WHITE GIRL
What about your father?

ALMIGHTY VOICE
We'll find a way. My mother will help.

WHITE GIRL
You won't leave me?

ALMIGHTY VOICE
Hey, I'm here with you. In the dark of the moon. They can't get at us.

WHITE GIRL
Almighty Voice–

ALMIGHTY VOICE
Can't you be quiet, girl? Your husband doesn't want to sleep any more. He likes your hand here.

SCENE EIGHT

A projected title: "Scene Eight: The Hunting Moon." A gunshot. The social drum. Three more shots. ALMIGHTY VOICE with his Winchester at the last fire, the dead one. WHITE GIRL with a baby-sized bundle in her arms, still illuminated by the moon.

WHITE GIRL
You brought me home to your mother. It was time. Spotted Calf expected me. She took me into her new house. Other women were waiting. "Go

away," she said. "Young Dust will bring you news." Someone, the Rump's Daughter, might tell. It was dangerous. The Mounties – it was dangerous. You wanted to hide under the floor, under her bed like last winter. But she made you go. "You men shouldn't know women's stuff." You men. Little Salteau and Dubling came along. I heard you laughing. Off you rode to hunt somewhere, the grass new, blue green. I saw you through the glass in the window of that house. Going.

ALMIGHTY VOICE

Has he come? Tell him, wife, tell him how good a season it was everywhere along the Saskatchewan the winter before he was born. Tell him I always found game, never got cold. Till now. Say the ghost men shivered in their huts, too afraid of the wind to fire a shot. Tell him it can be like that again. Tell him, girl. Do you hear me? I wish you did.

Tell him how we visited and people would give his mother more to eat. Even people in the woods far up north. An old bull buffalo, chewy but sweet. You worried it might be their last one but ate anyway. Tell him Old Dust gave in, gave us lots of sugar for our tea, called me son, when he saw how fat you were. One day I remember. Cold, bright. Leather stiff as wood. Your belly had begun to curve. Your breath feathers, or smoke that fell, hugged the ground. I teased you, your belly like the iron stove at the store at Duck Lake. Tight as a drum. I felt him kick then. What a thump! I knew I had a son. I wanted to dance.

> *ALMIGHTY VOICE dances with the drum in celebration. Then, as WHITE GIRL speaks, his steps turn into a war dance and then into stillness. The moon around WHITE GIRL turns bloody.*

WHITE GIRL

They tell me you came across another cow. They say you wanted to feast me and the baby. So you shot the stupid thing. Some farmer heard your guns, didn't mind his own business. Him and his sons gave chase. I can hear you laughing, leading them into this bluff of poplars. And suddenly there's Mounties, soldiers, farmers everywhere. And someone shoots someone. I hope it was that farmer. They tell me you got no food, no water all day. They say someone else got shot. Maybe a Mountie. Young Dust said he heard you singing. War songs. He says you were dancing. There were ghost men all around that night. Farmers, soldiers, priests of the glass god. Over a hundred against Little Salteau, Dubling and Almighty Voice by the end. And two big iron guns. I saw them myself the second day. Spotted Calf and I stood watching. I wanted you to be anywhere else. Young Dust held the baby, reminded me to feed his nephew. I didn't notice I was full, aching. I have no milk now. *(She puts her bundle down.)* That night I saw my husband Almighty Voice again against that moon I had tried to forget. Then those two guns started firing and firing. Firing and firing. It was cold and the smoke would not go away. I seemed to see you sometime in the night, in the smoke, but even before morning broke, your mother was singing her death song.

SCENE NINE

A projected title: "Scene Nine: His Vision." The drum beats in the night. The moon is low in the sky, pulsing. ALMIGHTY VOICE lies by the dead fire, his leg badly wounded. The spectral tipi appears and the drum goes silent. Inside the tipi are WHITE GIRL and her baby, mother and child, a destination. ALMIGHTY VOICE rises and uses his Winchester as a crutch to come to the tipi. WHITE GIRL comes out and shows him the baby and the baby cries. The moon turns white. ALMIGHTY VOICE dies.

ACT TWO

A follow spot finds a title placard: "Act Two: Ghost Dance."

SCENE ONE

The spot shifts to a second title placard: "Scene One: Overture," then fades. Spectral light from the dead fire. ALMIGHTY VOICE, now in white face as his own GHOST, continues his dance of celebration around the fire inside the last crescent of the moon. Scattered around the moon's half circle are ruined stools, three of which are still sturdy enough to be useful. On the one upright at the crescent's mid point a searching spot finds a seated figure and finding its head, finds white-gloved hands hiding its face. As the crescent moon fades, the hands open to reveal the white face that masks WHITE GIRL into the role of the INTERLOCUTOR, a Mountie and the Master of Ceremonies. In a glance their eyes meet. Sudden light shift to variety show lights, both the GHOST and the INTERLOCUTOR in follow spots. The INTERLOCUTOR adjusts her monocle.

INTERLOCUTOR
Here, here? I said "Here, here." Hey dead man! Hey red man! Hey Indian!

GHOST
Awas. Si-pwete. [Go away. Go on.]

INTERLOCUTOR
"Here, here", I said. What's the meaning of this? Come on, use the Queen's tongue, or I'll sell you to a cigar store.

GHOST
Awas kititin ni-nimihiton oma ota. [Go away. I'm dancing here.]

INTERLOCUTOR
You dare call these furtive foot steps, these frenzied flailings of arms like wings, dancing! Stop it. It's nonsense.

GHOST
Awena kiya? Kekwiy ka-ayimota-man? [Who are you? What are you talking about?]

INTERLOCUTOR
Snap out of it, chief. *(slapping him with the gloves four times)*

GHOST
Oweeya! Oweeya! Ya! Ya! Pakitinin awena kiya moya ki-kis-ke yimitin. [Ow! Ow! Ow! Ow! Let go of me. Who are you? I don't know you.]

INTERLOCUTOR

You know very well who the hell I am. I don't have to remind you no show can begin without its master. Here, here. Stop I say. How dare you go faster.

GHOST

Nahkee. Kawiya-(ekosi). Ponikawin poko ta kisisimoyan. [Stop. Let me alone. I have to finish my dance.]

INTERLOCUTOR

I'll break the other leg for you, Kisse-Manitou-Wayou.

GHOST

Tansi esi kiskeyitaman ni wiyowin? [How do you know my name?]

INTERLOCUTOR

Names, names, they're all the same. Crees all wear feathers. Dead man, red man, Indian, *Kisse-Manitou-Wayou*, Almighty Voice, *Jean Baptiste*! Geronimo, Tonto, Calijah. Or most simply, Mister Ghost.

GHOST

Ghost?

INTERLOCUTOR

Boo! Almighty Ghost, Chief. Now we're speaking English.

GHOST

What? Who are you?

INTERLOCUTOR

How. You're supposed to say "How." You know. Hey Pontiac, how's the engine? Can't you stick to the script? You're too new at this ghost schtick to go speaking *ad liberatum.*

GHOST

Let me go. I don't know you. Let me dance.

INTERLOCUTOR

Here here. Stop, I say. How dare you! Do I have to remind you this colourful display, these exotic ceremonials belong later on in the program? Listen to me, Chief. One doesn't begin with a climax, an end. Unmitigated foolishness, I'll have you know. If you begin at the end, then where do you go? Do you know? No. Well? What have you got to say for yourself?

GHOST

How–

INTERLOCUTOR

That's more like it!

GHOST

How did I get here? What's going on?

INTERLOCUTOR

What's going on! The show. The Red and White Victoria Regina Spirit Revival show! These fine, kind folks want to know the truth, the amazing details and circumstance behind your savagely beautiful appearance. They also want to be entertained and enlightened and maybe a tiny bit thrilled, just a goose of frightened. They want to laugh and cry. They want to know the facts. And it's up to you and me to try and lie that convincingly. And since all the rest of our company is late for the curtain, this is your chance, your big break for certain.

GHOST

No, I won't dance for you.

INTERLOCUTOR

But you have to toe the line, Chief. We all do. Here. Let me smell your breath. Bah! Like death warmed over. I've warned you before. You choose to booze and you're back on the street where I found you.

GHOST

Leave me alone. Go away.

INTERLOCUTOR

Don't you realize you could be internationally known, the most acclaimed magic act of the century?

GHOST

What do you mean?

INTERLOCUTOR

The Vanishing Indian!

GHOST

Poof?

INTERLOCUTOR

Forget about faggots.

GHOST

I want to know how I got here.

INTERLOCUTOR

Gutter. Does that sound mean anything to you? Gutter?

GHOST
All I remember–

INTERLOCUTOR
Answer me, you sotted fancy dancer.

GHOST
My leg was gone.

INTERLOCUTOR
Come on, Chief, be a friend.

GHOST
It was! I used a branch from a sapling.

INTERLOCUTOR
Be a pal, Chiefy, dear.

GHOST
No, it was my gun for a crutch.

INTERLOCUTOR
This is a bit much for this early in the proceedings.

GHOST
Sometime in the night–

INTERLOCUTOR
Wait wait wait. I'd like to apologize to the ladies in the audience and
suggest that this might be a prime opportunity to make use of our
theatre's other facilities. The details of the following story may be not
for the faint of heart, are in fact quite gory, and ordinarily it would be
our custom to warn you and ask your permission before we proceed.
However—how-ever—as you can see, my peer here feels he must thrust the
entire tale upon us. Once again, I apologize. Thank you for your attention.
All right. Proceed.

GHOST
My legs were gone.

INTERLOCUTOR
His leg was gone!

GHOST
I must have screamed.

INTERLOCUTOR
Talk about Wounded Knee.

GHOST
But my throat was too dry.

INTERLOCUTOR
The bones were shattered, pulp. Not that that mattered.

GHOST
There was no sound in my mouth.

INTERLOCUTOR
Quite the come down for Almighty Vocal Cords.

GHOST
I couldn't sing my song.

INTERLOCUTOR
Oh lord, talented, too!

GHOST
My death song. I crawled out of the pit.

INTERLOCUTOR
And we're not talking orchestra pits out here in the sticks.

GHOST
We had dug it in the ground to protect us from the gunfire.

INTERLOCUTOR
Not much good compared to a couple of cannons, was it?

GHOST
There was smoke close to the ground.

INTERLOCUTOR
From the fires all around?

GHOST
I thought I might be able to make it across the open space.

INTERLOCUTOR
And was it really over a hundred men by then?

GHOST
Against Little Salteau, Dubling and me.

INTERLOCUTOR
Imagine. Red coats and wild Indians. What a spectacle! Where are my glasses?

GHOST
It was the middle of the night. I might get by if the watch was asleep.

INTERLOCUTOR
Not on duty? Now that's not very funny.

GHOST
I had seen her watching, many times that day, beyond their lines. I got halfway across.

INTERLOCUTOR
And amazingly, no one saw him then. He might have made good his escape. Think about that. However—how-ever—he was bleeding a lot. Red blood oozing from red skin. Oh what a thrill! I'm not offending you, am I?

GHOST
She came to meet me.

INTERLOCUTOR
(á la "Indian Love Call") When I'm calling you-oo-oo-oo-oo-oo-oo!

GHOST
No one could see her. My wife had denied their glass-eyed god. It was her medicine to be invisible.

INTERLOCUTOR
Wish my wife could do that. That's really interesting. Kissy Kisse-Manitou-Wayou? Did you give her some tongue!

GHOST
She told me about my son. She told me I would not be forgotten.

INTERLOCUTOR
How can I put this delicately? Your last meeting, your last touch. Your life dribbling out of you, hot and sticky. Big strong buck like you used to be. Was it savage love? Did you have a last quickie?

GHOST
I knew I could die then.

INTERLOCUTOR
She was some babe, eh?

GHOST
People would remember me.

INTERLOCUTOR
Give me some of the juicy details, Chief.

GHOST
My people would remember me.

INTERLOCUTOR
One must always strive for accuracy. Do you have documentation?

GHOST
I knew I could die then.

INTERLOCUTOR
Come on, Chief, speak up. Anybody got a cigar? Never mind.

GHOST
I could hear my mother, off on the hill, singing her song.

INTERLOCUTOR
Talent just runs in that family!

GHOST
Her death song.

INTERLOCUTOR
So does manic depression! Do we feel better now? We do remember you, Mister Almighty Ghost. The angry young man, the passionate lover, the wild and crazy Indian kid. A shocking but true tale of the frontier. Now don't you think this is just too touching, ladies and gentlemen? Too much for my refined sensibilities, that's a certainty. That wasn't too bad, Chief, considering. And now– *(She changes the title placard.)*

SCENE TWO

The new placard reads: "Scene Two. Baritone Solo."

INTERLOCUTOR
Ladies and gentlemen, for your further edification and delight, a musical selection. Mister Almighty Ghost, the famous Aboriginal voice, will now render for you the sweet ballad, "Lament of the Redskin Lover." Mister Ghost?

GHOST
(in a spotlight) What are you talking about?

INTERLOCUTOR
Go on, Mister Ghost. We wait upon you, sir. Sing. Sing.

GHOST
I don't know this.

INTERLOCUTOR
No memory at all? Here. It's number two on your lyric sheet, sir.

GHOST
Who are you?

INTERLOCUTOR
This is it, your last show. You're back on the street in the morning. The gutter? Here we go.

> *The INTERLOCUTOR stands behind the GHOST and guides him through the accompanying mime.*

GHOST
(to the tune of "Oh! Susanna")
I track the winter prairie for the little squaw I lost.
I'm missing all the kissing I had afore the frost.
I'm moping, oh I'm hoping oh, to hold her hand in mine.
My flower of Saskatchewan, oh we were doing fine.

GHOST & INTERLOCUTOR
In our tipi, oh we were so in love,
One Arrow was too narrow for my little squaw and me.

GHOST
I had a dream the other night, I saw her on a hill.

INTERLOCUTOR
My little squaw was shaking, the wind was standing still.

GHOST
The banic bread was in her mouth, and blood was in her eye.
The moon so bright I lost my sight–

INTERLOCUTOR
–I pray she didn't die!

GHOST
On the prairie, oh how the white does blow!
Who makes it through the winter?
                    Not my little squaw or me.

INTERLOCUTOR
Nicely done. Thank you, thank you, Mister Ghost. You were almost your spooky self again.

GHOST
Thank you, Mister Interlocutor.

INTERLOCUTOR

Buck up, Mister Ghost. Isn't this all familiar? Might not, say, Buck and Squaw be the latest dance craze?

INTERLOCUTOR pulls GHOST into a short Hollywood Indian War Dance. GHOST resists. At the end GHOST grabs INTERLOCUTOR and looks into her eyes.

GHOST

This is what they've done to you.

INTERLOCUTOR

Thank you, thank you, Mister Ghost. A most original interpretation of the material. Gentle listeners, Mister Bones will now perform for you–

GHOST

Mister Bones? He the one with the dice?

INTERLOCUTOR

No, Mister Ghost. He's the one who's got rhythm.

GHOST

There's no one like that backstage, sir.

INTERLOCUTOR

No? Perhaps our friend Mister Tambo waits in the wings.

GHOST

That the Tamborine Man? Not even in the flies, sir. Nor, sir, is Mister Drum lurking below the trapdoor.

INTERLOCUTOR

No Mister Drum? Well, Mister Ghost – no! Wait!

The GHOST changes the placard.

SCENE THREE

The new placard reads "Scene Three: The Stump."

GHOST

Ladies and gentlemen, boys and girls, dogs and cats, we of the Pale-Faced Band of the Sweet Saskatchewaners are pleased to present for your information and concern our own Mister Interlocutor in the role of Mister Drum, a loyal citizen of our territory.

INTERLOCUTOR

Wait a moment, Mister Ghost. That is not my part.

GHOST

But you do know it by heart. This is your chance, sir, your big break for certain. Ladies and gentlemen, please welcome Mister Drum.

INTERLOCUTOR

Ahem. Ahem. I come before you this evening, my dear friends, full, full of concern. We have ourselves a problem, dear friends, an Indian problem. Dare I say an indigent Indian problem? Dear friends, the pampered redskins, they are the bad ones. Those tribes that have been cared for as if they were our equals, they, dear friends, are the first to turn and shed the blood of their benefactors. Noisemaker was petted, yes, even feted, my friends, and now raids our farms. Pricky Pinecone was paid to come up to our fine territory and what, dear friends, is his pursuit nowadays? Carnage! Large Prairie Dog who for years has sharpened his teeth by chewing on the bone of idleness, shows his gratitude by killing his priests for their holy wine. That is not communion, friends. Little Dump, a non-treaty Indian, has been, friends, provisioned with all necessaries and so gets to spend all his days gallivanting about the territory, shouting loudly and plotting mischief. And now, my dear friends, this Almighty Gas character joins in on the season's carnival of ruin. Oh friends, the petted Indians have proved the bad ones and this gives weight to the wise adage, friends, that the only good Indians are the dead ones.

GHOST

Bravo! Bravo, Mister Interlocutor, sir. Mister Drum could not have said it better.

INTERLOCUTOR

Thank you, Mister Ghost.

GHOST

No, thank *you*, Mister Interlocutor. I take your words to heart. My heart soars! We all thank you, sir. Don't we, ladies and gentles? Never a truer word was said. It is to our great benefit to know of this dread red threat to our well-beings and livelihoods, this deadly hood, this Almighty Fart character. Dead Indians would be even better, sir, if they didn't stink that way.

INTERLOCUTOR

Thank you again, Mister Ghost, thank you again. I thank you too, ladies and gentle sirs. We will now return to the sequence of events as listed in your programs.

GHOST

But sir, there's still no sign of Messers Bone, Tambo, Drum, or any one. The entire company, sir, seems to be running on Indian Time!

INTERLOCUTOR
Would you now consider performing, Mister Ghost, for our attentive
friends that charming curiosity you called a dance?

GHOST
No.

INTERLOCUTOR
Surely, Mister Ghost–

GHOST
Call me the late Almighty Voice. Call me an early redman. Call me, yes,
even call me a ghost – but don't call me Shirley!

INTERLOCUTOR
You're the most spirited ghost I've ever met.

GHOST
You better believe it. There's a stir of dissatisfaction, sir, in the audience.
Perhaps number seven?

INTERLOCUTOR
An excellent suggestion, Mister Ghost. An excellent selection, I assure you,
my friends.

GHOST
But, sir, it calls for the entire company. And we, sir, are the skeleton crew!

SCENE FOUR

*The INTERLOCUTOR changes the title placard to: "Scene Four: The
Walkaround."*

INTERLOCUTOR
Ladies and gentlemen, for your delight and encouragement, Mister Ghost
and Yours Truly will now present a martial interlude. In honour of all our
heroic boys in uniform!

GHOST
I'll even honour those boys out of uniform.

INTERLOCUTOR
I appear first in the role of Mister Allan, leading the charge through the
bluff. After the renegade!

GHOST
Hurrah! We're beating the bushes.

INTERLOCUTOR
Where are the cowards?

GHOST
Moo? Pow, pow!

INTERLOCUTOR
Ambush, vicious ambush!

GHOST
It appears Mister Allan's fallen off his horse!

INTERLOCUTOR
A bullet! A bullet shattered my arm.

GHOST
Bull! The bottle did him in.

INTERLOCUTOR
Then I take the part of the brave second in command, Mister Raven.

GHOST
Already shot on the wing.

INTERLOCUTOR
What?

GHOST
In his private parts!

INTERLOCUTOR
Not my leg?

GHOST
Groin, groin, gone!

INTERLOCUTOR
Oh where is the rest of my happy company?

GHOST
Retreat! Retreat! Buck up, my friend, there are but three of them.

INTERLOCUTOR
We've got them outnumbered. I, Mister Hockin, take charge. Surround the bluff!

GHOST
But are you nine and the settlers enough?

INTERLOCUTOR
Postmaster Grundy here, volunteer, sir. We'll all of us beat them bushes again.

GHOST
March then. March south, men. They can't hide from you.

INTERLOCUTOR
Where have they gone? We had them surrounded.

GHOST
This could be embarrassing.

INTERLOCUTOR
East to west now. Shoulder to shoulder.

GHOST
Nothing. No one. Again?

INTERLOCUTOR
Here we go. These darn trees.

GHOST
Unpopular poplars?

INTERLOCUTOR
If they weren't so green. Fire would force them out.

GHOST
Say again.

INTERLOCUTOR
Fire!

GHOST
Bang bang! Bang bang, bang bang, bang bang! The mail comes late.

INTERLOCUTOR
Why?

GHOST
Postmaster Grundy got shot in the gut.

INTERLOCUTOR
What about Hockin?

GHOST
His heart got broken.

INTERLOCUTOR
And Kerr?

GHOST
Sorry, sir. Retreat! Retreat!

INTERLOCUTOR
I don't want to wait all day and all night.

GHOST
Too late.

INTERLOCUTOR
I could have got them.

GHOST
Reinforcements arrive!

INTERLOCUTOR
I could have got them alive!

GHOST
So can I play the one little, two little dozen Mounties?

INTERLOCUTOR
I'll take the roles of the two big guns!

GHOST
Bang bang? Boom boom. Doom doom!

INTERLOCUTOR
As well as the crowd of concerned civilians, including the disappointed–

GHOST
–I do so much for those ungrateful wretches–

INTERLOCUTOR
–farm instructor and his friend the ever hopeful–

GHOST
–Spare the rod and spoil the child!–

INTERLOCUTOR
–missionary priest. Well?

GHOST
It will be the least I can do then and an honour to represent the man's wife and mother as well as others from the One Arrow Reserve, Treaty Number Six.

INTERLOCUTOR

Perhaps, then, you will do the parts then of the young man and his ill-fated companions? Yes?

GHOST

No.

INTERLOCUTOR

Mister Ghost, sure – please listen to me and consider–

GHOST

Fuck you. I'm not going through that again for your entertainment.

INTERLOCUTOR

Mister Ghost–

GHOST

You do it.

INTERLOCUTOR

(to the tune of "Derry Down")
Who is fighting the battle for everyone,–

GHOST

–is fighting the battle for everyone,–

INTERLOCUTOR

–fights blood-thirsty redskins and wears a grin,–

GHOST

–not afeard of anything?–

GHOST & INTERLOCUTOR

Who rides high in the saddle and shoots a gun,
rides high in the saddle and shoots a gun,
shoots blood-thirsty redskins and wears a grin,
not afeard of anything?
We have the guns, the guts, the wit.
We know that you are stinking shit.
We did it to the buffalo.
Want to be next? Yes or no?
We are the men with guns and bucks.
We know that you are stupid fucks.
We did it to the buffalo.
Want to be next? Yes or no?

INTERLOCUTOR

Who is fighting the battle for everyone,
is fighting the battle for everyone,

shoots blood thirsty redskins and wears a grin,
not afeard of anything?

GHOST

We have the guns, the guts, the wit.
We know that you are stupid shit.
We did it to the buffalo.
Want to be next? Yes or no?

GHOST & INTERLOCUTOR

We are the men,
well let's say it again,
to get them heathen Indians.
We are the ones,
oh let's do it with guns,
let's kill them stinking Indians.
We are the ones,
well let's do it with rum,
let's get them redskin Indians.
We are the men,
oh let's say it again,
to kill them damn dead Indians.

GHOST

Who rides high in the saddle and shoots a gun,
rides high in the saddle and shoots a gun,
shoots blood-thirsty redskins and wears a grin,
not afeard of anything?

INTERLOCUTOR

We have the guns, the guts, the wit.
We know that you are stinking shit.
We did it to the buffalo.
Want to be next? Yes or No?

GHOST & INTERLOCUTOR

We have the bucks and you do not.
Is it a wonder that you got shot?
We have the bucks and you do not.
Is it a wonder that you got shot?
We have the bucks and you do not.
Is it a wonder that you got shot?
We have the bucks and you do not.
Is it a wonder that you got shot?

We have the blankets and the rum.
Oh did you say that you want some?

GHOST
Well, Mister Interlocutor, how do you feel now?

INTERLOCUTOR
No, Mister Ghost, how do you feel now?

GHOST
Well, Mister Interlocutor, I feel somewhat like a newspaper.

INTERLOCUTOR
You feel like a newspaper? How is that, Mister Ghost?

GHOST
I'm pale as a sheet of paper.

INTERLOCUTOR
A sheet of paper? With black eyes, Mister Ghost?

GHOST
Every one dotted, sir.

INTERLOCUTOR hits GHOST.

And ultimately, sir, I am like a newspaper in that I am read all over – the countryside.

INTERLOCUTOR
Red all over, sir? A most colourful conceit. Bloody good, as our cousins would have it. Newspapers are our pass to an understanding of the reserve and the life of its denizens.

GHOST
And we don't have to go to the Indian agent to get them. The passes.

INTERLOCUTOR
Are you making one at me, sir? *(hitting him)* Did you read how we're teaching our primitive friends agriculture?

GHOST
That'll bring them down to earth.

INTERLOCUTOR
And we're giving them the benefit of our modern tongue.

GHOST
They'll need no other one, our kingdom come.

INTERLOCUTOR
Did you read how tranquil and subordinate they've become under our wise and humane government?

The GHOST claps a "gunshot."

Was that a gun? A shot?

GHOST
Likely not. The Indian Agent won't give them any more ammunition until they put in a crop.

INTERLOCUTOR
What will they eat in the meantime?

GHOST
(hitting himself) Off to the hoose-gow with them! Lazy is as lazy does. So it says in the newspaper. Or the Bible. *(reprising "Derry Down")*

Who is shooting in battle at every one
is shooting in battle at everyone,–

GHOST & INTERLOCUTOR
–fights blood-thirsty redskins and wears a grin,
not afeard of anything?–

GHOST
–We have the words, the pens, the laws.
We know that treaties are for fools.
We did it to the buffalo.
You want to be next?

SCENE FIVE

The GHOST reveals the next placard: "Scene Five: Tenor Solo."

GHOST
And now, for the particular delectation of the ladies in the audience–

INTERLOCUTOR
What are you doing?

GHOST
–Mister Interlocutor will render in his most famous transvestatory manner–

INTERLOCUTOR
I won't do this.

GHOST
-as the Princess Porkly Haunches, he now sings "The Sioux Song."

INTERLOCUTOR
This is not a regular part of the program, ladies and gentlemen.

GHOST
And therefore we must show our gratitude to the Princess. Let us further encourage her, ladies and gentle sirs.

INTERLOCUTOR
(to the tune of "Amazing Grace")
How beautiful
A man the moon.
I am what I am.
I'm not above
A buck for love.
What good is it? Sioux me.

A sparkling place
The city is.
My face is my face.
I must go far
Below zero.
What good is it? Sioux me.

My name is Sioux.
What did I do?
I never ever said
That red is what
I want to drink.
It goes right to my head.

How beautiful
A place the past.
We are where we are.
The redskin race
Finishes last.
What good is it? Sioux me.

GHOST
Thank you, thank you, Mister Interlocutor. An astonishingly touching masquerade. It seemed almost real. Is this a tear here, washing the war paint?

INTERLOCUTOR
Unhand me, sir. I'm not afraid of you.

GHOST
Boo is no go then. So how do you feel, Mister Interlocutor?

INTERLOCUTOR
I'm the Interlocutor here!

GHOST
How do you feel now?

INTERLOCUTOR
I know what to do. I know the order of the show.

GHOST
You do, do you?

INTERLOCUTOR
I want my happy company.

GHOST
They're even later than I am, sir. It's curtains for all of us!

INTERLOCUTOR
No, the show must go on.

GHOST
The audience is waiting. Mister Interlocutor?

INTERLOCUTOR
The playlet.

SCENE SIX

The INTERLOCUTOR reveals the placard: "Scene Six: The Playlet."

GHOST
The playlet!

INTERLOCUTOR
Ladies and gentlemen, as a public service to the citizens at the forefront of our civilization, we now present a short drama of spiritual significance.

GHOST
Mister Interlocutor, in the continued absence of Mister Bones, will now render the role of Sweet Sioux.

INTERLOCUTOR

I dream. I dream, I do, of the bright lights of the city. Regina, she's the finest, the queen city of my dreams. But I promised Daddy, Daddy dear, I would keep up the homestead, I would be his little red pioneer. This on his deathbed. Sigh. Gangrene from an arrow. Oh horror!

GHOST

Shot by me, ha ha, in error. Oops!

INTERLOCUTOR

Mister Ghost now appears, in the infelicitous absence of Mister Tambo, in the role of the villainous Chief Magistrate.

GHOST

Ahem. Ahem. Give me some rum or I'll shoot you in the bum. I need fire water for a starter. Then off I go on a hunt or to court. Order, order, I say to the buffalo. Right between the eyes, I warn the prisoners. Tonight it's too late, too late for her.

INTERLOCUTOR

It is the eleventh hour. It is beyond my power to pay the mortgage on my daddy's farm. Oh I am losing courage.

GHOST

Knocka knocka, Sweet Sioux.

INTERLOCUTOR

Who's there? At this hour.

GHOST

Knocka knocka.

INTERLOCUTOR

What would Daddy do?

GHOST

Answer the door.

INTERLOCUTOR

You think so?

GHOST

Knocka knocka, Sioux!

INTERLOCUTOR

Hello. Who's there?

GHOST
It is I, my dear. Your sweetheart, Chief Magistrate.

INTERLOCUTOR
You're no sweetheart to me.

GHOST
She's not all there up here. Sometimes she believes me.

INTERLOCUTOR
Stay away. What is it you want?

GHOST
The time is short. The deed on this land is about to come due. I was
worried, my dear, about you.

INTERLOCUTOR
You were? Really?

GHOST
Do you have the necessary dollars?

INTERLOCUTOR
No–

GHOST
–Hooray!–

INTERLOCUTOR
–I'm sorry to say.

GHOST
I mean to say I'm here to help you.

INTERLOCUTOR
But at what price? A Chief doesn't become Magistrate without vice.

GHOST
Oh Sweet Sioux.

INTERLOCUTOR
What's a girl to do?

GHOST
Oh sweet Sweet Sioux.

INTERLOCUTOR
Oh, no, Chief Magistrate. I couldn't do that.

GHOST
Why not, my dear? She's done it before.

INTERLOCUTOR
I'm not that kind of girl. I only do it for love and/or marriage.

GHOST
Why buy the moo cow?

INTERLOCUTOR
I won't do it for meat anymore.

GHOST
I'll give the deed to you.

INTERLOCUTOR
Oh no. I couldn't do that. That would make me one of those women, nothing more than a squaw.

GHOST
A squaw? You mean like Buck and Squaw?

> *The GHOST pulls the INTERLOCUTOR into a reprise of the Hollywood Indian War Dance. The INTERLOCUTOR complies but keeps it short.*

INTERLOCUTOR
Midnight is about to strike!

GHOST
There goes the farm.

INTERLOCUTOR
But I keep my honour.

GHOST
Midnight strikes. The farm is mine. And what the hell, so are you!

INTERLOCUTOR
Oh no no! That would be – rape!

GHOST
Right you are! You're more intelligent than you appear.

INTERLOCUTOR
Rape, oh no!

GHOST
Oh yes, yes, Sweet Sioux! Talk about the Almighty Buck.

INTERLOCUTOR

Corporal? Corporal Coat? Mister Tambo? Mister Drum! Anybody!

GHOST

There's no one here to come to your aid.

INTERLOCUTOR

Stop! Stop, I know. It is I, I, Corporal Red Coat of the Mounted Police–

GHOST

–Aye, aye!–

INTERLOCUTOR

–cleverly disguised as Sweet Sioux in order to tempt the evil Chief Magistrate to show his true colours.

GHOST

Blast you, Corporal Red Coat. Talk about an Indian giver. Your feminine innocence, your eyes, had me completely convinced.

INTERLOCUTOR

It is now my duty to arrest you, Chief Magistrate.

GHOST

Corporal Coat, could I make you an offer?

INTERLOCUTOR

Oh more villainy. You're trying to bribe me.

GHOST

I offer you the deed to the farm for a taste of your feminine charms.

INTERLOCUTOR

How dare you, sir! Bang bang!

GHOST

Oh I am wounded, I am dying, mortifying, I am dead.

INTERLOCUTOR

Oh Corporal Coat.

GHOST

As my soul slips toward hell, I repent. Is it too late?

INTERLOCUTOR

Call me Red, miss.

GHOST
What a sorry end this is!

INTERLOCUTOR
I want to thank you.

GHOST
Jesus loves me!

INTERLOCUTOR
We can talk about that later on, Sioux.

GHOST
And suddenly my skin is white.

INTERLOCUTOR
Oh, Red, may I offer you some apple cider?

GHOST
Oh miracle! I'm heaven sent!

INTERLOCUTOR
I love you.

GHOST
Or are those wedding bells I hear?

INTERLOCUTOR
I love you, too, my dear. I'm beside myself with love.

GHOST
And as I say *adieu* to those two united souls, choirs of angels remind me
how true it is said that the only good Indians are the ones who are sainted.

INTERLOCUTOR
Bravo, Mister Ghost. What a wonderful halo.

GHOST
It's old paint, Mister Interlocutor. Bravo to you, too, sir. I love your Sweet
Sioux.

INTERLOCUTOR
As you were. Thank you, thank you, ladies and gentlemen. You're too kind.

GHOST
They're deaf, dumb and blinded by the light of the heavenly Ghost, sir.

INTERLOCUTOR
We hope our tale encouraged all and offended none.

GHOST
There ain't no nuns I can see out there, sir.

INTERLOCUTOR
We give you laughter and tears. We give hope to all who toil and are laden.

GHOST
For every girl, there is a guy.

INTERLOCUTOR
For every man, a maiden.

GHOST
For every nun, a holy Ghost.

SCENE SEVEN

The GHOST, on his way to the footlights, bumps into the placard stand and "Scene Seven: Duet" turns up.

GHOST
Hi, my name's Almighty. Do you come here much?

INTERLOCUTOR
Mister Ghost, where are you going?

GHOST
I want to get in touch with the audience.

INTERLOCUTOR
Our final curtain has yet to descend, Mister Ghost.

GHOST
Speak for yourself. I want to make some new friends in the pit.

INTERLOCUTOR
You can't leave me too.

GHOST
Hiya. Will you help me down?

INTERLOCUTOR
Mister Ghost, I implore you.

GHOST

Mister Interlocutor, sir, or madam, I was forgetting about you.

INTERLOCUTOR

You can't go. I mean we do have some few ensuing numbers, Mister Ghost.

GHOST

The two of us? Go on without me.

INTERLOCUTOR

None of the rest of our happy company has come along.

GHOST

Look me in the eyes and ask.

INTERLOCUTOR

Please, Mister Ghost. Please.

GHOST

Mister Interlocutor, sir, how do you feel?

INTERLOCUTOR

How do I feel? With my hands! No, Mister Ghost, I feel this evening like the moon.

GHOST

You feel like the moon, Mister Interlocutor. How is that?

INTERLOCUTOR

Envious and pale of face and alone, Mister Ghost.

GHOST

I know how you feel, but you are mistaken.

INTERLOCUTOR

How am I mistaken, Mister Ghost?

GHOST

The Moon's an old woman. We call her Grandmother. (*to the tune of "God Save The Queen"*)
The Moon's an old woman
A very wise woman.
She's made of light!

GHOST & INTERLOCUTOR

She watches over us,
Over the children
Each of us is a child again
In the coldest night.

INTERLOCUTOR

The Moon's a young woman
A very new woman
Made out of dark
She's waiting for the light
Just as a child might
Wrapped warmly in a blanket and
Not at all afraid.

GHOST

Well how do you feel now, Mister Interlocutor? Mister?

SCENE EIGHT

*The INTERLOCUTOR, fleeing the GHOST, bumps into the placard stand.
"Scene Eight: Standup" turns up.*

GHOST

Sir!

INTERLOCUTOR

Did you know, Mister Ghost, that marriage is an institution?

GHOST

Yes, sir, I had heard that said.

INTERLOCUTOR

Well, sir, so is an insane asylum! Did you know, Mister Ghost, that love
makes the world go round? Well, sir, so does a sock in the jaw! Which
reminds me, sir. An Indian from Batoche came up to me the other day and
said he hadn't had a bite in days. So I bit him! Do you know, sir, how many
Indians it takes to screw in a light bulb?

GHOST

What's a light bulb?

INTERLOCUTOR

Good one, Mister Ghost, a very good one. Well then, sir, if it's night time
here, it must be winter in Regina. Nothing could be finah than Regina in
the wintah, sir. Am I making myself clear? Does this bear repeating? Does
this buffalo repeating? Almighty Gas, you say! Answer me, Mister Ghost.
Answer! What! A fine time to demand a medium! It's very small of you,
sir. I promise you I will large this in your face if you do not choose to
co-operate. Tell me, is it true that the Indian brave will marry his wife's
sister so he doesn't have to break in a new mother-in-law? Does it therefore
follow, sir, that our good and great Queen Victoria keeps her Prince Albert
in a can? That's where she keeps the Indians! Hear ye, hear ye! Don't knock

off her bonnet and stick her in her royal rump with a sword, sir. The word, sir, is treason. Or are you drunk? Besotted! Be seated, sir. No! Standup! You, sir, you, I recognize you now. You're that redskin! You're that wagon burner! That feather head, Chief Bullshit. No, Chief Shitting Bull! Oh, no, no. Blood-thirsty savage. Yes, you're primitive, uncivilized, a cantankerous cannibal! Unruly redman, you lack human intelligence! Stupidly stoic, sick, demented, foaming at the maws! Weirdly mad and dangerous, alcoholic, diseased, dirty, filthy, stinking, ill-fated degenerate race, vanishing, dying, lazy, mortifying, fierce, fierce and crazy, crazy, shit, shit, shit, shit...

GHOST
What's a light bulb?

INTERLOCUTOR
Who are you? Who the hell are you?

GHOST
I'm a dead Indian. I eat crow instead of buffalo.

INTERLOCUTOR
That's good. That's very good.

SCENE NINE

The lights shift from variety to spectral as the spotlight finds the placard: "Scene Nine: Finale."

INTERLOCUTOR
Who am I? Do you know?

GHOST
I recognized you by your eyes.

INTERLOCUTOR
Who am I?

GHOST
White Girl, my White Girl.

INTERLOCUTOR
Who? Who is that?

GHOST
My fierce, crazy little girl. My wife. *Ni-wikimakan.* [My wife.]

The INTERLOCUTOR touches her face with her gloved hands as the GHOST embraces and releases her. The spotlight finds her face as her gloved hands begin to wipe the white face off, unmasking the woman inside. The GHOST removes one glove and throws it on the dead fire, she does the same with the other. The fire rekindles.

GHOST

Piko ta-ta-wi kisisomoyan ekwo. [I have to go finish dancing now.]

INTERLOCUTOR

Patima, Kisse-Manitou-Wayou. [Goodbye, Almighty Voice.]

The GHOST goes and dances in celebration to a drum. The woman removes the rest of the white face and costume, becoming WHITE GIRL again. She gathers the costume in her arms as the spotlight drifts away to become a full moon in the night. WHITE GIRL lifts a baby-sized bundle to the audience as the GHOST continues to dance in the fading lights.

The end.

JOB'S WIFE
OR
THE DELIVERY OF GRACE

YVETTE NOLAN

YVETTE NOLAN

photo by Michael Cooper

INTRODUCTION TO *JOB'S WIFE,*
OR *THE DELIVERY OF GRACE*

Yvette Nolan is a playwright, director, dramaturg, and teacher born in Prince Albert, Saskatchewan to an Algonquin mother and Irish immigrant father. She has worked as a director of plays by Miche Genest, Drew Hayden Taylor, and Philip Adams, and as a dramaturg on work by Bev Brett, Catherine Banks, Donna Smyth, and Sharon Shorty. She is a member and past President of Playwrights Union of Canada (now Playwrights Guild of Canada) and the current MAD (Managing Artistic Director) of Native Earth Performing Arts. Her first play, *Blade*, was produced in 1990, and since then she has written a dozen works for the theatre, including *A Marginal Man, Annie Mae's Movement, Child, Donne In,* the AIDS musical *Everybody's Business, Job's Wife, Shakedown Shakespeare* (co-written with Philip Adams), and *Video*.

Job's Wife was first produced in February 1992 by Theatre Projects Manitoba under Nolan's own direction, with Tiffany Taylor, Gerry Martin, and D-Anne Kuby in the cast. A play that is at different times funny, wistful, and very sad, it is framed by a prologue representing the fruitless prayers of its central character, Grace, addressed to an indifferent white God. But then something unexpected happens. "Grace. I'm here. You're here. Let's talk." So begins a strange encounter between Grace, a middle-class, Roman Catholic, non-Native woman pregnant with the child of a Native man—"the kind of person your mother is used to helping, with her church group or whatever"—and God, or "Josh," who turns out to be a large Native man in a rag-and-bone cape. As Grace says, "I wake up and there's a large half-naked – person – in my room, telling me he is the answer to my prayers." That encounter, which is constituted as the playing out of Grace's life, is effectively punctuated by the "Baby-Spirit" in her womb, whose words lightly echo those of Grace, Josh, her father, doctor, partner, and priest – this last providing one of the short play's nicest touches, as the priest's empty "my child" is underscored by the baby's insistent "Mychildmychildmychild.... Chi-i-i-l-l-d!" The male roles are all doubled by the actor playing Josh, who operates as a kind of spirit guide, taking Grace back through the history of her pregnancy, confronting her with her own ambivalences and responsibilities for the "troubles" that she and her partner Paul are having (like Northern Ireland) in their relationship and that she is currently having in her pregnancy.

Josh doesn't like the term "religion," but his intervention effectively introduces Grace to the spiritual realm in which her baby lives, and where she must learn to take responsibility for her choices, including her "sins of omission ("white words for lying"). And ironically, as the play's subtitle suggests, it is Grace herself who is delivered at the end of her pregnancy. In the Bible, Job's wife breaks down under the terrible tests of faith imposed on her by a patriarchal God and husband, including the loss of her children. In this play, facing a different kind of God but a similar trial, Job's wife achieves a new name.

CHARACTERS

GRACE
BABY-SPIRIT
HIM
   Josh
   Doctor
   Father
   Priest
   Paul

JOB'S WIFE
OR THE DELIVERY OF GRACE

YVETTE NOLAN

GRACE on her knees DS in a pool of light with a rosary, probably praying.

Lights warm on BABY-SPIRIT in its hanging chair USL. It is singing.

BABY-SPIRIT
Oooh ooooh ooh omm omm omm mlak mlalk mlalk umumumum umum ooh ooh oooh... *(smacking wet warm sounds)*

Lights down on BABY-SPIRIT as its humming song goes out.

GRACE continues to tell her rosary. Her lips move. She becomes more distressed the more beads she tells.

The light warms on the "white god" on the scaffolding USR. He holds a white neutral mask before his face. He appears to be watching GRACE, or perhaps not.

GRACE
Oh please where are you? Why can't I find you *now*?

The "white god" turns his face away from GRACE as his light fades.

GRACE
Please, are you there? It's me...

She listens, senses nothing, bows her head.

(whispering) Now I lay me down to sleep, I pray the Lord my soul to keep...

Lights fade on GRACE.

In the darkness, there is noise from slightly up and above, the sound of bones against bones and a rattle that sounds like a snake. The lights come up US on the scaffold. The figure is laid out flat on top of the scaffold. He wears a cape that is made of rags and bones. As he rises up the cape makes a rattling sound. He sits on the edge of the scaffold and watches the sleeping GRACE for a moment. He is a big man, obviously Native Indian. He points a finger at a light—gunshot style—and a light pops on to illuminate the sleeping GRACE. She moans a little, stirs, falls silent again.

HIM
(singsongy) Gra-ace. Gra-ace.

GRACE opens her eyes, freezes. She begins to moan in the back of her throat.

Grace. I'm here. You're here. Let's talk.

GRACE
What do you want? I have no money, but there's some jewellery, the stereo, the VCR, please...

HIM
Grace. You were praying. Well, I'm answering your prayers.

GRACE
I'm sorry?

HIM
You were praying. To me, I presume. Well, here I am. Let's talk.

GRACE
How – how did you get in here?

HIM
What do you mean? I'm everywhere. Always. You *know* this.

GRACE
I don't know what you're talking about. Please, take anything, take everything you want, but please, please just leave.

HIM
Grace, you're not listening. You were praying, yes?

GRACE
Yes. So?

HIM
Well, here I am. I'm answering your prayers.

GRACE
I know! I'm still asleep! And this is the most amazingly realistic dream.

    He smiles at her.

HIM
It's no dream, Grace. Well, no more than any other part of your life.

    GRACE screws up her eyes, pumps her arms.

GRACE
Wake up, wake up, wake up, wake up, wake up.

She opens her eyes.

HIM

You're having a hard time with this, I understand.

GRACE

No. Absolutely not. Not at all. I wake up – no! – I *dream* I wake up and there's a large half naked – person – in my room, telling me he is the answer to my prayers.

HIM

Grace, all this is wasting time. The night is short. Let's talk.

GRACE

What do you want to talk about?

HIM

Grace, *you* called *me*.

GRACE

Call you? I didn't call you. I didn't call anyone. I haven't spoken to anyone in days.

HIM

"Oh please where are you? Why can't I find you *now?*"

GRACE

What?

HIM

"Please, are you there? It's me..."

GRACE

You were listening!

HIM

Of course I was! I hear everything, every prayer, every curse.

GRACE

What are you saying? Are you trying to tell me that you're – you're–

HIM

Yes, now you're getting it.

GRACE

–that you're God?

He smiles. She begins to laugh.

But you're, you're...

HIM
Careful now.

GRACE
You're Native.

HIM
You know the old stories, how God was so bright that he blinded the prophets who looked at him?

She nods.

Well, for you I put on something dark.

GRACE
(*pause*) That's a joke.

HIM
That's very good, Grace.

GRACE
You're saying you're God.

HIM
Oh I so hate labels. Call me Josh.

GRACE
Josh.

HIM
I always kinda liked Josh.

GRACE
Josh.

HIM
Grace.

GRACE
Alright, *Josh*. If I did indeed call you, I mean, no offence, but I'm a Catholic, born and bred, and you're – you'll excuse my saying it – you're not exactly my idea of God.

HIM
Aren't I?

GRACE

Perhaps you have the wrong room. Paul is asleep in the other room. You'd probably measure up to his idea of a God.

HIM

Because he's Native, you mean.

GRACE

Yes. *(pause)* How'd you know that?

He gives her a "now, Grace" look.

Of course. You know everything. Perhaps you really want Paul?

HIM

No Grace, I am for you. Paul doesn't ask for things, he just gives thanks frequently.

GRACE

He does?

HIM

Speaking of which, have you got a little tobacco? A cigarette? Pipe? No? *(sighs)* But you, your prayers are full of need. So, tell me what you need.

GRACE

Paul, Paul, Paul, PAUL, PAUL!

HIM

Paul Paul Paul PAUL PAUL! Grace, he is sleeping, peacefully I might add, though I don't know how he can be comfortable on that couch. Why are you making him sleep out there anyway?

GRACE

I'm not making him sleep out there. He chooses to sleep out there. We're – we're having troubles.

HIM

Troubles?

GRACE

Yes, we're – why don't you know? I thought you knew everything.

HIM

I know what I know. Tell me your troubles. Tell me about the baby.

Lights warm on the BABY-SPIRIT. It gasps, more surprise than pain.

BABY-SPIRIT
Ah! Ah! Ah!

> *JOSH pulls on a white DOCTOR's coat; there is a stethoscope in the breast pocket.*

HIM
So tell me, Grace, is this a welcome pregnancy?

GRACE
I'm sorry, what do you mean?

HIM
Well, has there been tension about this pregnancy? Do you have a husband? No? Hmmm? A partner? Yes? How does he feel about it?

GRACE
Well, he's been very supportive...

HIM
Would you say that you have been looking forward to this pregnancy with excitement? Hmm? With dread? Mixed feelings, perhaps? Hmm? Yes?

GRACE
No, no, I've been looking forward to it...

BABY-SPIRIT
Ma. Mama. Mum.

HIM
Were you resentful in any way of the pregnancy? Has it made a big difference in your lifestyle? How about your partner?

GRACE
Well of course it's made a dif–

BABY-SPIRIT
(*chuckles*) Hee hee.

HIM
Did you have doubts about this pregnancy? Did you ever consider terminating it?

GRACE
No, no never, I'm Ca–

HIM

What you are experiencing is called a threatened abortion – the mild cramping, the spotting. Now in the olden days, doctors would have prescribed bed rest, but it has been my experience that if you are going to miscarry, you are going to miscarry. Usually, if you do miscarry, the foetus was already dead and all the bed rest in the world is not going to stop you from miscarrying. Now, sometimes pregnant women do spot and then stop and have a perfectly normal pregnancy and a perfectly normal baby, but sometimes not. Do you understand what I'm saying Grace?

She nods.

JOSH takes off the white DOCTOR's coat.

The BABY-SPIRIT is humming its hum song, punctuating it with gasps.

GRACE

Please, if you can help me... what am I doing? Why can't I wake up from this?

HIM

I don't understand you *people*. You all pray and pray, all infinity long, bless my mother, bless my father, intercede for me, help me get this job, help me find my wallet, make him love me back, save my baby's life and when I come to answer your prayers, suddenly you no longer believe...

GRACE

Oh I believe in God, alright, I just don't believe in you! You're not my God!

The BABY-SPIRIT begins to chant an Aboriginal chant. GRACE suddenly feels her abdomen.

BABY-SPIRIT

Ay-ay-ay-ayy...

GRACE

I – I – My baby! You're here for my baby. Oh please, if you are God, Paul's God, its God, then you can save my baby!

HIM

Say I am who you say I am–

GRACE

You are, you are, I believe you are, I really really do!

HIM

Whoa, slowly, daughter. Think about this now. If I really can work a little miracle, you could change the whole direction of your life right now. The fellow in the white coat–

GRACE

The doctor?

HIM

Yes, he had some points. Perhaps you have had second thoughts about the baby. This could be your chance to turn back the clock, go back to the way things were.

GRACE

No! Why would I want to do that?

HIM

Perhaps the obstacles are too many.

GRACE

No. No. Just because Paul and I are – we're just working some things out. These things would have happened without the baby.

HIM

And the rest of your family?

GRACE

I don't care. I don't care what they think.

HIM

What do they think? What did your mother say?

GRACE

I didn't tell my mother. I told my father.

JOSH grabs a cardigan sweater, puts it on, takes glasses out of the pocket puts them on. Opens the paper. GRACE enters, sits near her FATHER. He acknowledges her, she smiles at him. He goes back to his paper. After a long pause:

HIM

What's on your mind, Grace?

GRACE

I'm pregnant.

Pause.

Daddy? Did you hear me? I said...

HIM

I heard you, Grace. Are you sure?

GRACE nods.

This is going to kill your mother.

Pause.

I suppose it was that Paul.

GRACE
Yes, of course.

HIM
This is going to kill your mother.

GRACE
Never mind Ma for a moment, Daddy. Tell me what you think.

HIM
It's a bit late for thinking now, isn't it Grace.

GRACE
Daddy.

HIM
I think this is going to kill your mother.

GRACE
I don't think it's going to kill her. Daddy, I know she was pregnant when you got married.

HIM
That was different.

GRACE
Why?

HIM
Grace, your mother and I were in love. We were probably going to get married anyway. I wasn't too pleased at first, but.... But, Gracie, you've got to understand how your mother sees things. Paul is not the kind of person she is ever going to welcome into this family with open arms.

GRACE
Because he's Native.

HIM
Grace, he's the kind of person your mother is used to helping, with her church group or whatever.

He reaches into his pocket and finds a pipe. He is quite excited by this discovery, keeps feeling the other pockets for tobacco, but there is none. Puts the pipe between his teeth.

What are you going to do about it?

GRACE
What do you mean?

During this the BABY-SPIRIT does "grandchildy" things, bouncing, singing "O-pa O-pa O-pa..."

HIM
It's not going to bother me, having a daughter in the family way. In fact, I'm probably getting on to the age where I should be a grandfather, I don't mind, those old biddies in the Catholic Women's League can cackle 'til the cows come home, but this is going to be very hard your mother. They are her friends, and maybe you should think about her feelings. I mean, Grace, if you're not sure about this, then there are alternatives.

GRACE
Like abortion, you mean?

The BABY-SPIRIT stops abruptly.

HIM
No, no, not that. I'm an old man and any way I look at it, church or no church, it's murder. But there are people, couples, good, happily married churchgoing people who can't, for whatever reason have babies, and they'd be happy to take a baby, any baby. Why, some of those people are so desperate for babies that they're taking those foreign babies with AIDS, so...

GRACE
So there's no reason why they wouldn't take a little half-breed child.

HIM
Grace, try to think about someone else's feelings for a change. Are you really sure you want to do this?

GRACE
Whose feelings? Ma's feelings? Ma's embarrassment that I got knocked up by an Indian?

During this her FATHER leaves, and she yells after him.

That's Ma's problem, Daddy, not my problem. I don't care, I'm going to have this baby, I don't care what Ma and her stupid cronies say, I want this baby!

HIM
(*from behind her*) You don't want it.

GRACE
What? I do, I do! Of course I do! Haven't you been listening? I want this baby! More than anything!

HIM
You don't want it, Grace. You said you wanted a healthy baby. Well, it's not healthy. You don't want it.

BABY-SPIRIT
Ah! Ah! Ah!

GRACE
(*hand to her belly*) What are you talking about?

HIM
The foetus – the body – is damaged. Not healthy. You don't want it.

BABY-SPIRIT
Oh oh.

GRACE
I don't care! I don't care! It's still my baby. I never said I didn't want it.

HIM
(*patient*) Every train bridge you passed under, every first star you saw, you wished *let my baby be healthy*. Well, it's not, and so I'm taking it away.

GRACE
I never meant that!

HIM
Be careful what you wish for.

GRACE
What the hell are you doing listening to wishes under bridges anyway? What kind of – almighty being – would listen to wishes made under bridges?

JOSH is not listening to her, but to something else, far off. The BABY-SPIRIT listens as well.

HIM

Sorry? A bird fell.

GRACE

A what? Oh, and I suppose you caught it.

HIM

No no. Just watched it. Especially graceful, especially divine, a plummeting, feathery spiral to the earth, there to become ironically food for worms.

GRACE

Shakespeare. You stole it.

HIM

Please. He borrowed it. He was inspired. Who made the worms?

GRACE

This is crazy. Please God make me wake up.

HIM

Grace. Grace. Your prayers are going nowhere.

GRACE

I believe in God the Father Almighty...

HIM

Catholics are the funniest. I am constantly amazed at the tenacity of the Catholics. So severe. Pantheists I understand, Buddhists I understand best. Jews, sure they got a history, but Catholics. All that free will and they choose Catholicism.... Between a rock and a hard place...

GRACE

You're punishing me.

HIM

Grace, I don't punish, it's not our way.

GRACE

Why are you punishing me? None of this is my fault. Not my fault that I got pregnant, not fault that I'm losing the baby. I ate well, I slept well, didn't drink, didn't smoke.... Why are you punishing me?

HIM

Grace, why would I want to punish you?

GRACE

Because you think I lied.

HIM
Do you think you lied?

GRACE
It doesn't matter what I think!

JOSH takes a jean jacket from the scaffolding, becomes PAUL, the boyfriend.

Maybe you should sit down.

HIM
I don't need to sit down.

GRACE
I'm pregnant *(she begins to hyperventilate)*.

HIM
Maybe you're the one who should sit down.

GRACE puts her head between her knees. PAUL pats her on the back awkwardly, waits, reaches into a pocket for a cigarette package, extracts a cigarette, puts it in his mouth, looks at her bent-over figure, decides better, puts the cigarette away. Waits. GRACE straightens up.

GRACE
So.

HIM
So.

GRACE
Well?

HIM
Well.

Pause.

HIM
Well, I guess we'll work it out somehow.

GRACE
You're not happy.

HIM
No, I can't say that I'm happy.

GRACE
Are you angry with me?

HIM
Did you do this on purpose?

GRACE
N-n-no.

HIM
Well, then I can't be angry with you for an accident.

> *Big pause.*

I'm going to go out... get some smokes. Do you need anything?

GRACE
No. I'll start dinner. It'll be about an hour.

> *She goes to him, tries to be held by him, it is very uncomfortable. After what PAUL thinks is long enough, he exits.*

I know. Sins of omission. I know all about sins of omission.

HIM
White words for lying.

GRACE
But I have confessed. I saw the priest.

HIM
How could you see in that dark little box?

GRACE
I mean, I confessed to the priest and he absolved me of my sins.

HIM
Did he?

GRACE
What do you mean, did he? Of course he did! That's his job! I've never gone to confession and not been absolved.

HIM
What did he say?

GRACE
Who?

HIM
The man in the little box.

GRACE
The priest?

JOSH snorts.

Well, he didn't say much really, mostly I did the talking.

HIM
What did you say?

GRACE
I said, you know, the usual *(crosses herself, kneeling)* Bless me Father, for I have sinned. It has been – um – eight months since my last confession.

HIM
Why so long, my child?

BABY-SPIRIT
mychildmychildmychild...

GRACE
I – I – don't know.

HIM
Liar.

GRACE
I'm sorry, Father?

HIM
Go on, child.

The PRIEST makes a motion like a baby in utero and the BABY-SPIRIT imitates him.

BABY-SPIRIT
childchildchild

GRACE
I – I have been having sexual relations outside of marriage.

HIM
(rolls his eyes) The church does not condone relations before marriage. *(lewdly)* How often?

GRACE
Often, Father. And...

HIM
Go on.

GRACE
(whispers) I'm pregnant.

HIM
Speak up child.

BABY-SPIRIT
Chi-i-i-l-l-d!

GRACE
I'm pregnant!

Pause.

Father? Father? Are you there? What should I do?

HIM
You made your bed, you lie in it.

The BABY-SPIRIT laughs.

The father, does he know?

GRACE
Yes.

HIM
Well, you will have to marry as quickly as possible. Go now and sin no more.

GRACE
Marry? I don't want to marry. He won't want to marry. Father, please. Father? (She goes to tap on the screen.)

HIM
What odd customs you have. Instead of apologizing to the one you have wronged and making restitution to that one, you go into a little box and whisper your mistakes to someone who doesn't know you and doesn't care about what you've done, and he tells you that's it's all right. No wonder you have such a hard time getting on in this world; you make it so hard for yourselves. (pause) Do you feel cleansed when you come out of that little box?

GRACE
Well... yes.

HIM
Really? Then what do you need me for?

GRACE
I don't need you! I never asked you here! I'm not even convinced that you are here. I know that I'm fast asleep and I'm just making you up. And now that I know I'm asleep, I can change this dream and get rid of you. *(closes her eyes)* I'm thinking about swimming, the water is warm and clear and refreshing. There's life in the water, little creatures. The water is calm, smooth, glassy, there's no current, no undertow that can grab my legs and start to pull me under, nothing to grab at my legs and start pulling at me so I have to fight *(getting visibly distressed)* I – can't – it's too – strong–

    JOSH reaches to her and grabs her wrist, pulls her up.

    She gasps and opens her eyes.

What are you doing to me?

HIM
Grace, *you* called *me*. You must have something very important indeed to tell me, because I'm here, aren't I?

GRACE
I don't know what it is I am supposed to do! I don't know anything about your kind of religion.

    JOSH cringes.

HIM
Please, we'd all get along a lot better if no one used that word...

GRACE
If I called you here, it was because I thought you could save my baby. You don't seem willing—or able—to do that, so I don't know what you're hanging around for! Go on! Ascend or whatever the hell it is a god does!

    GRACE turns from JOSH. Goes to her knees, begins to pray, ignoring JOSH. He shrugs, goes to the hanging chair. Pushes it a bit. From inside comes giggling. Pushes it a bit more.

BABY-SPIRIT
Hey!

The BABY-SPIRIT pokes her head out. Smiles at JOSH. He holds out his arms to her and she starts to climb out.

GRACE
No! Oh no! No, please. Oh God, oh please. Josh, please. Josh, come back.

JOSH and the BABY-SPIRIT pause.

BABY-SPIRIT
Come back come back come back come back...

JOSH gently pushes the BABY-SPIRIT back into the chair. He takes the PAUL jacket and puts it on and goes behind where GRACE is kneeling. Through this, he stands behind her.

HIM
Grace, get up.

GRACE
Paul. Please. I have a confession to make. I know this – this – child is driving us apart...

The BABY-SPIRIT reaches to PAUL who still stands behind GRACE.

BABY-SPIRIT
da

PAUL begins to exit.

GRACE
Where are you going?

HIM
Out for a smoke.

GRACE
You can smoke in here.

HIM
No, I don't think I can. It's not good for – for you.

BABY-SPIRIT
(gently) Da.

PAUL continues to exit.

GRACE
Paul, please.

PAUL stops. As GRACE makes her confession, he turns back to her, but GRACE never looks at him.

Paul, I'm so sorry about all this...

HIM

Grace, I don't want to...

GRACE

No, please, you have to let me talk first. Then you can say what you want, do what you have to. Paul, I thought I wanted to be pregnant, to have a child. I thought it would show the world what we are—what we were—to each other. Everyone kept asking when we were going to have a child. My friends, your friends, the people I work with... I mean, I'm thirty this year. Everyone is always waiting for you to take the next step, to prove the strength of your relationship, house, marriage, children... we never did any of those things.

HIM

You got pregnant on purpose?

GRACE

Not exactly on purpose. I stopped using birth control and I sort of left it up to fate. An act of God.

HIM

You told me you didn't do this on purpose.

GRACE

I lied. I lied, and I'm so sorry because it is costing me so much now.

HIM

You lied to me.

GRACE

I thought a child would guarantee the most precious thing to me. I thought a child would bind you to me forever. And now all it's doing is driving us apart. And once I saw the damage it was doing, I was so sorry, I wished I'd never done it. And now I am losing the baby and I may have lost you...

PAUL crosses US and hangs up the jean jacket.

GRACE

It was not the baby's fault.

BABY-SPIRIT

my fault my fault my fault

GRACE
My fault, my fault, all my fault. But *(pleading)* I never wished it harm. Please, oh please believe me, I never meant it.

BABY-SPIRIT
no no no no no

HIM
No, of course not.

GRACE
Oh God.

HIM
Oh Grace.

BABY-SPIRIT
Oh oh oh oh oh.

GRACE
I'm not sure now.

HIM
You didn't do this, Grace. You don't have control over it now.

GRACE
I can never make things go back the way they were.

HIM
No.

BABY-SPIRIT
(wistful) no.

GRACE
And now I'll lose everything.

HIM
No.

> The BABY-SPIRIT is silent.

GRACE
And the child?

BABY-SPIRIT
yes

HIM
What about the child?

GRACE
never to see light

BABY-SPIRIT
there is light where I go

GRACE
never to hear music

BABY-SPIRIT
I hear music mama

GRACE
never to experience love

BABY-SPIRIT
I am, mama

GRACE
never to hear you say mama

HIM
Ah.

BABY-SPIRIT
Mama.

GRACE
I will never see you

> *JOSH goes to the hanging chair, the BABY-SPIRIT climbs out onto JOSH. He carries her over to GRACE. She sees the BABY-SPIRIT. For a moment they do exactly the same motions: reach one hand to the other's face, touch, take the hand on their face in their other hand, drop hands.*

HIM
Bye now.

BABY-SPIRIT
Bye now.

GRACE
No.

HIM
Grace.

BABY-SPIRIT
Mama.

GRACE
(whispers) Bye now.

> *The BABY-SPIRIT climbs onto JOSH again, GRACE collapses slowly to the floor. JOSH walks to the scaffolding, the BABY-SPIRIT climbs off him onto the top of the scaffolding. JOSH puts PAUL's jean jacket on.*

PAUL
Grace? *(sees her collapsed)* Oh Grace, are you alright?

GRACE
Paul? I'm sorry, Paul.

PAUL
Sorry? What for? Grace, are you–

GRACE
What a mess I've made of all this...

PAUL
Don't. It's alright.

GRACE
No, no. I'll make it up to you. I promise.

PAUL
Grace. There's nothing to make up. I swear.

GRACE
I think we'd better go to the hospital now.

PAUL
Alright. Can you walk? I'll bring the car around, alright? Just wait here.

> *He starts to leave.*

GRACE
Paul? Can I have a cigarette?

PAUL
Uh – yeah – sure – I guess so.

He pulls out the cigarette package, gives her a cigarette and offers her the lighter.

GRACE
No, just the cigarette. Thanks.

He leaves. GRACE puts the cigarette on the floor. Looks at it, undecided. Picks it up, tears the paper off, piles the tobacco neatly, surveys this. Stands. Looks at the tobacco again, shrugs. Exits.

The end.

LADY OF SILENCES

FLOYD FAVEL

FLOYD FAVEL

photo by David LeReaney

INTRODUCTION TO *LADY OF SILENCES*

Floyd Favel is a Plains Cree from the Poundmaker Reserve in Saskatchewan. He trained as an actor first at the Native Theatre School in Toronto, and later at Tukaq Theatre in Denmark and at Jerzy Grotowski's renowned Centro per la Sperimentazione e la Ricera Teatrale in Italy, before returning to Canada. In 1991 he came full circle, returning to the Native Theatre School as its director, and founding the Centre for Indigenous Theatre. He has also trained in Japan with the Suzuki company and under Butoh master N. Nakajima. From 1991 to 1996 he led a creative, research, and training team, Native Culture Research (including at its core Muriel Miguel, of Spiderwoman Theater; Pura Fé, of Ulali, a North Carolina Tuscarora singer and songwriter; Sadie Buck, a Seneca clan mother and lead singer of the Six Nations Women's Singing Society; and Monique Mojica) to investigate common ways in which the indigenous peoples of North America use movement, oratory, song, story structure and symbol to create "Native Performance Culture." In the summer of 2001 he led a project at Brandon University, Manitoba, using Native Pictographs as dramaturgical models for First Nations theatre. He is Artistic Director of Takawakin Performance Laboratory. He has worked extensively as an actor, director, and choreographer, and on Tom King's CBC radio series, *Dead Dog Café*. As a playwright, in addition to a number of performances that he has co-created, he is author of *The House of Sonya* (a Native adaptation of Chekhov's *Uncle Vanya*), *Lady of Silences*, and *Governor of the Dew* (a play based on Cree legend about love, nostalgia, and culture linking the animal kingdom to the world of man) performed at the National Arts Centre and The Globe Theatre. In 2002, he led a theatre expedition to central Siberia to research his new play, *The Sleeping Land*.

Lady of Silences, which began as an exploration and adaptation of Jean Genet's *The Blacks*, was originally developed at the Catalyst Theatre in Edmonton in 1990, and it was performed there in March 1992 and again at Native Earth Performing Arts in April 1993. The version published here premiered at the Globe Theatre in Regina in the Fall of 1998, directed by Floyd Favel himself, dramaturged by Ruth Smillie, and performed by Andrea Menard, Cecile Brass, Rhonda Cardinal, Kennetch Charlette, and Richard Moonias. The play takes huge risks. It addresses the always vexed question of interracial sexual relationships in ways that are perhaps comparable to Djanet Sears' treatment of the same subject in her play *Harlem Duet*. It addresses the equally vexed question of internalized racism among Native peoples, graduated by colour, as when the central character, Village (whose name represents his allegorical status in the aboriginal global village), speaks to the mixed-race Sheila, one of his Native lovers, as "the whitest one out of this beautiful lot," or when he prays to "God, Father of all, Timakinowin," to pity him and give him "blonde hair, blue eyes and, and – white skin." And it addresses the even more vexed question of the vicious murder of a white woman (represented only by a dress) by a trio of Native women – a murder that includes, risking the worst of racist stereotypes, a scalping. Exploring and exposing what Robert Appleford calls "the self-hatred suffered by

Native peoples living in an environment where the ideals of beauty and worth are determined by non-Native dominant culture" (242), *Lady of Silences* is a painful play. "It hurts me to tell this story," says its Native detective/narrator Belmondo at the outset. He proceeds, nevertheless, to frame the play as at once a black *film noir* parody, an investigation, and a healing, metatheatrical ritual (re)playing—a "daily repetition of performance, a spectacle"—of the murder of Village's white lover, Linda, by his three Native lovers: "with that device," Belmondo says, "the revealing of your life, and of your peoples', will shine as bright as shame, as fiery as injustice." "Each night" he says, "they [the women] perform to free themselves from their hate. That is their task. Each night you [Village] perform to free yourself of your desire [for 'white skin']."

Village presents himself as "only a scapegoat," a pawn, perhaps, in the exorcism of hundreds of years of the history of colonization that have produced both that hate and that desire. Sheila, the mixed-race Native woman whose near-white beauty could only have been produced by "centuries and centuries of intermarriage," pleads not to be left alone with those "centuries of pain." Belmondo presents the Native women's acts of ritual murder as "redemptive deeds... slowly exposing so many truths," but he eventually abandons his stance as objective investigator and interlocutor to run raging from the room "in memory of [him]self and [his] beloved people," ashamed of his own complicity, as investigator, in what he is investigating, and the role that his objectifying, detective stance has played in their subjection.

The object of Balmudo's investigation has turned out to be less significant as a revelation of "who done" the murder of Linda than as an exposition of the sources of the Native violence and self-hatred that have led to the murder. This is a tough-minded play. It pulls few punches, and lets few members of its audience, Native or non-Native, off the hook. But it exposes the poison, and, like the play that is its inspiration, Genet's *The Blacks*, it perhaps foreshadows a potential, and not very pretty, revolution.

Notes:
Appleford, Robert. "Making Relations Visible in Native Canadian Performance." *Siting the Other: Re-visions of Marginality in Australian and English-Canadian Drama.* Ed. Marc Maufort and Franda Bellarsi. Bruxelles: P.I.E. Peter Lang, 2001. 233-46.

CHARACTERS

BELMONDO
VILLAGE
RUTH
SHEILA
LISA

NOTES

The title *Lady of Silences* is taken from T.S. Elliot's poem, "The Wasteland." *Lady of Silences* initially began as a three-month exploration and adaptation of Jean Genet's drama, *The Blacks*.

An Indian is a role like any other role. We are all actors, children of colonizations. Of each other and our true natures.

THANKS

The author would like to thank the following for their help and friendship: Tanya Kappo, Peter Feld, Allan Macinnis, Kent Monkman, Sharon Starr, Brenda O'Donnell, Thom Sokoloski, and most importantly Ruth Smillie.

LADY OF SILENCES

FLOYD FAVEL

ACT I

A Native male, VILLAGE, is sprawled on the stage. BELMONDO stands in the shadows, casually smoking a cigarette.

BELMONDO
Friends, Nitootamitik, *aha hil*
It hurts me to tell this story, the story of a great love which came here to die.
This love, ascended dove-like, a victim of murderous love.
She was happy to be free, free from her prison where she caused much unspoken grief.
Little did we know that here death would plunge this man into darkness – for all he held dear to him was lost. Lost? Lost!
He – he was born to dire circumstances.
And, from this glory, he crawled his way to life, a life so common to these people.
A life exemplified in this male who now lays before me, innocent as the day he lay swinging in this mother's tipi. Unknown!
He was not yet known. He was not recognized as he grew up among us, a dirty Indian boy who would shoulder our troubles and be broken by them!
A courageous act, a courageous man.

VILLAGE
Who're you?

BELMONDO
Detective Belmondo, Homicide.

VILLAGE
Homicide? Who's the victim, me?

He laughs.

BELMONDO
Yes, and what a pity! Another wasted life!

VILLAGE
I suppose I'm dead?

BELMONDO nods and calms himself.

Oh, am I in Hell where Father Marchand used to say that sinners like me roast?

He laughs.

Ouch! Boy, I got a hangover. Hey, man, you got a beer?

BELMONDO
You're not in Hell yet. This is Purgatory.

VILLAGE
Purgatory? Looks like downtown to me. I just love these bars, the smells, the unpredictability.

BELMONDO
Recognize the twilight and the endless sands, the constant horizon from which comes no relief.

VILLAGE
Twilight? Endless sands?

BELMONDO
This is a play.

VILLAGE
Oh, I get it. I can picture it now.

BELMONDO
You'll stay here until you're cleansed of your sin.

VILLAGE
My sin? Which one?

BELMONDO
Your desire for the White Woman.

VILLAGE
Linda...

BELMONDO
Until this cancerous desire is burned from the cells of your body, you will remain here, in Purgatory.

VILLAGE
My desire – cancer? Linda? It's none of your business! How do you know about me and her?

BELMONDO
I have my sources. That's what makes me a detective.

VILLAGE

Suppose this did happen, this desire, this lust you spoke about. Maybe you're jealous.

BELMONDO

Your treatment and eventual cure will depend on your daily repetition of a performance, a spectacle. With that device, the revealing of your life, and of your people's, will shine as bright as shame, as fiery injustice.

VILLAGE

Is this a joke? A sick joke? Hey, I want a lawyer! I want a lawyer right now!

BELMONDO

If you are successful, you can proceed to Heaven, to Our Father's house, where there is a room even for one as sinful as yourself.
But first you must pay. The desire must be expunged from the marrow of your bones. If not, then it is down to the Inferno! You will derive no pleasure there, I assure you.

VILLAGE

Oh my God, please, don't let me be dead – let me be alive! I'm begging you, on my knees, with sincerity in my eyes! I'm sorry for what I have done. I promise to be good. I want to live. I want to awaken and hear the birds chirping at dawn – chirp, chirp! Smell the dew upon the grass, sniff, sniff. Hear the mooing of the cows. moo, moo? I want a lawyer! I am entitled to seek counsel.

BELMONDO

It's too late. You had only one chance at life. Sure, the circumstances you were born into were not ideal. Illegitimate, Native, a reserve. Who can blame you for wanting to rise out of this misery to glorious white splendour?

VILLAGE

Right, who can blame me for that? I was within my rights.

BELMONDO

Look !

The three women enter. They sing "Kyrie Elision."

SHEILA

I've done a lot of shit in my time, but that morning, I've never felt so scared before.
The fear burnt a hole in my stomach and we could not look each other in the eye.

RUTH

We drank to dull the fear, but conscience is cruel, driving us as we roamed the streets in the pre-dawn hours.

SHEILA

We carried a case of beer, and it rattled and jangled as we stumbled and fell.

RUTH & LISA

Hey, watch out! Don't break the beer! Jeez you!

SHEILA

We walked down the streets until we reached the house, so cold and grey, untouched by sun and laughter.

LISA

Our house, untouched by sun and laughter.

RUTH

The bitch. She didn't have to do that.

SHEILA

I think she deserved it, doing what she did. I mean, you just don't do that.

LISA

What, chum?

RUTH

Do you think they'll catch us?

SHEILA

Yeah.

RUTH

Let's run away to the States so we don't get caught.

SHEILA

No, the Mounties always get their man.

RUTH

So what are we going to do?

SHEILA

We're all going to have to take the rap.

RUTH

Sheila?

SHEILA
What?

RUTH
I'm scared.

SHEILA
So am I.

RUTH
Sheila?

SHEILA
Keekwiya!

RUTH
No matter what, we'll always be friends okay?

SHEILA
Yeah, okay.

RUTH
Promise me.

SHEILA
Cross my heart and hope to die.

RUTH
Don't say that! Don't say that! I don't want to die ! Sheila!

SHEILA
Ruth!

> *RUTH gets hysterical and SHEILA slaps her.*

LISA
Shut up! It could only have happened this way, we are only fulfilling what has been destined. After all, a great love came here to die by our hands, for only by our hands, for only by our hands could this love have died... this love would not have died of its own accord, for this is not the nature of sacrifice.

BELMONDO
Heard enough?

VILLAGE
That doesn't prove anything. Is it illegal to see someone?

BELMONDO

She wasn't just "someone."

VILLAGE

What is the problem? I'm a man, she was a woman. We were only doing what comes natural.

BELMONDO

She was white, did that have anything to do with... your relationship?

VILLAGE

No, her whiteness had nothing to do with it.

BELMONDO

You think I'm stupid? Huh? Again! Did her whiteness have anything to do with it?

VILLAGE

You would've done the same thing. Who wouldn't in our positions?

BELMONDO

Leave me out of this. I am removed from your drama!

VILLAGE

I'm only a scapegoat. By trying to establish some guilt through this performance you will only show the guilt that is in all of us, guys such as ourselves, *neechees*. Who are you trying to kid? It's innate. It's in our blood.

BELMONDO

I will not stand for this! I am the detective! I am Detective Belmondo. Homicide squad. I ask the questions around here. I'm in charge! Do you see any other detective around here?

VILLAGE

I don't think so.

BELMONDO

You know, I could do anything I want with you, and there isn't a damn thing you could do about it.

VILLAGE

If it weren't for your cheap suit you'd be just like me. Give an Indian a suit and he thinks he runs the joint... okay, big man... the floor is yours!

BELMONDO

Each night, they perform, to free themselves of their hate. That is their task. Each night, you perform, to free yourself of your desire.

VILLAGE
I suppose they're dead too?

BELMONDO
Unfortunately, yes.

VILLAGE
No!

BELMONDO
The Lord giveth, and the Lord taketh away.
Soon your sentences are up, and you can leave this place and the performance behind to serenity and harps and angelic voices. There are no miracles here, only sweat and toil and endless repetition, and repentance that will lead us to some vague from of absolution.

VILLAGE
Let they who are without sin cast the first stone.

BELMONDO
As you say.

VILLAGE turns and approaches the WOMEN.

RUTH
Well, well. Hark, my lover comes, bounding across the plains, leaping across the hills. My lover is like a gazelle, or a young stag – that wretch!

VILLAGE
Hey girls, where's the party?

SHEILA
So how was she? Was she good? Better than me?

RUTH
Or me? Crawling back like a dog with his tail between his legs. How dare you show your face? Get the hell out of here!

LISA
Save it. Save your anger for the performance.

RUTH
Even here, our fates are still intertwined.

SHEILA
What a tangled web we weave–

VILLAGE
Hey, what're you talking about? I didn't do nothing.

RUTH
I knew you were bad news the minute you laid your shifty eyes on me in the welfare office.

VILLAGE
You wanted it as much as I did.

SHEILA
And me, when we met in the hall, bashful like school kids, and you came to my apartment, acting all innocent. I had no idea it would end like this, absolutely no idea! Why did you ever enter my life?

VILLAGE
You also wanted it as much as I did. Perhaps more.

LISA
You made a mockery of love. The countless times you whispered "I love you." You left me pregnant.

VILLAGE
How was I supposed to know it would end like this? I made mistakes. We're all entitled to some mistakes. All the times I held you in my tattooed arms and whispered "I love you," I meant it every time. All the promises I made, I meant to keep all of them.

SHEILA
Yeah, right.

RUTH
What do you think we are, Village, stupid?

LISA
Pathetic. Stop your lying, Village.

VILLAGE
Hey, come on. Give me a break.

LISA
You know why we're here? I imagine he told you.

VILLAGE
About my desire for the White Woman? Yeah, he told me.

RUTH
And about our hate!

SHEILA
Always thinking about yourself. What about us and our hate? Think about us for once! We want to get out of here too.

VILLAGE
You guys make it sound like a crime. I was within my rights.

LISA
Explain that, Village.

VILLAGE
I was born on a reserve. Never had new shoes. Two pants a year. One bath a week. I was born poor! My parents never loved me! No one ever loved me! I had every reason to seek love and, if I harmed anyone in that search, I'm sorry.
I repent – it'll never happen again! Have some mercy and pity for me, lowly Indian that I am.
There, can I go now? Did I do that right?

BELMONDO
Ladies, was he believable? Did his words arouse compassion?

LISA
He has no pity here – only our contempt!

BELMONDO
Very well. We have to continue with the performance. Begin.

VILLAGE
Come on. what do you want from me? Didn't you see how my tears came from the bottom of my heart! Look at them. Taste them! Please, you guys, come on. Pity me. Pity me!

The WOMEN spit at VILLAGE with disgust.

BELMONDO
We must establish the circumstances that will reveal the malaise permeating the centre of your soul. What is the cause? Oppression? Colonization? Does colonization create him? Or does he create colonization? What are the symptoms? We shall see them all in relief, in impression, through the performance. Let's proceed.

The WOMEN sing. BELMONDO unfolds the dress like a relic and carries it like an icon around the performance space.

WOMEN
Katowaytahkosit
Kasaywatisit

Kimeeyewsit mana
Nimitay Katoowake
Seepee Kamichowa
Peeyaseesak Kanikamochik
kameeyewsit man
kameeyewsit kakikay

> *As the song ends, BELMONDO drapes the dress on the altar, creating an effigy of the White Woman. Then he rings the bell.*

SHEILA

She was born among the marble ruins of a foreign civilization, chalk-white and stately as a cypress tree. Her eyes sparkled a Nordic blue. Lips blew kisses soft as dandelions and the warm Mediterranean wind. Against her whiteness, our hate pounded its teeth and nails until there was no more teeth and nails, only blood and shreds of Red skin. Our screams died to hoarse whispers as we realized in our dazed oppression that silence descended on us, cloaking us, and there was only the beating of our hearts like tribal tomtoms—tom, tom, tom, tom!—and the wind of our breaths.

LISA

Linda, why did you come into my life to take away the only man I ever loved? He was all I ever had. I tried to tell you to leave us in Peace, but you came anyway and shamed my man in front of my eyes. Harmed him with his desire for your white skin.

SHEILA

My hate would not allow me to sit back and watch. I have been silent too long.
My hate, sharpened by schoolyard taunts, unleashed its fury and I tried to stop you, but your blue eyes only laughed silently. So silent and deafening in the face of my anguish. We warned you but you didn't listen. I hope you rest in Peace.

RUTH

Why did you have to take my man? He belonged to me. I was lonely until I met him. You have no idea of the depths of my loneliness. I hated you, and I repent for this sin, but now, it is too late. You're dead. Your life is gone. But your memory will never leave me. That is your legacy to me. Love, Ruth.

VILLAGE

Staring upon her body that had pleasured me so many times, I felt no remorse that no more would we wile away the cold winter nights entangled in each others' limbs, that no more would our sweet breaths mingle.
Yes, no remorse, only release that I was freed from my suffering.
No more was my heart burdened by my lust for her.

Rather I felt a duty to my people and the children who will come after us.
I was innocent and pure, proud. I laughed in the cold night air, my breath
an icy white cloud – and I blew smoke rings! I looked into the pools of her
blood to slick back my hair, and I saw my heavy Indian features reflected
back at me. I thought that surely I was made in the image of God.

RUTH
Really now!

LISA
What was it, Village, that brought you to her?

VILLAGE
Do you want a detailed description of the humiliations she made me feel?

LISA
She never made you feel anything Village, she was just a poor innocent girl.
She was a victim in the same way that we are all victims.

VILLAGE
You want me to say that, because I felt shame, I went after this woman?
Well, I said it. How else do you want me to say it?

WOMEN
With honesty, Village!

VILLAGE
Do we have to go through it all again?

BELMONDO nods.

All right. My love was based on self-hate. I confess. That's what you want,
right?

BELMONDO
It's not that easy. We will relive that day, all that was destined and the night
of the murder. And one of the women will play the part of the White
Woman.

RUTH
She had a name, Belmondo!

SHEILA
Like we all have names.

LISA
We aren't just the "Native women!"

BELMONDO
Yes, of course she had a name. I didn't mean to further desecrate her memory or dehumanize her by my references to her as the "White Woman." Yes, I agree, agreed?

WOMEN
Agreed.

VILLAGE
Yes.

BELMONDO
It was a bar...

> *The WOMEN enter a bar elegantly, humming the "Blue Danube Waltz."*

...a filthy downtown bar–

> *The WOMEN start to stagger around the street, drunkenly singing the "Blue Danube Waltz."*

VILLAGE
No way! This is bullshit! I'm not taking part in this performance anymore.

> *VILLAGE heads towards an exit but the WOMEN block his way.*

SHEILA & RUTH
Oh Village, Village, please stay!

SHEILA
Just this once more for old times sake.

LISA
I'll cook you your favourite dinner.

VILLAGE
Kraft dinner?

LISA
No just kidding, *cha*, no really I will Village.

RUTH
Please, please, please, please, please, please, please...

SHEILA
Oh Village, we love you.

WOMEN
With all of our hearts, *cha*! ever stupid.

LISA
Be a man Village, for once in your life.

RUTH
A Man? I don't think I've ever met one.

SHEILA
What is a "man?"

VILLAGE
All right then, you asked for it!

The WOMEN dance and sing in celebration.

BELMONDO
Let's proceed, orderly and systematically, with the night, then the day proceeding that night. Who's going to be the White Woman?

RUTH
Me, me, I'll do it!

SHEILA
Pick me, pick me! I can, I know I can!

RUTH
Please, please, please!

LISA
Oh, Village!

RUTH
Come on, I want to be the White Woman. See, I've been practising.

RUTH parades around like the White Woman.

SHEILA
Nah, that's nothing. You still look like you're fresh off the reserve. Anyways, look at this.

SHEILA parades around like the White Woman.

RUTH
Holy! Ever gross.

SHEILA
Better than you anyways.

BELMONDO
Well?

VILLAGE
(VILLAGE points with his lips to LISA.) You do it.

RUTH
Cho. She's always the White Woman.

SHEILA
Nach, why always her? What's wrong with me, hunh?

RUTH
Just for this one time, let someone else be the White Woman.

SHEILA
Are we too black or something? I can do better than that bitch.

LISA
Who are you calling a bitch!

> *They start to fight.*

RUTH
Go for it, Sheila! She's getting too good for us anyways! I'll back you up anyways!

> *RUTH joins the fight against LISA.*

VILLAGE
(VILLAGE breaks them up.) Hey, hey, girls, come on! Chill out! Wait your turns. What I say goes, okay?

> *The WOMEN lunge for each other again.*

What I say goes! Lisa is the White Woman, and that's that!

RUTH
I don't want to do this anymore. Every twilight the same damn thing. Nothing is going to change. Lisa always gets to be the White Woman. Pretty soon she's going to think she is one. She's beginning to act like one too with all her pleases and thank you's. *Mooniasquao*. Makes me sick. This is all getting to her head, *skanak*.

BELMONDO

Are you all finished? Feel much better? And now, the night at the filthy bar.

VILLAGE and LISA move aside, leaving SHEILA and RUTH in "the street" scene.

It was a dark and stormy night.

The WOMEN make storm sounds, insolently.

No! It was cold and dark, and there was a moon.

The WOMEN start to walk down the street.

SHEILA

It was our night on the town. Ladies night! Welfare night!

RUTH

At least for me. I got mine early.

SHEILA

We had nothing better to do that night to break our boredom except go drinking.

RUTH

We went cruising down the streets, causing heads to turn. They wish! We entered the bar.

SHEILA & RUTH

That filthy bar!

RUTH

Sheila, order up some beer. Molson light. You're buying.

SHEILA

Cho, what do you mean I'm buying? I bought last time. It's your turn tonight.

RUTH

Just joking. Holy! You don't have to get all rank on me.

SHEILA

Cho, who's getting rank here?

RUTH

I told you I was joking. You don't have to try and spoil the night. You always do that. You don't even know how to have a good time.

SHEILA
Who was it that threw the TV out the window last time?

RUTH
That doesn't count.

SHEILA
Why not?

RUTH
Because I don't remember doing it, that's why.

SHEILA
Well, either way, you don't know how to party.

RUTH
You're one to talk. I don't think going out with the first guy who even looks at you is knowing how to party.

SHEILA
Well, let's just drop this whole discussion. We'll just end up crying anyways and I don't feel like crying tonight.

RUTH
You're right, Sheila. You're my sister.

SHEILA
My blood sister, remember?

RUTH
Oh yeah – when we slashed up in the Youth Detention Centre and we thought we'd become sisters before we died.

SHEILA
And we came to – in the hospital!

RUTH
Those were the days! Let's drink to that. Waitress, where're those beers? It's on me sister. I got my welfare cheque.

SHEILA
How'd you get yours so soon?

RUTH
Direct deposit.

SHEILA
I should get that too. Why don't you lend me twenty bucks, chum, just until Monday?

RUTH

Nah, you don't even have to ask. You're my best friend. I was just going to give it to you. What do you think I am, tight?

SHEILA

Everyone knows that you're not tight.

RUTH

Cho, I didn't mean it like that.

>*LISA as the White Woman sweeps into the bar.*

VILLAGE

Oh, there she was! Oh God. Such glorious magnificence. She turned her head and my eyes fell upon her white marble classical features. Oh Venus, Athena, let me hold your thin waist. I was not myself as I walked towards her, my muscular legs trembling with desire. In my fantasies, I never thought this would happen to me, me. Village!

>*VILLAGE approaches the White Woman and, as the WOMEN sing the following lyrics to the melody of "The Blue Danube Waltz," dances with her.*

WOMEN

Pimatisiwin
Kaasawaytahma
Sakeetowin
Kasawaytahma
pimatisiwin
Kaasawaytahma
Sakeetowin
Kakeyo
Kamamtoonaytahma

VILLAGE

(speaking over the singing) I was holding a White Woman! I saw all the Indian guys looking at me real jealous, wishing they were in my shoes. I pressed her close to me and she was strangely warm like any other woman, my hands moved to the small of her back. I felt her body responding–

>*LISA continues singing the melody wordlessly. SHEILA and RUTH start to circle the dancing couple like wolves.*

SHEILA

Look at them dancing real close.

RUTH

What's she doing to Village? That's our man!

SHEILA
Jeez, he's just slobbering all over her. Come on. Let's go show her who's boss around here.

RUTH
Yeah. This is our bar. We don't go into their bars.

SHEILA
She might as well walk right into our bedrooms.

RUTH
Let's take her outside.

> *LISA breaks away from VILLAGE and dances violently alone.*

SHEILA
Hum makka.

> *LISA picks up the knife and dances the fight with it.*

Grab her hair.

RUTH
Give her the boots! Not so stuck up now, eh, you bitch? You like that? How does that feel? This is for every Indian that's ever been kicked around by you people.

SHEILA
Punch her! Pull her hair!

RUTH
Drag her outside! Come on, hit her! She's still moving!

SHEILA
Cut that pretty little nose off.

> *LISA plunges the knife into the floor. SHEILA and RUTH give a tremolo. Everyone is silent.*

> *BELMONDO lights a cigarette. He blows the match out.*

BELMONDO
She was never so beautiful as in death. Death, lips so cold, why did you plant your lips on lips so fair?
Did you die for our sins? Was it written in the stars that a simple girl, born in humble surroundings, who was loved, took ballet lessons, and did well in school, would die a lonely death outside of a downtown bar at the hands of our mothers and sisters? Why?

God, can you answer me? Can I hear your voice which has spoken to others in their need.

Silence.

I am sure that God does not approve. Neither does he disapprove. He is uninvolved, only watching, as I am now watching the memory of the congealing blood upon the cold winter morning.
Did she die for our sins?
You have never meant so much for the world as you do in your death. Only in death do you take on the necessary symbolic proportions.
Yes, I am a detective. That is my job, Detective Belmondo, Homicide, Precinct One Oh Nine.
I remember my tracks circled the body that morning, around and around, bigger and bigger, until I was circling this wind-swept prairie city.

He spins in the wind, his jacket opening like wings.

The circle widened, and soon I was circumambulating the world – which was round.
It is round! Below me I hear the sounds of humanity in its random existence. I circle, and soon I am a star. A star falling, falling from the Grace of Heaven where I was once an angel, a light. The light pierces me like nails and I am not sure of who I am, and that knowledge sends a shudder through my body... and the joy is excruciating.

He hangs on the wind in the sky.

SHEILA
Did you see the way she looked when I grabbed her?

RUTH
Yeah, I saw! Did you see what I did to her?

SHEILA
No, what did you do?

RUTH
I just grabbed her by the hair, brought her down – and kneed her right in the face!

SHEILA
Holy! But did you see what Lisa did? She just–

RUTH
She didn't have to do that!

LISA
Dreams, I had dreams. I wanted to be a dancer, and teachers were always telling me, "Lisa, if you believe in yourself and believe in your dreams, all of your dreams will come true." Well, I knew that, and I worked very hard and I became a dancer, and a very good one at that.
But that wasn't good enough for me. I wanted more out of life. I wanted – I wanted to be white. To have the fair skin, the blue eyes, the blond hair and, of course, the grace of a swan.

> *SHEILA and RUTH hiss her.*

LISA
I realize that this is not possible, and I know that I am not white. But I want to be white!

> *LISA stabs the knife again into the floor.*

SHEILA
Oweeya!

RUTH
Hoocah!

LISA
Deep down inside of me, there is a little part of me that is white. If that little part of me would just grow and grow and, finally, just come out, I'd be so perfect! I'd have blond hair, my blue eyes and, of course, my grace of a swan.

WOMEN
(they sing) Katowaytahkosit
Kasaywatisit
Kameeyesit mana
kapay wahpa
kipaytahkosin
Nimitay Katookwake
Seepee Kamichowa
Peeyaseesak Kanikamochik
kameeyewsit mana
kameeyewsit kakikay

> *SHEILA and RUTH as warrior horsewomen, begin to gallop and circle LISA as the White Woman.*

SHEILA & RUTH
The thunder of the horses' hooves shakes the earth, and the dust and action is as thick as the battle of the Little Big Horn. A massacre is in the

air – our nostrils dilate with the smell of blood, our eyes roll white with anticipation! We attack with prayers and hate in our savage red hearts.

RUTH jumps off her horse and catches the knife SHEILA tosses her. The White Woman is terrified. Then RUTH, knife clenched in her teeth, attacks the White Woman. Throwing the White Woman to the ground, RUTH stabs her repeatedly and scalps her.

RUTH

Watatootis! My a name is *Watatootis!* "White Woman killer."
Two summers ago, I killed a White Woman in battle, like this! Like this!
I stabbed her many times and I heard her cries.
I like White Women. Their thin fragile veins, delicate like spider webs, arouse me.
Their blue eyes tempt me – to kill, kill, kill!
I love the smell of death and victory.
Later on that evening I saw a rabbit, and I sneaked up on it. I killed it. I ate it all, fur and everything. I never cook my rabbit. Later on, I celebrated.

She dances and sings.

I went to a mountain and I prayed.

She prays.

After my prayers, I went to another mountain and I yelled my name for everything to hear. *Watatootis! Watatootis!*

She runs to her horse, leaps on it and she and SHEILA start to gallop wildly away. SHEILA and RUTH stop in their tracks, LISA rises from the dead White Woman. Now they circle VILLAGE.

Why, Village, why did you choose her over us?

LISA

Did you, every time we were making mad passionate love, imagine I was blond and blue-eyed?

RUTH

Why did you make me feel so unworthy? I thought I was special.

VILLAGE

No, girls, it's not like that at all.

SHEILA

Girls, Village doesn't make love to Indian girls.

The WOMEN hiss him.

RUTH

Is that right, Village? Look at me! I gave you my heart and you stepped all over it!

SHEILA

Maybe, by having their women, he was getting back at all the humiliations they have inflicted on him. The manhood they stole from him!

VILLAGE

I'm a warrior and I love you, okay? I love all of you!

SHEILA

Then why her over us? She wasn't even pretty – white trash.

RUTH

That's how mixed up you are Village. You choose them over us.

VILLAGE

What are you talking about, Sheila? You're the whitest one out of this beautiful lot.

The WOMEN start to beat VILLAGE.

SHEILA

Is that why you came after me, because of my white skin, my light eyes?

RUTH

You used us! You could have bought a prostitute!

VILLAGE

How could I? I was always broke!

SHEILA

Why were you ever born? We should've left you on the street.

LISA

You're a disgrace to your people! Just like the rest of our men!

The WOMEN finish beating him.

VILLAGE

Oweeya! Oweeya! Oweeya! Stop it! That's enough. It's not my fault. What do you want me to do about it now? The past is the past! Let sleeping dogs lie!

RUTH

Yeah right, sleeping dog!

WOMEN leave the stage. BELMONDO rings the bell to get their attention.

BELMONDO

He cursed the day he entered the world against his wishes on some lonely prairie reserve.

As he watched his old grandmother crushing chokecherries with her stones, the window reflected back to him his dark eyes, and he wanted to take his eyes out to feed the crow. "Take back my eyes because I don't wish to see anymore!"

"Why, son?"

"Because it is too hard!"

So he took a fork – but his mother stopped him! Never before had he felt so much hatred towards her, and he yelled, "I hate you! I hate you! I hate you!" Until he had no voice, just like a crow.

VILLAGE

Oh please God, Father of all, Timakinowin, pity me. Have mercy on me, your humble servant. Let me be white. Please let it be that when I wake up in the morning, I will have blond hair, blue eyes and, and – white skin. I beg this of you, hear my cry. Grant me my humble request – to be white.

BELMONDO

In his school, there was a blond girl. He wished to be white, so he could sit beside her and not be afraid to soil her prettiness.

VILLAGE

Indians on one side! Lice check!

We stood in a line at the front of the class, reserve Indians all. Teacher searched our heads for lice with the eraser ends of two lead pencils. Rosy-cheeked children witnessed our lousiness.

I see an open school book in front of the little blond girl. I imagine I disappear into the book, and I am Dick and she is Sally. My hand creeps up her thigh, to the edge of her yellow skirt. All the time I am wishing, "Please don't let me have lice! Please don't let me have lice!" I want to disappear under her skirt to a secret garden where only her and I will roam without shame like First Man and First Woman. See Sally run! See Sally run!

LISA

Our poor boy, our poor man. Sometime a mother brought you into this world and had high hopes for you. My boy will be a good dancer, he will be a good singer and he will be generous, just and kind. All will speak well of him, and he will be known far and wide for his Power. She brought you to her breast and gave you milk, lulling a beautiful brown baby to sleep.

She begins to sing a lullaby. The other WOMEN join.

a tootoo beebee a mama
a tootoo beebee a papa
mpi sakeehawow nitooskineekeem
a too too beebee a mama
a tootoo beebee a papa
mpi sakeehawow nitooskineekeem.

WOMEN
Good night. Sweet dreams. Happy nightmares.

ACT II

BELMONDO
And now the day in question that led you to commit your redemptive
deeds.
Take heart as we relive that day so often lived and treasured.
When we struggled from sleep to the light of day, like newborn babies,
tired with living, we did not know the day would unravel, slowly exposing
so many truths.
We were not used to days such as these.
Aha hi! Akamaymook nitootemitik! Take heart, my friends!

> *BELMONDO turns through the wind like a circling hawk.*

The night before, they were all sleeping, even Village.

> *BELMONDO intones a low, dark prayer in Latin.*

WOMEN
The dog was howling that night, a bad omen.

RUTH
Evil forces and lost souls that only a dog can see, were about.

WOMEN
We clung together, whispering prayers of protection and, around us in the
darkness, we felt the battle between the Good and Evil forces.

LISA
The nightingales were whispering "*Keepa*, it's time, *keepa*, it's time."

WOMEN
And we heard that dog howl again.

> *VILLAGE howls.*

Good and evil were waging a war for our souls, and our medicine was weak.
We found that our eyes were opened.

SHEILA
My blanket had been torn back, exposing my body to the darkness. I felt
someone kiss me last night. Their lips were cold.

> *VILLAGE howls again.*

WOMEN
And we shivered. Only the Evil One has the power to open our eyes. We
drifted back to sleep, sleep, sleep, clutching the memory of our rosary
beads and mumbling forgotten prayers. And we dreamt.

BELMONDO
Prior to the day in question, I, of course, dreamt a detective dream. In
the dream, I awoke late. The stale taste of scotch and cigarettes filled my
mouth. The residues from last night's debaucheries. I had been doing what
all good detectives do late at night, drinking scotch, smoking cigarettes,
cruising the bars, and suffering existential angst. I had been staring at the
wall for a few hours when the phone rang.

RUTH & LISA
Ring! Ring! Ring!

BELMONDO
"Hello." It was the Chief of Police and he said–

SHEILA
"Hello, Belmondo, it's me, the Chief. The Chief of Police! Get your brown
ass over here. I got a case for you."

BELMONDO
"Oh Chief, what kind of case?"

RUTH & LISA
A case of beer, *cha*!

SHEILA
No! "I got a murder case for you. White girl. Looks like Indians really did a
job on her. St. Regis Hotel. Get over there quick." Click!

BELMONDO
Click! So I jumped out of bed, slicked back my hair, got dressed and rushed
out the door.

> *The WOMEN sing the melody of "The Blue Danube Waltz" and waltzing,
> carry over the white dress and lay it in the middle of the floor.*

BELMONDO
In the dream, the traffic was just picking up and the narrow cobble-stoned
streets were blanketed with fog. A perfect setting for a murder. I didn't
recognize anyone on the busy streets.
The desire for a cappuccino grabs me, but I must go on. That's my job.
I arrive, and the hotel is swarming with detectives. Homicide Squad.
"Good morning, Detective Belmondo, Homicide." I came to the body
underneath a white sheet. I lifted the sheet. Multiple stab wounds, severe
contusions around the face. The frozen blood kind of like a halo around
her head.
This looks like the work of Indians.
What brought her down here last night? Was it a drug deal gone wrong?
Or was she just slumming?

"Where's the murder weapon? Off to the lab, huh? Get any prints?"
The hunter has to think like his prey. This is my job. I'm a detective. My
eyes wandered up and down her blood streaked legs and her mangled face
and I thought, "A human being is never so beautiful as in lovemaking, sleep,
and death."

BELMONDO carries the dress over to the altar.

I imagined her horror and terror as I sat and lit a cigarette.
What a waste, what a pity!
Got to keep myself together. I'm the hunter. Become their shadow – yes,
that's it.

WOMEN
Ten AM in this windy prairie city. We awoke, bothered by our dreams
lingering with us as we went about our daily business. It's a jungle out
there.

LISA
I – as a sweet innocent girl who would be aged and matured like fine wine
by heartbreak and deception.

SHEILA
I – as the luckless tenant, going from room to room, caught in the endless
round of waiting for welfare cheques and my school funding. And that day,
my cheque never arrived – to my great sorrow!

RUTH
I – as the lonely woman who fell for the first man who made her feel
special and wanted. She thought this might be the one man who would
be different – but I guess not.

WOMEN
All Indians, of course!

BELMONDO
I began my hunt, acting on my hunches.

VILLAGE
I awoke that day, bothered by my dreams, but who the hell cares about
dreams anyways, they belong to another time and place where dreams have
meaning. I went about my daily business, looking for an easy score. I roam,
I strut, bouncing like a pinball from one day to the next. It's the Indian
way. Live for the moment, intensely and beautifully, the moments are so
precious. It's a good day to die, *meeyasin* boy. What is life? Life is the breath
of a buffalo in the cold morning air. Gone, just like that!

LISA

No! I told you that I can't come and see you, I don't have a ride and I don't have bus fare. No, don't call me again, the only time you ever call me is when you're in trouble or have no money. Why don't you call your other girlfriends. Don't be like what? Yes, I still love you, but I can't go on like this... I have to get my life together. I'm trying to go to school, yeah, I'm just on a waiting list for my funding right now... you know how Chief and Council are... I'll know soon... how much? Oh, alright...

BELMONDO

Inner city. Chinese herb stores, pawn shops, informal street churches, around the corner there are low rent apartments and run down bungalows occupied by Natives looking for a break, or escaping the boredom and politics of their reserves. Sioux's, Crees, Saulteaux's, poverty has made them indistinguishable from each other. After midnight, they are all equally dangerous. Maybe I've been too long on the job, a little jaded, worn around the edges.... Typical prairie city, seen them all.

BELMONDO circles the stage, investigating.

SHEILA

(She knocks at a door.) Hello, it's me Sheila, the one who lives down the hall? remember me, I just moved in last week. Which reserve you from? You know, we're probably related, you and I. Me, I'm from up north there, you know Pelican Lake? Well not there! *(laughs) cha...* I'm just joking, I'm from there. Hey cousin, let me in. I know you're home because I can see somebody moving inside.

When I was young we lived by the lake. In the spring the pelicans would return and I often marvelled at how sleek and primordial they looked. The shape and consistency of their bodies and beaks, the swift swoosh of the air as they flew low overhead in formation...

Oh hi. I just wanted to know if I could borrow some stuff? Like sugar, yeah sugar to sweeten my teeth. Also, maybe some flour, and jam for my bannock, after I make the bannock of course from the flour I'm borrowing off you. Come on cousin, don't be stingy, I'll pay you back anyways. O jeez, thank you very much.

BELMONDO

I went walking further. I reach the end of the street and come to a transit stop. I look in my cool pockets for a bus token, finding none, I settle for a deuce, my donation to the transit authority. The bus comes and I clamber on, a bit flustered and I check out the denizens and doyens of this city. It's a microcosm of this city. A few poor people, some not so poor... middle-class, yeah that's it. A blond girl who looks like an office girl or bank clerk sits reading a book cool as a cucumber. Lady Chatterly's Lover... D.H. Lawrence, good taste for a broad. I grab a seat where I can listen to snatches of conversation, might pick up a few leads, tips, this is my job...

RUTH

Yeah, hi there, my name is Ruth and I'm HH, head of household. I want to apply for social assistance. I just got in from the reserve. I'm so impressed, it's so cool here, the plants look so nice too, look like plastic and I didn't expect to see so many here. *Tansi.* Anyways, what's this? A rent report? You want me to go get this signed and come back tomorrow? Where am I going to stay? I got no money, no friends, lots of relatives but I don't want to see them! I'm tired of them, I see so many relatives back home... Lady? She just called me a Lady...

BELMONDO

The eighth floor in a downtown highrise around the corner from "hooker corner" and a pizza joint. The welfare office, late afternoon. Dying plants, demoralized lonely social workers who would be hard up for a date, lord it over their clients, fractured syllables hang in the air, conversations that vaguely remind us of "the gift of speech," shuffles and coughs... diabetic bodies where was once the nomads' sensual body and grace...

VILLAGE begins to strut around.

Aha, an obvious suspect. Native male, six feet, two hundred and ten pounds. Muscular body going to flab. Scars on both wrists, tattooed upper body, needle track marks. Outstanding charges for assault and armed robbery. No fixed address.

This FBI is a real customer, a real item, a classic. They make too many of these kinds of guys, it's getting stale, like my cigarettes.

VILLAGE leaps gracefully to the centre of the stage.

VILLAGE

The city is my domain. I am the once proud chieftain of a brave warrior band who struck terror in the hearts of timid Presbyterian politicians and French priests. Legs made strong by centuries of bounding over prairie grasses and knolls, remind me of my inherent regency.

RUTH

He came walking in and I thought, "Holy" "Ever!" I didn't think he'd notice me, just sitting there all anonymous and plain. I didn't even do my hair or nothing. Hi, *tanisi.*

VILLAGE

Monanto, monanto, how about you? *Wahwa,* you're looking good, real good.

RUTH

Nah... *awis,* ever bold you...

VILLAGE

Cho, don't you know how to take a compliment?

RUTH
Just new in town?

VILLAGE
Yeah, I just got out of jail and I'm on a waiting list for a life skills course. It's quite the town.

RUTH
Yeah, I know.
He was so – so – so thick! His hips were squeezed into these tight, tight pants, showing off every nerve and muscle. It was too early in the morning for this! I had a hard time to deal with this. His arms so big and brown, tattooed, and I just wanted him to put those arms around me and squeeze me so tight, squeeze my shoulders together.

VILLAGE
So, ah, what are you doing later?

RUTH
Nothing much. Why do you ask? Got something in mind?

VILLAGE
Holy. Nice body.

RUTH
Cho, awis, ever bold.

VILLAGE
I was thinking of maybe heading downtown later, have a couple of cool ones. Wanna come?

RUTH
Well, I don't know. Maybe.

VILLAGE
Come on, we'll have a good time.

RUTH
Maybe. What time?

VILLAGE
How about midnight?

RUTH
That sounds okay.

VILLAGE
See you there then. Catch you later.

RUTH

Hey, which bar?

VILLAGE

The St. Regis.

RUTH

That sounds good. See ya.

VILLAGE

You bet.

VILLAGE struts away.

SHEILA

She is at the door again.

Hello, it's me Sheila again. The one just down the hall, remember? I want to borrow some tomatoes and lettuce, and – and cucumbers. Maybe some salt and pepper to go with that, and mustard. Oh yeah – and some cheese and crackers.

BELMONDO

Is there no moral that these people uphold? It seems they hold nothing sacred. This man seems to disappear into the darkness. Excuse me, Miss. Detective Belmondo, Homicide. Have you seen this man?

RUTH

Never saw him in my life.

BELMONDO

When did you last see him?

SHEILA

Who?

BELMONDO

Has he called or anything?

LISA

I don't even have a phone!

BELMONDO

Indians! They just clam up!

BELMONDO continues to circle and investigate.

RUTH

When he walked out of that welfare office, I knew that this was the one. The man I had waited for all my life. I knew he liked me, the way he sized me up and down. His eyes were like hands, hungry hands.

SHEILA

I seen him in the hall and I liked the way he smiled and walked. I didn't know what to make of him. He kind of looked like one of those fool-around type of guys. They just have that look about them. I can't explain it. You know what I mean? I guess I was right. It's pretty hard to fool me.

LISA

I used to get collect calls from him every day when he was in jail. Now I don't think it was to talk to me but it was more like something to do, just someone to break the boredom. When they picked him up, he'd been staying with me for a few weeks. Had his little gym bag in the corner.

WOMEN

A strange smell began to rise out of his ears, eyes, and nostrils. We couldn't stand it!

> *VILLAGE interrupts the dance, grabbing LISA's arm*

VILLAGE

Stop! I said stop right there!

LISA

No, get away from me!

VILLAGE

Lisa, baby, what? What's the matter?

LISA

I know about you and that other woman. I know about you and that White Woman!

VILLAGE

Who? What? What're you talking about?

LISA

Don't try and hide it. You know and I know. It's true isn't it! Isn't it!

VILLAGE

Well, it was just once.

LISA

Then it's true? Oh Village, I'm so happy for you. I mean, think of all the doors that will open for you, all of the opportunities, all because of her.

VILLAGE

No, Lisa. It was a mistake. Don't leave me. I love you.

LISA

Go to her, Village. I don't want you to have anything to do with me or our child.

VILLAGE

Our child!

LISA

Yes, Village – and I'm going to give him a good life. Bye, Village.

VILLAGE

Lisa, don't leave me. I'll change. I'll be a good father, a good husband! I love you! I love you! I love you!

VILLAGE, alone, breaks down in grief. WOMEN begin to sing "Dies Irae."

During the song, VILLAGE and RUTH mime the "dysfunctional relationship" scene. RUTH and VILLAGE see each other. He catches a butterfly and shyly shows it to her. He releases the butterfly and shyly puts his arm around her. He sees a flower and, running to pick it, falls, embarrassed. He picks the flower and places it behind her ear. He tries to kiss her and she refuses coyly. He becomes more aggressive and ends up beating RUTH and walking away, leaving RUTH on the floor crying.

BELMONDO

Hey you there, you got a minute? I'd like a few words with you, boy. Hey! Come back here!

VILLAGE runs guiltily from BELMONDO. BELMONDO begins to pursue calmly and malevolently.

SHEILA

As a young girl, they used to call me *mooniasquao*. Grandmother used to say, "*Tapwe mpi meeyewsoo, tapiskooch mooniasquao*. Is she ever pretty! Just like a white girl." I hated that because I could see the looks of disappointment in my sisters' eyes.

VILLAGE knocks at SHEILA's door.

Yes?

VILLAGE

Um, I saw you earlier, down the hall, and I just thought...

SHEILA

Can I help you?

VILLAGE
Well, when I first saw you, I couldn't help but think...

SHEILA
Well, get on with it!

VILLAGE
I just thought that I'd come by to tell you that, pardon me for being such a lout, but I've never been with a woman with – I mean, met a lady like you before. So I took it upon myself to... you know, since I don't think you'd ever look me up...

SHEILA
May I have your hat?

VILLAGE
No, that's okay.

SHEILA
Give me your hat.

VILLAGE
No thanks.

SHEILA
Give me your hat!

She grabs his hat and whips it to the floor.

Would you care for some tea?

VILLAGE
No thanks.

SHEILA
You'll have some tea!

VILLAGE
Yeah, sure, tea would be just fine, just fine.

SHEILA goes to the kitchen and returns with a mimed cup of tea and the knife.

I see you got a nice place here. Set yourself up pretty good here.

SHEILA raises the knife to his turned back.

VILLAGE
Those pictures on the wall, that family of yours?

He turns and SHEILA hides the knife behind her back.

SHEILA
Here's your tea. Some cookies?

VILLAGE
Cookies would be perfect.

SHEILA
Please, make yourself comfortable.

> *SHEILA goes to the kitchen again and returns carrying imaginary cookies and the knife. Again she raises the knife to his turned back but again he turns to face her in time to save himself, to force her to again hide the knife.*

VILLAGE
Well, anyways, as I said earlier, I saw you before in the hall. When I saw your eyes, I couldn't help but think that your eyes reminded me of my mother's.

SHEILA
I am the Métis Belle of the West. Only centuries and centuries of inter-marriage could achieve such a miracle. Exotic, pleasing to the eye, the body and the soul. My pale eyes framed by the duskiness of the evening, the furtive *metissage* of prairie desires. Oh eyes of mine, delicately hued iris, greenish iris, iris of the mountain glacier, violet and amber, grey green.

VILLAGE
That's beautiful. Who wrote that, Shakespeare?

SHEILA
No, I did! For all the times I have been loved simply for the sake of my colour! For all the times I have been chosen over sisters duskier than I. For that—and only that—do men like you seek me.

> *She makes her points with the knife.*

VILLAGE
Well, will you look at that! I got to be going. Thank you for your tea.

SHEILA
No, don't go!

VILLAGE
I really must be going.

SHEILA
Don't leave me here alone with my pain. Centuries of pain! I cannot bear it! I simply can't!

She grabs his arms.

I'll make you dinner like the kind your mother made, rabbit stew and bannock, Saskatoon berry soup! Stay here with me!

VILLAGE
Please, no.

She jumps on his back.

SHEILA
Don't leave me! Stay here and love me for who I am and not who I remind you of. Don't leave me.

VILLAGE throws her off.

SHEILA
(She crawls and grabs his leg.) Stay here with me! You'll love it here. Only you and I and our love. What else do we need? We'll be together forever and forever and nothing will come between us – not even my whiteness!

VILLAGE breaks free and runs away. She wails.

BELMONDO flies into the scene. He investigates the WOMEN.

BELMONDO
Hot on his trail. He leaves strewn behind him wreckage, wreckage. Surely what he had done to them, he has done to himself tenfold. I walk into the room to administer to their needs and offer words of solace.

RUTH
Don't touch me!

SHEILA
Please take me away from all this! I can't live anymore!

BELMONDO
Their pain drives me away. "I can't do anything for you!" I turn and run out of the room, down the hall, stairs, the street and my strides get longer.
Soon, I am loping like a wolf, and my rage grows and guides me like a light. I have never felt such hate before, a hate so evil, I can feel it transforming in my body to love, a love that burns my soul.
I see him in the distance.
I am running in memory to myself and to my beloved people. My people, what have I done to you! I live in shame – I am shamed before the sun!
I run in memory of who I once was, and who he once was, and it is dark, so dark.
The impulse of Evil and Good, have become One – and it is good.

VILLAGE is staggering along, destroyed.

VILLAGE
That day I awoke pretty early – around noon.
I began to plan my evening rendezvous.
I dressed for the occasion and slipped out on the street. Smell the gas,
the city air, so far from home, sage and spring winds. "It's a good night,"
I thought, "a good night to do something great to be remembered by."

*VILLAGE notices BELMONDO behind him. VILLAGE tries to run away
but BELMONDO catches up and jumps on VILLAGE, and they fall to the
ground.*

RUTH
Are we dead yet?

LISA
We don't want to go there.

She points upward.

SHEILA
We want to go there.

*She points downwards. They stand and sing "Requiem" and cross the space in
procession. The men fight during the song, then finish as it ends.*

BELMONDO
Show us your truth.

VILLAGE walks on his knees to the centre of the space.

VILLAGE
I walked into the smoke-filled bar and I was hot. And there she was. Linda,
Linda, on the other side of the dance floor, all radiant and white. My dark
eyes met her blue eyes. I walked across the floor and it felt like an eternity.
I can't go on. Please.

VILLAGE is crying.

BELMONDO
No, go on. We're with you.

BELMONDO crosses to the altar, opens the scotch and drinks from the bottle.

VILLAGE
In this Eternity, only her and I dwelled. I asked her to dance, and we
danced. Angels sang and the sky opened up. A beam of white light

illuminated us. I pulled her warm body close to mine and buried my face
in her hair. I kissed her beautiful skin. I was drunk, drunk on salvation.
I was saved. Then – then they tore her from my arms like wild beasts. "Hey,
what are you doing, stop that!" Then they dragged her outside by the hair,
leaving a trail of blood. She looked at me and there was nothing I could do.
"This is how it must be, my love." They kept kicking her! Then I saw one
of them pull out a knife, saw the glint of metal. "Cut her pretty little nose
off!" One of them said. "Linda, oh jeez. Look what they've done to you! My
pretty little bird, all broken and dead like a doll." "Linda, don't leave me!
I need you. Save me! Don't die. Everything will be all right. I'll just go and
call a doctor. Linda, don't leave me please. I love you, Linda–"
They killed her! May the Lord forgive them!

> *VILLAGE collapses. The WOMEN give a victorious tremolo.*

> *BELMONDO is drinking heavily now. The WOMEN sing.*

Katowaytahkosit
Kasaywatsit
Kameeyewsit mana
Kapay wahpa
Kipaytahkosin
Nimitay Katoowake
Seepee Kamichowa
Peeyaseesak Kanikamochik
Kameeyewsit mana
kameeyewsit kakikay

> *BELMONDO rings the bell and the WOMEN, in a procession, exeunt the
> space.*

> *BELMONDO sits, lights a cigarette, observes the effigy of the White Woman
> and VILLAGE, back where he began the performance. BELMONDO takes
> another stiff drink.*

> *The end.*

CREE TRANSLATION FOR *LADY OF SILENCES*

I wish to thank Jean Okimāsis and Arok Wolvengrey of the Department of Indian Languages at the Saskatchewan Indian Federated College, Regina, SK, for their aid in providing the written form of the Cree songs and dialogue. The Plains Cree words found herein have been written in the Standard Roman Orthography, with a pronunciation guide for non-speakers, and a translation for those who wish to stage the play incorporating another First Nations language.

—FF

Cree [Pronunciation]	*Translation*
Song 1	
kā-towēhtākosit [kaa-toe-wayh-TAA-ko-sit]	*one whose voice impacts*
mistahi ē-kisēwātisit [MIS-tu-hay ki-say-WAA-t'sit]	*she's very kind*
kā-miyosit māna [kaa-MEE-yo-sit MAA-nu]	*always beautiful*
kā-pē-wāpahk [kaa-PAY-waa-PUHK]	*as dawn comes*
kā-pēhtākosin [kaa-payh-TAA-ko-sin]	*she is heard*
nitēh kā-towēk [ni-TAY KAA-toe-WAKE]	*my heart beats loudly*
sīpiy kā-pimiciwahk [see-PEE kaa-p'MI-tso-wuhk]	*the river flows*
piyēsīsak kā-nikamocik [pee-YAY-see-suk kaa-ni-KU-mo-tsik]	*the birds sing*
kā-miyosit māna [kaa-MEE-yo-sit MAA-na]	*always beautiful*
kā-miyosit kākikē [kaa-MEE-yo-sit KAA-ki-kay]	*forever beautiful*
Song 2	
ēy, tōtō, pēpī a māmā [AY too-too bay-BEE u-maa-mAA]	*ah, the breast, the baby, the mom*
ēy, tōtō, pēpī a pāpā [AY too-too bay-BEE u-baa-BAA]	*ah, the breast, the baby, the dad*
ninipahi-sākihāw awa nitoskinīkīm	
[nim-PIE SAA-ki-how n-toe-SKIN-nee-keem)	*I love my young man greatly*
nitoskinīkīm awa nipepim	
[n-toe-SKIN-nee-keem u-WU M-pay-peem]	*my young man, this baby of mine*
Dialogue	
nitōtēmitik, ahā hay! [n-toe-TAY-mi-tik u-HAA HIE]	*my friends, greetings!*
kīkwāy? [kee-GWHY]	*what?*
cā [CHAA]	*expression of disgust or joking*
mwāc [MWAACH]	*NO WAY!*
mōniyāskwēw [moe-NEE-yaas-kwayoo]	*white woman*
'skanak [sku-NUK]	*bitch*
pimātisiwin [pi-maa-TI-si-win]	*life*

kā-sawēyihtamahk [kaa-su-WAYIH-tu-muhk] *which we love and respect*

sākihitowin [saa-ki-HI-to-win) *love*

kahkiyaw, kahkiyaw [KUH-kee-yow KUH-kee-yow] *all, everything*

kā-māmitonēyihtamahk [kaa-MAAM-to-NAYIH-tum-muhk] *that we think about*

hāw, māka [HOW MAA-ku] *okay, then*

awiyā! [OW-we-yaa] *owtch*

hoka! [HO-kaa] *(Lakhota battle cry)*

Watatoosis *(a made-up name - used in the play with vicious sarcasm)*

kitimākinawin [ki-ti-maa-KIN-nu-win] *pity me*

nōhkom [NOH-koom] *my grandma*

tanisi [TAAN-si) *hello, how are you*

mōy nānitaw [mo-NAAN-tow] *fine*

wahwā [wuh-WAA] *oh my*

nā, awas [NAA, u-WUS] *ah, go on*

tāpwē nipahi-miyosiw [taa-PWAY m'PIE MEE-yo-so] *she's truly very beautiful*

tāpiskōc mōniyāskwēw [TAA-p'skoats moe-NEE-yaas-kwayoo] *like a white woman*

nīcī [NEE-chee] *my fellow, my compadre*

GIRL WHO LOVED
HER HORSES

DREW HAYDEN TAYLOR

DREW HAYDEN TAYLOR

INTRODUCTION TO *GIRL WHO LOVED HER HORSES*

Drew Hayden Taylor is an Ojibway from Ontario's Curve Lake First Nations. In the ten years since he won the Chalmers Canadian Play Award for his first play, *Toronto at Dreamer's Rock*, he has established himself as one of the country's most prolific and most frequently produced playwrights as well as a respected television, film, short story, and essay writer. His plays include a trilogy (*Someday, Only Drunks and Children Tell the Truth*, and *400 Kilometers*); a projected "blues" tetralogy (which so far includes *The Bootlegger Blues, The Baby Blues*, and *Bus'gem Blues*); a wicked intercultural satire of, among other things, higher education (*AlterNatives*); an adaptation of Bertholt Brecht's *Mohogany* (*Sucker Falls*); four plays for young audiences (*The Boy in the Treehouse, Toronto at Dreamer's Rock* and its sequel, *Toronto @ Dreamer's Rock.com*, and *Girl Who Loved Her Horses*); and a sort of agit-prop *Christmas Carol* about funding Native education (*Education is Our Right*). Most of these are published, remain in print, and are regularly produced across the country. He has also published three popular collections of essays under the title, *Funny, You Don't Look Like One: Observations of a Blue-Eyed Ojibway*, and he has served for a time as Artistic Director of Native Earth Performing Arts.

In his best-known plays Taylor adopts, adapts, and rings variations on the sit-com genre, and the apparent familiarity of the form has gained him access to theatres across the country that are not noted for producing Native work. These plays use a subversive brand of satiric humour to probe some of the most sensitive cultural and intercultural issues of our time. But there is another, more spiritual side to Taylor's dramatic work that is most apparent in his plays for young audiences, including of course *Girl Who Loved Her Horses*, which in the preface to its TalonBooks publication Taylor calls "my personal favourite of everything I have ever written." First produced by Theatre Direct Canada in April 1995 at the Theatre Centre in Toronto under the direction of Richard Greenblatt, *Girl* is perhaps most readily classifiable as a memory play. The central action is framed by the contemporary stories of three adult characters, Shelley, Ralph, and William, and their memories of events fifteen years earlier, triggered by the appearance, as graffiti on an old brick wall, of the worn but still startling image of a horse, its eyes terrifying, animalistic, and angry. But this play does not function like the memory play of western tradition. It doesn't explain away disturbing or traumatic childhood events, bringing satisfying and therapeutic resolutions to the tensions and conflicts of the past and leaving both the characters and the audience refreshed and ready to return to the quotidian world purged of their discontents. In this play the calm and complacent surface of the everyday life of the past and present, as well as of the audience, is ruptured by the insistent intrusion of the numinous.

Girl Who Loved Her Horses might also be read as a "loss of innocence" narrative about art and identity, a flashback to simpler times when, as to "the traditionally minded Inuit, the purpose of carving was to let free the image that was trapped within the stone," and "once the image was free, and the stone carved, they would move on." In this reading, the adult characters remember the "wild and free eyes" of the childhood drawing of the horse almost with nostalgia. They conjure for themselves a time before Ralph started studying to be a cop, before William learned to defraud the band to fund his business, and before Shelley learned to give up on troubled students – a time "way back when," when "Indian names said something about who you were or what you did," and when honouring the spirit of the fish one was about to hunt may have been more than an "old Indian line" used to lure or detour tourists. This reading, focusing on a stunning final image that "nobody's there to see," might consider the play to be a lament for an irrecoverably lost time when the world of spirit and that of everyday life were inextricably intertwined.

But the play won't quite sit still for either of these readings. Not only has this playwright, so clever with words and dialogue, daringly placed at the play's centre an almost silent title character, a troubled but magical young girl whom we never see in the present tense of the frame story (and who therefore remains an unknown rupture in its close), but he also relies for his opening and closing scenes, and for the most meaningful moments in between, on a wordless visual image brought to life through movement and dance. This is not a comfortable, sweetly nostalgic, or cathartic image, and it explains nothing away; rather it is a startling and visceral picture filled with energy and frustration – even rage. And it may be infectious, for of course it is not true that nobody is there to see it: effectively performed, the play's final image will haunt the imaginations of audiences for whom it might serve as a reminder of a still vibrant, angry, and powerful spirit realm. Audiences, indeed, might leave the theatre newly charged.

CHARACTERS

THE HORSE
RALPH
SHELLEY
WILLIAM
DANIELLE

GIRL WHO LOVED HER HORSES

DREW HAYDEN TAYLOR

SCENE ONE

The lights come up on a cold and stark rundown city street. Along one side of the set is an aged and worn brick wall, covered in bills and posters. A young Native man, RALPH, makes his way across the street in no particular hurry.

His attention is caught by the posters advertising a Native rally or festival, and he goes over to investigate. He reads them as he walks along the wall, when something from above grabs his eye, perhaps a flash of light or colour.

Backing up and looking above the posters, he freezes in recognition, awed and overcome. There, peeking above the posters, is the outline of what appears to be an old and faded mural. The only easily identifiable elements in the mural are the terrifying and angry animalistic eyes, barely above the paper posters, staring down at the silent RALPH. There is also the hint of a mane framing what might be the head. The colours and savagery of the mural trigger something in the stunned RALPH.

He approaches the wall again and rips away a few handfuls of posters and bills to reveal more of THE HORSE. The mural is drawn from chalk but half of it has been washed away by rains, leaving it blurry in places, giving the impression that part of the animal has been melted by heat. It is an old beat-up image on an equally beat-up wall, but there is still power.

RALPH
Ho-lee!

The lights go down on RALPH and up on THE HORSE at another part of the stage. THE HORSE, alone on the stage, executes through dance and movement, an expression of its raging anger. Both it and the dance should be terrifying and bold.

SCENE TWO

A typical Reserve household three hours from the city. It is early evening and the room is dark. At the table sits a depressed SHELLEY. She remains unmoving in the shadows, barely breathing. Then footsteps are heard and somebody whistling. A door is thrown open with gusto and WILLIAM enters the room, covered in grease, dirt and paint.

WILLIAM
I'm gonna kill that American. I just need one more thing to push me over the edge. That's all. Do you know what he wants now? He wants sharks on

that damn boat. Sharks! What the hell do I know about painting sharks! I tried to explain to the guy that muskies make better sense. The lake's full of them and that's what he wants to go out and catch. Gave him the old Indian line about honouring the spirit of the fish he's about to hunt. Didn't buy it. Sharks or nothing on the hull of that boat he said. I can paint a lot of things but only stuff that makes sense, you know. Sharks in these fresh-water lakes, I mean think about it buddy. Actually he heard me saying that to myself and well, it looks like he's not going to buy the 20-footer. There goes $30,000. So how was your day?

SHELLEY
I quit.

WILLIAM
Quit what?

SHELLEY
Work. I quit work.

WILLIAM
What do you mean you quit work!? You can't quit work!

SHELLEY
I've just had it. I can't take the daycare another day. The kids yelling, the staff, everything. I have reached a point of no return. And that means I am definitely not returning.

WILLIAM
But Shelley...

SHELLEY
That kid was the last straw. I couldn't take anymore.

WILLIAM
What kid?

SHELLEY
That Benojee kid. You know, the one I've been telling you about. The one that draws all these black pictures. Not even pictures, just covers the paper in a coating of black crayon. One right after the other. Weirdest thing I ever saw.

WILLIAM
You quit over that?

SHELLEY
He bit me today when I tried to get him to draw with a different colour. Bit me! Right there! All because I put a red crayon in his hand. That was it. I said to myself, "I don't need this anymore." So I quit.

WILLIAM

We need the money.

SHELLEY

Sell the marina.

WILLIAM

Not my marina. I love this marina.

SHELLEY

Then learn to run it properly. That American was practically drooling over that boat. That $30,000 could get us through the winter and I happen to be quite fond of being warm.

WILLIAM

So am I but sweetie, I can't draw a shark. Tried and tried. Ended up looking like a pickerel with an attitude. It just wasn't meant to be. Sorry, no sale.

SHELLEY

You no sale, me no job, we no eat.

WILLIAM

Maybe you'll reconsider and go back to work tomorrow?

SHELLEY

Don't think so. Maybe you'll reconsider the shark?

WILLIAM

Don't think so.

SHELLEY

Welfare's sounding better and better.

WILLIAM

I can't go on welfare. I used to be the Chief of this Reserve. How will that look?

SHELLEY

Don't give me that. You didn't care how things looked when you were Chief. You misappropriated funds to build this damn place. People are calling it William's Watergate Marina.

WILLIAM

Hey, I'm gonna pay them back. In a few more years when the marina...

SHELLEY

"In a few years, in a few years." You know how many times I've heard that? Or "next spring when the boats are in the water we'll start making real

money." It's going to take more than a few years. I do the books remember?
Nobody comes here from the village. They don't trust you.

WILLIAM begins to hunt through the cupboards.

WILLIAM
I think you're being a little selfish.

SHELLEY
Selfish! I'm being selfish. You won't paint a stupid shark on a $30,000 boat
to keep us warm this winter and I'm selfish! *(pause)* William, I'm tired of
being underpaid, understaffed, and overwhelmed. The council doesn't
appreciate what I do there, some of the kids would just as soon take a
chunk out of you as take a nap and... oh why am I talking to you anyways?
It's like talking to a three-year-old.

WILLIAM
We got any cookies? I'm tellin' ya, Ralph should have gone into business
with me like I asked him. Boy we would have really had this place rockin'
then. Me doin' the boats, you the books, he could handle all the people.
Folks like him. He'd have customers eating out of his hands. He'd have
convinced that American to keep the fish on the boat.

SHELLEY
Don't drag him into your fantasy world. He's happy studying to be a cop.
You know him, he always wanted to be one of the good guys.

WILLIAM
So what are we going to do about your job?

SHELLEY
I don't know. Maybe get another one.

WILLIAM
Your diploma says Early Childhood Education, it's either that or a
McDonald's. And the Reserve doesn't have a McDonald's.

SHELLEY
I am not going back to that place!

The door opens and RALPH enters.

RALPH
What place?

SHELLEY
Ralph!? What are you doing here?

RALPH drops his duffel bag on the floor, not answering. Instead, he approaches the far white wall.

Is something wrong? Are you okay?

RALPH
Yeah, I'm fine.

RALPH stops and gazes at the wall.

WILLIAM
That's a wall, Ralph.

RALPH
I know. I just wanted to come home. See the place.

SHELLEY
It's not like you to come home mid-week.

RALPH
It happens.

WILLIAM
Hey Ralph, Do you think sharks belong on the side of those boats out there?

RALPH
What?

SHELLEY
Stop trying to get him on your side.

WILLIAM
He's in college, he knows these things.

SHELLEY
I don't believe you're giving me a hard time on this. It's just paint on fibreglass. Last month somebody wanted a deer on a canoe. You didn't put up a fight then.

WILLIAM
The woods are full of deer. I've seen deer. You've seen deer. Even that American has seen deer. They belong here. But there's no point to drawing a shark. I don't know anything about sharks, I've never seen a shark, there are no sharks in these waters so there's no sharks on the boat.

RALPH
The Inuit.

SHELLEY
What?

RALPH
They're famous for their carvings.

SHELLEY
What are you talking about? *(to WILLIAM)* Do you know?

WILLIAM
Don't look at me, he's your brother.

RALPH
To the traditionally-minded Inuit, the purpose in carving was to let free the image or spirit trapped within the stone. Once the image was free, and the stone carved, they would move on. They were a nomadic people, the concept of carrying around big stone carvings just wasn't practical.

SHELLEY
Well, there's nothing more practical than eating and keeping warm.

RALPH
Like the wall.

WILLIAM
What wall? Pink Floyd's *The Wall?* The big one they have in China?

RALPH
We covered it over in layers and layers of paint like we were trying to hide or get rid of it. It's still there, like the hundreds and hundreds of Inuit carvings scattered all through the Arctic, almost forgotten, hidden behind that wall.

WILLIAM
What's hidden?

SHELLEY
Uh Ralph, are you okay?

RALPH
I'd almost forgotten all the things I'd seen on this wall, all the images, pictures, stories we had put on it. We used to kneel right there, by the refrigerator. Remember that?

SHELLEY
Ralph, are you talking about the Everything Wall?

RALPH
Right there, that's where the head would be, and over there was where the mane would extend to. That whole wall would be taken up, just flaming with colour. Remember how we used to just stand there and stare at it for hours. It gave me goosebumps.

WILLIAM
He's talking about that horse. The one that little girl did.

SHELLEY
Danielle.

RALPH
That's her name. Danielle. I haven't thought about her in years. Not until I saw that horse again. I saw it today. It was hard to tell it was a horse, let alone the same one. You couldn't look at those eyes and not remember it over there, on that wall. Except this time, it was different. It was as big as this house, drawn across a rundown brick building in a dirty part of town. It was something about the eyes. They used to be so, so wild and free, you remember them. But this time they were colder, darker. I wanted to see them the way they used to be, back when we were kids. That's why I came home.

SHELLEY
You came home to the Everything Wall?

RALPH
How old were we then? Ten, twelve...

SHELLEY
Yeah, something like that. I think you were in Grade Five. Wasn't that the year William failed?

WILLIAM
I didn't fail, I was left behind.

RALPH
Yeah, that was around the time of the Everything Wall.

SCENE THREE

The sound of crunching pervades the stage, little mouse-like chewing sounds as a petite girl, DANIELLE, walks across a playground eating from a bag of chips. She meticulously eats one after the other as she walks. She is tiny, even for an eleven-year-old, and walks slowly as if she has no place to go. She holds her school books across her body. She looks nervous for no apparent reason.

Then, from off-stage the sound of shouting and running can be heard. Two young boys rush on stage, one after the other.

RALPH
You run about as good as you smell. Awful.

WILLIAM
Let's see how good you smell when I break your nose.

WILLIAM lunges after RALPH and tackles him They go down in a pile of arm and legs. WILLIAM jumps up with a triumphant yell.

You're it!

RALPH races after him and is almost touching him when WILLIAM aims for DANIELLE and swerves at the last moment before RALPH has a chance to react. RALPH runs bang into DANIELLE, sending her, her books and her potato chips flying.

RALPH
Oh sorry, um here.

RALPH is embarrassed and a little concerned. He makes a token effort to pick up some of her books. RALPH quickly hands them, almost tossing them, to the fallen DANIELLE.

WILLIAM
You're still it, and you'll always be it.

WILLIAM darts away quickly as RALPH makes a lunge for him. DANIELLE is forgotten in the mayhem. The boys disappear off stage, running at full gallop, leaving DANIELLE alone on stage, books and chips askew.

DANIELLE
That's okay.

DANIELLE looks at the mess of spilled potato chips surrounding her. There is one left in the bag and she delicately eats it. Then she gets on her knees and picks up all the remaining chips on the ground and places them neatly in the bag, and then in a nearby garbage can. She gathers the rest of her stuff and walks to a nearby swing where she sits down and tries to put her books together.

There is silence for a moment then from the opposite end of the stage the sound of boyish yells gets gradually louder and closer until the two boys come racing out again, running flat out. This time RALPH is in the lead with WILLIAM behind him. RALPH then sees SHELLEY entering the playground. RALPH immediately stops, does a 180 to avoid her and runs directly into WILLIAM, heads knocking in a loud thud. They both, once again, go down in a heap. This

time however, they don't get up as fast, and moan in pain. SHELLEY
approaches them as they lie rolling on the ground. Behind them, DANIELLE
is swinging ever so slightly on the swing.

RALPH
Oh my head... I think I can feel my brain.

WILLIAM
Somebody look up my nose and tell me if it's bleeding.

SHELLEY
Oh gross. Get away from me. Ralph, Mom wants to know how many
people are coming over tonight.

WILLIAM
Coming over for what?

SHELLEY ignores him.

SHELLEY
I've invited Julia, Vanessa and Anita.

WILLIAM
To what?

RALPH
I didn't invite anybody.

SHELLEY
Why not?

RALPH
I didn't want to.

WILLIAM
Want to what? What am I missing here?

SHELLEY
You know Mom's looking forward to it. She's promised a prize and
everything to the best one.

WILLIAM
Prize!? There's a prize!? What do I have to do?

RALPH
Shelley, it might turn into something stupid like that time Mom bought
that cow.

WILLIAM

(*laughing*) I remember that. Your mom is so funny! She wanted to cut down on all the money she spent on milk and butter and cheese. So she bought that cow. And it wasn't even a milk cow.

SHELLEY

It wasn't even a female cow. Mom didn't even check.

RALPH

And then it ate everything in the vegetable garden. And it left behind those huge piles of green smelly cow sh...

SHELLEY

It was so embarrassing. I stayed at Grandma's for two weeks till things died down.

RALPH

Oh Mom's okay. She makes life interesting.

WILLIAM

I'll say.

SHELLEY

So you better invite some people over, for Mom's sake.

WILLIAM

Invite them to what?

RALPH

Mom wants us to draw things on our kitchen wall. She's calling it the Everything Wall because we're supposed to put everything we can think of on it.

WILLIAM

Everything?

SHELLEY

You behave. This is my mother's wall and I don't want you embarrassing us any more than you already do.

WILLIAM

Hey Ralph, I saw this great movie on television where this guy had this painting of himself that kept getting older and older while he stayed looking the same. Let's draw paintings of how Shelley will look when she's really old, with things falling off, drool coming down her chin, big wrinkles all over the place. You know, five years down the road.

SHELLEY
You're so immature. That's probably why you failed.

WILLIAM
I didn't fail. I was left behind.

SHELLEY
Big difference.

RALPH
Let's not do it, Shell. We'll tell Mom we forgot or something. Maybe she'll forget about it in a few days.

SHELLEY
We have to do it. She's made room on that whole wall for this. Even moved the refrigerator over. Now my friends will be finished around eight, then you can have it. I guess you'll have to bring him to draw with.

WILLIAM
Sure I'll go, what's for dinner?

SHELLEY
Liver.

WILLIAM
I'll come later.

SHELLEY
Mom's counting on us, Ralph.

> *SHELLEY turns to leave. RALPH and WILLIAM start walking in a different direction.*

RALPH
Why does Mom do these things?

WILLIAM
Are you really having liver?

> *DANIELLE stops swinging.*

DANIELLE
The Everything Wall.

SCENE FOUR

DANIELLE leaves the swings and journeys home in her typical meek manner. She arrives at her front door and stops, nervous. Loud and angry noises can be heard, and DANIELLE hears them and appears afraid to enter. She finally musters up the nerve and enters her house, making a quick beeline for her room where she immediately crawls into bed, letting the books fall to the ground. The noises seem to get louder and louder, and DANIELLE crawls under the covers seeking protection.

DANIELLE wraps the blankets around her tiny body and crawls into a corner, her body racked with shivers. The noise of a violent argument can be heard on the other side of the wall. Each loud bellow makes her shiver in fear. As the yelling gets louder, DANIELLE pulls the blanket higher and higher until she disappears beneath the covers. Occasionally, the covers hiding her continue to tremble.

Then a blurred or not-quite-realized image of THE HORSE appears on the wall, or more accurately, behind the wall. He moves along the length of the wall, behind DANIELLE, as if seeking an opening. He tries to reach out to the little girl but is prevented from making contact by the wall.

SCENE FIVE

SHELLEY is sitting at the kitchen table playing solitaire when WILLIAM and RALPH enter. They immediately grab pop from the refrigerator. The Everything Wall is partially covered in designs of various things and levels of talent.

WILLIAM
Hey Shelley, where are your friends? Didn't show huh?

SHELLEY
Oh they were here, and Ralph, you should have heard the things they were telling me about William.

WILLIAM
What? What did they say?

SHELLEY
Wouldn't you like to know?

WILLIAM
Well... yeah...

RALPH
You actually drew on this thing huh?

SHELLEY
(*pointing*) That's mine. Wait till you see what I have in mind for next week. It's so great. Wanna know?

RALPH
Nah.

WILLIAM surveys the range of art and starts to laugh.

WILLIAM
You call this art?! Come on, I've seen better drawings in kindergarten. What's this supposed to be?

SHELLEY
None of your business.

WILLIAM
Tell me.

SHELLEY
It's that cow we used to own. Happy?

WILLIAM
This is yours! How'd you remember what it looked like? Use a mirror?

RALPH
What is it with you? She's my sister, not yours. I should be the one always fighting with her.

WILLIAM
Nah, it's always open season on your sister. I'm just lucky enough to get in the first shots. What do you call it, a turkey shoot?

SHELLEY makes a jump for WILLIAM, wanting to punch him. RALPH holds her back.

SHELLEY
Just one shot, Ralph, that's all I want. That's all I need.

RALPH
Mom!!

SHELLEY
Forget it, she's not here. She's driving my friends home.

SHELLEY goes back to her cards while WILLIAM surveys the wall.

WILLIAM
My mother would have put me up for adoption if she saw me doing stuff like that on our kitchen wall.

RALPH
Well, have fun. We're going down to the lake.

SHELLEY
You're not going to draw anything?

RALPH
I can't be bothered.

SHELLEY
You'd better draw something. Maybe it will help you in art class.

> *RALPH approaches the wall, grabbing a pencil crayon. He draws a one-foot long vertical line, studies it for a moment, then draws another one parallelling it. He quickly adds two horizontal lines thereby making a tic-tac-toe.*

RALPH
Wanna play?

WILLIAM
Only if I can win.

> *They begin to play games while SHELLEY continues with her card game. WILLIAM cheats by putting an extra X on the wall when RALPH isn't looking.*

So Shelley, what did Vanessa and Julia say about me?

SHELLEY
Nothing much. It was what Anita said that was interesting.

> *WILLIAM gets all embarrassed and turns away from SHELLEY and RALPH.*

RALPH
Just go.

> *WILLIAM starts a new game.*

WILLIAM
How come you're doing so bad in Art? It's easy.

RALPH
It's boring. That and the fact I can't draw might have something to do with it.

WILLIAM
Everybody can draw. You just put lines on paper.

SHELLEY finishes her card game and walks over to take a look at what the boys are doing.

SHELLEY
Not exactly great art boys. Unlike these masterpieces. And William, Anita drew that one.

WILLIAM
So what? Looks like a strangled chicken.

SHELLEY
It's a dog.

WILLIAM
You can prove this?

RALPH
You're doing it again.

WILLIAM
Ralph, the rain falls, dogs bark, we fight. Get used to it.

RALPH
Well, I'll say one thing. I think Shelley's going to win the prize.

SHELLEY
Get used to it.

Like a challenge being thrown down, WILLIAM grabs a pencil and draws in a few quick strokes, a startlingly good image of a realistic teepee.

WILLIAM
Now what was this you were saying about a prize?

SHELLEY
Big deal.

There is a quiet knock, so quiet nobody hears it except RALPH. He cocks his head.

WILLIAM
Jealous?

SHELLEY
In your dreams.

WILLIAM
Wanna try your hand at some real cards?

SHELLEY
No.

WILLIAM
Afraid I'll beat you at that too?

SHELLEY
Oh drop dead and die.

WILLIAM
Aren't those two the same thing? Hey Ralph, wanna play some cards?

RALPH
Huh? Oh sure.

WILLIAM
Last chance there, Shell.

SHELLEY
Oh very well, just to teach you a lesson.

WILLIAM
Crazy Eights. My deal.

> *They sit down at the table. WILLIAM starts to deal. Then there is a very quiet, barely audible scratching/knocking. RALPH is the only one that hears it.*

RALPH
Hey, did you guys hear something?

WILLIAM
Like what?

RALPH
I don't know. It was just something out of the corner of my ear.

WILLIAM
(laughing) Corner of your ear? Good one Ralph. So what do you think my prize is gonna be?

SHELLEY
You're so sure it's you, aren't you? There's some other good stuff up there too. You're not the only one who can draw.

WILLIAM
I hope it's money.

The same noise repeats, this time just a little bit louder.

SHELLEY
I heard it that time.

RALPH
The door maybe?

WILLIAM
Awful wimpy knock if it is.

SHELLEY goes to investigate the door. She pulls it open to reveal DANIELLE standing there, looking smaller than ever.

SHELLEY
Hello, who are you?

DANIELLE, the poster girl for shyness, doesn't respond. The other kids look surprised to see her.

WILLIAM
(secretly to RALPH) Oh man, Ralph, look who it is. The dumb girl.

RALPH
She's not dumb.

WILLIAM
Sure acts like it sometimes.

SHELLEY
Aren't you gonna say something?

RALPH
She doesn't talk much. Doesn't do much of anything,

DANIELLE just stands there, looking more and more like the proverbial shrinking violet.

SHELLEY
Well, you coming in?

DANIELLE hesitates for a moment.

What are you afraid of? I said "come in."

DANIELLE manages to enter the kitchen.

RALPH
Hey Danielle.

SHELLEY
Danielle, that's a pretty name. I was thinking of changing my name to Kateri, you know, after the Indian saint when I got older. Better than Shelley. So what do you want, kid?

DANIELLE mumbles something but it's impossible to make it out.

SHELLEY
Tell me, I won't bite.

WILLIAM
Don't believe it.

DANIELLE struggles to speak louder.

DANIELLE
I heard you could draw here.

SHELLEY
Yeah, do you wanna?

DANIELLE shyly nods her head.

SHELLEY
Well, okay, the pencil crayons are over there. There's still a lot of room left, big space over there. *(pointing)* That's my house there, don't you just love the tulips? I saw this house once when we went to the city. That's where I want to live when I get out of school. So draw what you want, my mom gives a prize every Monday night to the best picture. She won't tell us what the prize is though. And then she washes it off for Tuesday. Okay?

DANIELLE
Thank you.

DANIELLE shyly approaches the Everything Wall. She walks around the card players and tries to reach the pencil crayons but they are too high for her. She jumps up but still can't reach them.

WILLIAM
Will you hurry up Shelley, it's your turn.

SHELLEY grabs the pencils and gives them to her.

SHELLEY
Here. *(to RALPH)* Did you watch him? He didn't cheat did he?

DANIELLE
(in an unnoticed voice) Thank you.

She examines her pencils closely, and removes five specific colours. The others she puts on the counter. She stands there and looks at the wall.

SHELLEY
Danielle? You live around here?

DANIELLE
My mom and I live across the tracks.

SHELLEY
Oh, so you aren't part of the Reserve?

DANIELLE
No.

SHELLEY
Who's your mom?

WILLIAM
Elsie Fiddler.

SHELLEY reacts to that. It does not look like good news. She speaks to RALPH in hushed tones.

SHELLEY
Ohh. You in her class?

RALPH
Yeah but that's about it. We don't hang around with her or anything. I don't think I've ever seen her hang out with anybody.

SHELLEY
No friends? Do you guys pick on her or tease her?

WILLIAM
No, you've got to have a personality to be picked on.

SHELLEY
What?

WILLIAM
Something for people to make fun of. She doesn't have enough to tease.

RALPH
She's sort of like a shadow.

WILLIAM
Just a dull blob, not making any noise or drawing attention to herself.

SHELLEY
Oh how sad.

WILLIAM
Yeah I guess, can we go back to the game now?

SHELLEY, WILLIAM and RALPH focus on the card game completely unaware of DANIELLE and what she's about to go through. DANIELLE puts pencil crayon to wall and THE HORSE comes through the wall slowly. He is skittish around her, checking out his space. She moves towards him. He looks slightly dangerous, but she's not afraid.

THE HORSE glows with energy, radiating everything that DANIELLE isn't. It has strength, confidence, freedom. Power. DANIELLE slowly, carefully continues to approach THE HORSE. She reaches out, her hands desperate to touch him, and at the same time afraid he'll disappear the moment they make contact. He swings her around, fast and amazing at first, then tenderly. She slides down the front of THE HORSE slowly, her back against him, her face glowing. She makes a huge sound of joy and release. She laughs and giggles like the child she has a right to be.

DANIELLE
I knew you'd be there. I knew it.

She closes her eyes, still radiant. THE HORSE slips away from her and back through the wall. She turns to find him gone. There is a moment of sadness as she allows the power to leave her. She goes towards the wall.

A large, magnificent creation of THE HORSE is on the wall. DANIELLE puts the last touch on her creation and then neatly puts the remaining pencil crayons back into the package.

SHELLEY
Ralph, I think he was cheating but I don't know how.

WILLIAM
(*cocky*) Too fast for you huh?

DANIELLE
Thank you.

> *She exits.*

RALPH
So you were cheating!

WILLIAM
I never said that. You can't prove it.

> *Upset, SHELLEY throws the cards on the table and storms away. She is the first to see THE HORSE.*

SHELLEY
Uh guys...

> *The two boys follow SHELLEY's line of sight and see THE HORSE. They get up to get a better view. They all stand there, eyes wide, amazed and silent for a few moments.*

RALPH
Nice horse!

SHELLEY
Amazing!

WILLIAM
Ultra-amazing! That was Danielle, wasn't it?

> *They all approach the wall, RALPH reaches out and touches the wall to make sure it's real.*

SHELLEY
That shy little girl...

WILLIAM
It's almost like it's alive. Where'd she learn that?

RALPH
Not with our art teacher. I think it's looking at me.

SHELLEY
This can't be washed off. It would be a sin, like painting over the Sixteen Chapel.

RALPH
That's Sistine Chapel.

SHELLEY
A sin's a sin Ralph, no matter what you call it. I think I want to look at this every day.

WILLIAM
Gotta admit, it is beautiful.

SHELLEY
We should put a frame around it.

WILLIAM
Maybe charge admission.

SHELLEY
I'll ask Mom if we can keep it.

> *The three stand there and look at it for a ridiculously long time.*

RALPH
Nice horse.

WILLIAM
I'm not gonna win, am I?

> *In unison, RALPH and SHELLEY shake their heads, their eyes never leaving THE HORSE.*

SCENE SIX

> *The next day at the school yard, DANIELLE is walking when RALPH and SHELLEY approach her and bar her way. Instantly she goes back into shrinking violet mode.*

SHELLEY
Hey Danielle, that was some horse you drew.

RALPH
Yep, never seen one like it before.

DANIELLE
Thank you.

SHELLEY
Um, my mom says you're welcome over at our place anytime you want.

DANIELLE
Thank you.

There is an uncomfortable silence. RALPH nudges SHELLEY.

SHELLEY
Oh and this is for you.

SHELLEY takes something out of her knapsack and hands it to DANIELLE who timidly takes it. It is the prize, a book of pretty but cheap paintings.

DANIELLE
Thank you.

SHELLEY
Do you, like, ever say anything other than "thank you?"

DANIELLE is thumbing through the book.

DANIELLE
Pretty pictures. Look, a horse.

She continues to leaf through the book, oblivious to SHELLEY and RALPH.

SHELLEY
Well...

No reaction from DANIELLE.

RALPH
I guess we should be going now.

No reaction.

SHELLEY
Okay...?! Bye.

RALPH
Bye Danielle.

They turn to leave. DANIELLE doesn't acknowledge them.

SHELLEY
That is one strange puppy.

They exit.

After a few seconds, DANIELLE closes the book, a smile on her face. She continues her journey across the playground, the book held tightly in her hands. Lights come up on WILLIAM straddling a swing and eating an apple. DANIELLE crosses in front of him. WILLIAM watches her for a moment, bored.

WILLIAM

Hey Danielle...

DANIELLE freezes instantly, not looking up, her lowered face hidden by her hair. She stays frozen in place as WILLIAM watches. Slightly amused, WILLIAM finishes his apple and tosses it at her feet, in disdain at her strangeness. He dismounts the swing like it was a horse and walks away from her. DANIELLE does not move until WILLIAM has disappeared, then she picks up the apple core, walks a few feet and deposits it in a trash can.

SCENE SEVEN

Later that week. The Everything Wall is covered with horses of every shape, description, colour and level of talent. RALPH is quietly doing his homework on the kitchen table while SHELLEY is doing hers on the counter while talking on the phone.

SHELLEY

Yeah, you should see it Julia. It's really amazing. There are horses everywhere. Everybody's drawing horses now. Pretty soon we'll need a corral.

Occasionally RALPH gives SHELLEY an annoyed look.

No, Danielle hasn't been here all week. *(pause)* Who knows. But I think it's between William and Vanessa's cousin for best horse, next to Danielle's of course but she can't win twice for the same picture. They both look really good but don't tell William I said that.

There is a quiet knock on the door.

Julia, somebody's at the door, I'll call you right back.

She hangs up the phone to open the door, revealing DANIELLE.

Hey, come in, do you want a pop or anything?

DANIELLE shakes her head as she enters.

Boy, you really started something with that horse of yours, take a look.

DANIELLE sees the wall of horses but has eyes only for hers.

DANIELLE
It's still here.

SHELLEY
I know.

DANIELLE
But you said you would get rid of them so we could do new ones. That's what you're supposed to do. It's still here.

SHELLEY
But it's so cool, we...

DANIELLE
I'm sorry. Thank you.

> *DANIELLE turns and leaves immediately, leaving behind a surprised household.*

SHELLEY
Danielle?! Wait. What's wrong?

> *DANIELLE is long gone. RALPH approaches the wall.*

RALPH
Model airplanes.

SHELLEY
What?

RALPH
Model airplanes. Like if someone gave me a model airplane, I wouldn't want to be given a finished one, I'd wanna put it together myself. After that they get kind of boring. It's drawing the picture she likes, not the picture itself.

> *SHELLEY dials the phone.*

SHELLEY
Well I think it's stupid. Julia? Yeah, that was her. She is so weird. She looked like she was insulted or something, or didn't want to see the horse. There's still room for her to draw something else. Like, what's her problem? Anyway, I'll be right over. Don't do anything till I get there, okay? Bye.

> *Hanging up, SHELLEY throws her jacket on.*

I'm going to Julia's. Tell Mom I'll be home for dinner.

She exits. RALPH, still looking at the wall, makes a mental decision. He locates a bucket of water, some soap and a sponge. He takes one last look at THE HORSE.

RALPH
Bye.

SCENE EIGHT

SHELLEY, WILLIAM and RALPH are back in the kitchen playing cards. SHELLEY is looking out the kitchen window at the miserable rainy weather and WILLIAM is waiting for RALPH to deal.

SHELLEY
What a horrible day. I was going over to Vanessa's. I bet her and Julia are having fun.

WILLIAM
Who cares? Are we playing or what?

RALPH starts to deal the cards.

RALPH
Mom asked about Danielle again.

SHELLEY
Did you tell Danielle you washed it off?

RALPH
Course I did. She said "thank you" then walked away.

WILLIAM
I think it has something to do with her mother, that Elsie Fiddler lady.

SHELLEY
What does?

WILLIAM
Her weirdo-ness. That's what my mom thinks. I heard her talkin' with my dad about all these parties she had and all her boyfriends. They say the police have even been over there a couple times.

RALPH
What about her father?

WILLIAM
They didn't say but I heard Elsie's new boyfriend just got out of jail.

SHELLEY
You're kidding!

WILLIAM
Nope, heard it myself. Beat up some woman over in Barrie.

SHELLEY
Really? But guys, we really shouldn't be talking about her behind her back.

WILLIAM
Okay, let's do it in front of her.

Nobody laughs.

It was a joke.

There is a quiet knock at the door. SHELLEY gets up and opens the door to reveal a wet, drowned-looking DANIELLE, but there is still a spark in her eye.

SHELLEY
Hey, it's you.

SHELLEY ushers the dripping girl into the kitchen and takes her coat. SHELLEY then grabs a dishtowel and tries to dry DANIELLE's hair.

You are a wet one, aren't you? You know where the pencil crayons are. Go to it.

DANIELLE approaches the wall but is deliberately blocked by WILLIAM. She can't get around him and he pretends to be busy looking at his cards. He feels SHELLEY and RALPH staring at him in disgust and annoyance making him reluctantly move out of her way.

DANIELLE picks up the pencil crayons. She removes five of them and studies a large blank section of the wall. RALPH watches her while SHELLEY and WILLIAM continue playing cards. DANIELLE selects her first pencil crayon and stares at the wall.

Whose turn is it?

WILLIAM
It's Ralph's. Hey, snap out of it. Are we playing or what?

RALPH
I don't wanna play anymore.

RALPH leaves, obviously fascinated with DANIELLE and her drawing process. WILLIAM is frustrated at RALPH for leaving the game.

WILLIAM
What's with this stupid picture anyway? It's just some lines on the wall.

SHELLEY
William, shh.

WILLIAM
I just don't see what all the fuss is about.

SHELLEY
You wouldn't.

WILLIAM
Come on, Ralph, let's at least finish the game.

RALPH
Play without me.

WILLIAM
I'm sick of that horse. If she's such a great artist let's see her do something else. Danielle, as a favour to me, please, draw me a... a... dog. Yeah a dog.

SHELLEY
Maybe she doesn't want to.

WILLIAM
Sure she does. If she's an artist like everybody says, she should be able to draw anything. Oh come on, there's more to life than just horses. I'm waiting for a dog!

DANIELLE shakes her head.

DANIELLE
No. They bark.

SHELLEY
William, leave her alone.

WILLIAM
We were having a fun game of cards till she showed up. Did you know Ralph gave her a cute little nickname?

SHELLEY
Shut up William or I'm gonna...

WILLIAM
Girl Who Loved Her Horses. Should be Girl Who's Afraid to Draw a Stupid Dog. I wanna see a dog.

RALPH
William!

WILLIAM
I know my name. Danielle, draw a dog right there. *(He points.)*

> *DANIELLE turns hesitantly to the wall. There is a long pause as she tries to imagine the dog.*

SHELLEY
Leave her alone.

WILLIAM
I'm not hurting her. I just want to see a dog. Horses are easy, dogs are harder.

> *Startled and nervous, she starts to draw but her movements lack the grace of the drawing of the horse. It is jerky, very unartistic. WILLIAM is watching her with fascination, then amusement. It is a very poor image of a dog.*

That's a dog? Boy they must have some funny looking dogs across the tracks. Looks like a cross between a chicken and a rhinoceros. Draw me something else. Draw me a... duck.

> *WILLIAM is laughing and DANIELLE is starting to cry softly.*

SHELLEY
That's enough. You leave her alone this minute. Just get out.

WILLIAM
Fine, you want her for a friend, then have her. I got better things to do than this. I just wanted to show you she isn't all that hot. Come on Ralph, let's get out of here.

RALPH
You go without me.

WILLIAM
(surprised) Ralph...?

RALPH
Just go, William.

WILLIAM
Fine, I didn't want to stay here anyway.

> *Angry and embarrassed, WILLIAM storms to the door and flings it open to make a dramatic exit. As the door opens, there is a bright flash of lightning and*

a loud crack of thunder making him pause at the door, but instead of turning around and losing face, he stubbornly gathers himself up and walks out into the pouring rain, slamming the door behind him.

SHELLEY
What a goof.

RALPH
I wonder what made him do that?

SHELLEY
I don't know. He's your friend.

RALPH
Hey...

They are so engrossed in their conversation they barely hear the quiet crying of DANIELLE. Instantly concerned, SHELLEY and RALPH rush to her side. DANIELLE tries to crawl away and ends up in the corner.

SHELLEY
Hey, take it easy. He's gone.

RALPH
Are you okay?

DANIELLE doesn't say anything, just cries more.

What should we do?

SHELLEY
I don't know. What an idiot.

DANIELLE looks up.

No, not you. William. You're okay.

DANIELLE
He scares me.

SHELLEY
He pisses me off. Come on, let's get you up off the floor.

They place her in a chair and SHELLEY wipes her eyes and nose.

He's usually not as bad as that but I think he's a little jealous of you.

DANIELLE
Me?

SHELLEY
Yep. Eh Ralph?

RALPH
He's kinda used to being the centre of attention.

> *RALPH runs to the refrigerator and gets DANIELLE a pop. He pours it into a glass and hands it to DANIELLE.*

DANIELLE
Thank you.

RALPH
Can I ask you a question?

> *DANIELLE shrugs nervously.*

Why do you draw that horse? I mean, that's an amazing horse.

> *DANIELLE shrugs again.*

Like, that's a bad dog. But your horse...

DANIELLE
He's a beautiful horse, huh?

SHELLEY
Never saw one like it.

DANIELLE
That's my horse. Mine. He wasn't always there, but now he's there whenever I want him.

RALPH
Where'd it come from?

DANIELLE
Campbellford I guess.

SHELLEY
Campbellford?! That town past Marmora?

DANIELLE
Uh huh.

SHELLEY
Why there?

> *DANIELLE shrugs again.*

You can tell us. Really.

DANIELLE
When I was six, back when my dad was alive, he took me to that fair they have in Campbellford. They had pony rides there. I remember this big line-up of kids, and there was only one pony for all those kids.

SHELLEY
Yeah, we had one of those at Indian Days, remember Ralph?

DANIELLE
We had to stand in line for a long time before I got a chance to ride, and I kept watching that pony. They put one kid after another on its back and it would go around in a circle, and around and around, wearing out a path in the grass. Sometimes its eyes weren't even open. That's all it ever did. Just went around in a circle all day, every day. And I felt sad for it. It looked old, unhappy, and its back was bent. When it was my turn to ride, I started crying. I felt so sorry for that poor pony, I didn't want to ride it.

RALPH
What's that got to do with your horse?

DANIELLE
A couple months later my dad died. And things got different at home. And I never stopped thinking of that pony, thinking how sad its life must be. I wondered if it dreamed of better things when his eyes were closed. Then it began to change. When I'd think of him, he grew bigger, got stronger, got real beautiful. And I began to wonder if all things could change, be different if they had better places to live, people who loved them. That makes me want to draw the horse even more. It makes the horse happy.

RALPH
Geez, your art teacher must really love you.

DANIELLE
It doesn't work when it's on a small piece of paper. Then it becomes the pony again. It has to be someplace big, it has to be special. Your house is special. I tried it once on our wall. Mommy didn't like that. I got punished for that. That's why I wanted to come here.

RALPH
Maybe we can come over to your place sometime.

DANIELLE shakes her head vigourously.

DANIELLE
No. Can't. Mommy's boyfriend is there. Doesn't like people coming to visit. *(She is quiet for a moment.)* I miss my dad. I miss my mommy.

RALPH
But your mom's still alive.

DANIELLE
It's not my same mommy. She's changed. She used to be so nice. Now I'm afraid.

SHELLEY
Afraid of what?

DANIELLE
Mommy. Her boyfriend. They make fun of me. I don't like being made fun of. Mommys aren't supposed to do that. Yours doesn't.

SHELLEY
Maybe she's just teasing.

DANIELLE
No.

There is an awkward silence, followed by a peal of thunder.

SHELLEY
It's really getting bad out there.

DANIELLE
I'm cold.

SHELLEY
Oh my gosh, your clothes are still all wet. You must be freezing.

RALPH
Should I get a blanket?

SHELLEY
I'll get it, and I think I know where Mom put some of the clothes I outgrew. Maybe there's something in there that would fit you. I'll be back in a moment.

SHELLEY gets up and leaves the two sitting at the table.

RALPH
When you draw, do you actually see the horse?

DANIELLE
Sort of. He kinda sees me too.

RALPH
Wow.

DANIELLE
Sometimes he's there. Sometimes I have to call him.

RALPH
How do you call him?

DANIELLE
I do it with the colour. I just hold it up to the wall and if I wish hard enough, he'll come.

> *RALPH picks up a pencil crayon and holds it up to the wall. He stands there for a moment.*

RALPH
Nope, nothing.

DANIELLE
It's not that easy.

> *DANIELLE hesitates for a moment, then takes RALPH's pencil crayon and holds it up to the wall. She is motionless for a moment. Then her hand slowly begins to move as she begins to sketch the familiar pattern of THE HORSE on the wall. Her gestures have a familiar welcoming feel to them. She starts to smile as the image of THE HORSE begins to come through the wall. Alive once more, it goes to DANIELLE and once again dances with her in a gorgeous ballet.*

> *Only this time, RALPH is watching. He is in her world and can see the three-dimensional horse and the dance they are doing together. At one point THE HORSE comes close to RALPH, beckoning him to take part in their dance. Hesitantly, RALPH lifts his hand, unsure of what to do. They are about to touch when DANIELLE notices this and shouts.*

NO!

> *The mood and magic are broken and THE HORSE disappears. RALPH is left in the kitchen with his hand outstretched and an angry DANIELLE standing in front of him.*

No! It's my horse. Mine. You can't have him.

RALPH
Uh, I was...

DANIELLE
Mine. Please, I don't have anything else. Get your own horse.

SHELLEY walks in at this moment, with an armful of clothes.

SHELLEY
What's...?

DANIELLE bolts out the door and out into the rain. SHELLEY runs to the door.

Danielle! Danielle! Wait!

There is no response.

What was that all about?

RALPH looks at his hand.

RALPH
I almost touched him.

SCENE NINE

SHELLEY is sitting on the floor, an open box of clothes beside her. She is sorting the clothes. RALPH enters through the kitchen door, one side of his body covered in mud.

SHELLEY
What happened to you? Are you okay?

RALPH
Elsie Fiddler threw a beer bottle at me and I had to run as fast as I could to get out of range.

SHELLEY
You're kidding! Why?

RALPH
I just went there to see if Danielle had come home yet. I guess all those calls Mom made about trying to adopt her sort of made it back to Elsie. Told me to tell Mom to mind her own business or she'd come over here and punch her in the face. I think she'd been drinking.

SHELLEY
Well, considering she threw a beer bottle at you, you're probably right.

RALPH notices all the clothes.

RALPH
What are you doing?

SHELLEY
These are my old clothes. I was gonna give them to Danielle if she came to live with us. I think she'd look pretty in blue, don't you? I always wanted a sister.

RALPH
It would have been kinda nice, huh? Having her here.

SHELLEY
Why won't her mother let her come stay with us? Maybe if we told the police about her throwing that bottle at you they'd change their minds and Danielle could...

RALPH
Shelley, she can't. Mom tried. Elsie's her mother.

SHELLEY
Some mother.

RALPH
Maybe, but there's nothing we can do. We're just kids.

SHELLEY
Ralph, there's gotta be something...

RALPH just shakes his head silently. SHELLEY continues sorting the clothes in silence, with RALPH trying to clean himself off. There's a loud knocking at the door. It's WILLIAM.

(disappointed) Oh.

RALPH
Haven't seen you in a while.

WILLIAM
Didn't think you wanted to.

SHELLEY
You got that right.

WILLIAM
Well, um, I guess I kinda got carried away the other day. A little maybe.

SHELLEY
No *little* about it William.

WILLIAM
Well look, I'm sorry. I blew up. I didn't mean to. I don't know why I did. It just happened.

SHELLEY
You scared her.

WILLIAM
I know. I didn't mean to. Really. Just everybody was talking about that stupid picture.

SHELLEY
She's missing, William. Nobody's seen her for two days.

WILLIAM
I know. I think I know where she is.

RALPH & SHELLEY
You do?

WILLIAM
Yeah, I was heading down to the lake. Gonna spend the day out on our boat, been kinda bored since... even brought my lunch for the day. So I was cutting across your backyard and through the woods. That's when I saw her in the doorway of the fort. You know, the one we hang out at during the summer.

SHELLEY
Just behind the house.

WILLIAM
I'm pretty sure it was her. Anyway, I thought you might like to know.

WILLIAM turns to leave, but SHELLEY and RALPH prevent him, grabbing their coats and boots.

SHELLEY
Not yet, William, you're coming with us.

Delighted that he's part of the gang again, he brightens up.

WILLIAM
Yeah, okay. Follow me.

He dashes out the door with the other two following.

SCENE TEN

The location is that of a ramshackle fort that has been put together over years by young boys. Across the sloped and planked ceiling is the drawing of THE HORSE, majestic and strong, and perhaps bigger. In the corner of the fort on the floor is DANIELLE, nestled happily in the presence of THE HORSE. It is a relationship of love and security. She is singing, or more accurately, mumbling an inaudible song as she basks in the warmth of THE HORSE. They are playing a hand game.

Then from outside the fort the voices of RALPH, SHELLEY, and WILLIAM are heard approaching. Instantly THE HORSE disengages himself from the now agitated DANIELLE and re-enters the wall only to disappear. Desperately, DANIELLE tries to follow him into the wall but fails. She has been left behind. The door of the fort is opened and DANIELLE quickly hides under an old ratty sleeping bag that has probably been there for years.

She hides silently as the trio enters. They look around and WILLIAM spots the huddled mass in the corner. He silently points to her and SHELLEY approaches, signalling the others to stay behind.

SHELLEY
Danielle? It's me, Shelley.

WILLIAM is first to notice the image on the ceiling and nudges RALPH. No response from DANIELLE. SHELLEY sits beside her.

Boy it's cold in here. You can't be warm underneath that ratty thing. Come on, let's take you inside.

SHELLEY tries to remove the sleeping bag but DANIELLE won't let go. From across the room RALPH speaks.

RALPH
Danielle, I'm sorry.

WILLIAM
What have you got to be sorry for?

DANIELLE whimpers at the sound of WILLIAM's voice.

Oh, um, Danielle, it's me, William. Well, I guess you know that. But I'm really sorry for all those things I said. I really like your horse. Honest.

DANIELLE peeks out from under the sleeping bag.

DANIELLE
Then why did you call him stupid?

WILLIAM
Um... because... I don't know Danielle.

SHELLEY pulls the ratty sleeping bag away. Slowly DANIELLE slides towards her.

I guess I just wish I could draw like that.

SHELLEY
We've been looking all over the village for you.

DANIELLE
They were yelling again. All night. I don't wanna live there anymore. I wanna stay with you guys. I like your place.

SHELLEY
Did they hurt you or anything?

DANIELLE
No. Mommy's boyfriend got a job in Toronto. We're moving there but I don't want to go. I wanna stay here. *(pause)* He scares me. Can I stay with you guys? Please.

SHELLEY
Well, um Danielle, we already thought of that.

DANIELLE
(to RALPH) I'll let you meet him. My horse.

SHELLEY
But your mom said no. We tried everything. Really we did. Mom tried with the Children's Aid Society, the band office, everything. Nobody would help.

DANIELLE
I didn't think so.

RALPH
When are you going? To Toronto.

DANIELLE
Monday.

RALPH
So soon?

DANIELLE nods.

DANIELLE
What time is it?

WILLIAM
Almost lunchtime.

DANIELLE
I'm awful hungry.

> *Realizing she hasn't eaten in two days, SHELLEY and RALPH search through their pockets for food of any kind. No luck until WILLIAM pulls his paper bag lunch out of his coat pocket.*

WILLIAM
Do you want my lunch?

> *Nervous of WILLIAM but very hungry, she grabs it from his hand.*

DANIELLE
Thank you.

WILLIAM
It's just some sandwiches.

> *She proceeds to eat as fast as she can.*

DANIELLE
Did my mother call looking for me? Was she worried about me?

SHELLEY
Yeah. She called. Of course she's worried. Wasn't she?

WILLIAM
Real worried.

RALPH
No, she didn't call.

DANIELLE
I didn't think so.

> *DANIELLE gets up to leave.*

RALPH
Danielle, I'm sorry.

DANIELLE
That's okay. *(pause)* That was a pretty name you gave me. Girl Who Loved Her Horses. Pretty. I liked it.

RALPH
Way back when, Indian names said something about who you were or what you did. That's who I think you are.

DANIELLE
Thank you.

As she walks out the door, she has one final sentence for RALPH.

I should have let you touch him. I should learn to share more. I'm sorry.

DANIELLE exits. The three remaining kids look miserable.

SCENE ELEVEN

The now older RALPH, SHELLEY and WILLIAM enter the alleyway where the graffiti of THE HORSE is located.

SHELLEY
You know, to this day, every time I see a red pickup, I can see her and that family of hers driving by the school for the last time.

RALPH
I remember running to the window waving goodbye.

WILLIAM
I spent that whole summer sitting in that fort looking at that horse.

RALPH
There it is.

RALPH points to the half-covered horse on the wall.

SHELLEY
Could be hers but it doesn't look like the one I remember.

RALPH
It's older, bigger, like us. It's gotta be her.

SHELLEY
Ralph, that was more than fifteen years ago. People don't go around
drawing horses on walls for that long. That could be anybody.

RALPH
And how many people do you know suddenly stop and say "Gee, I feel like
drawing a horse on a wall today for no particular reason."

SHELLEY
Maybe it's just wishful thinking Ralph. Maybe you'd just like to believe she's
out there still drawing that horse of hers.

WILLIAM
It's her.

SHELLEY
How do you know?

WILLIAM
That's the horse. I know it.

*WILLIAM approaches the wall and starts to pull at the flyers, grabbing
handfuls and tossing them to the ground. Soon RALPH, then SHELLEY join
him in a ripping frenzy. Soon, most of the drawing is free. They step back to
appraise the bigger image.*

SHELLEY
It's almost scary.

WILLIAM
Are you going to look for her?

RALPH
I don't know. Maybe she doesn't want to be found.

WILLIAM
You should never bring horses to the city. They don't belong here.

SHELLEY
So what now?

RALPH
I don't know.

SHELLEY
We can't just stand here looking at it all night.

WILLIAM
Let's go get something to eat. Maybe we can come up with some ideas on how to find her. We let her get away once. And that happened.

RALPH
(to SHELLEY) What do you say?

SHELLEY
I agree. And maybe we can stop somewhere and pick up some black crayons.

RALPH
What for?

SHELLEY
There's this kid in my class. I'm not going to give up again.

WILLIAM
Let's go eat.

> *They turn and leave. RALPH lags behind, turns and approaches the drawing on the wall. He reaches out and touches the horse image for a moment.*

SHELLEY & WILLIAM
Ralph!

RALPH
Okay.

> *He joins the others off stage.*

> *From inside the wall on the empty stage, THE HORSE appears, an angry frustrated one. Still filled with rage, he dances and raises his arms to the wall, still facing the audience, as if calling forth a power. The wall begins to radiate and pulsate, then the image of THE HORSE painted on the wall begins to glow, solidify and take shape at his urging. The picture of the horse gets brighter, stronger, and more brilliant until the wall is seething in colour and presence. The magic and power of THE HORSE has returned.*

> *But unfortunately nobody's there to see it. The lights go down.*

> *The end.*

THE UNNATURAL AND ACCIDENTAL WOMEN

MARIE CLEMENTS

MARIE CLEMENTS

INTRODUCTION TO *THE UNNATURAL AND ACCIDENTAL WOMEN*

Marie Clements is an award-winning writer, performer, and artistic director of urban ink productions. Her eight plays, including *Age of Iron, Now look what you made me do, The Unnatural and Accidental Women* and *Urban Tattoo*, have been produced and presented on stages across Canada, the United States and Europe, and published in a variety of anthologies and other books. Her latest play, *Burning Vision*, was commissioned by Rumble Theatre and developed in collaboration with Playwrights Workshop Montreal and produced by Rumble Theatre in association with urban ink, and it was nominated for five Jessie Awards. It was presented at the prestigious Festival des Ameriques in Montreal and the Magnetic North Festival, Ottawa, Spring 2003. *Burning Vision* and *Copper Thunderbird* (a commission by Les Ondinnok Theatre) have evolved over the last two years through writer's residences at Rumble Theatre, Playwrights Workshop Montreal, The National Theatre School, Banff Playwrights Colony and Firehall Arts Centre. In 2002, Marie worked in the writing department of the television series "Davinci's Inquest," and she is currently working on the film adaptation of her stage play, *The Unnatural and Accidental Women* through a fellowship with the BC Film commission.

The Unnatural and Accidental Women is a stunning, complex, and multi-layered piece of theatre, drawing upon a range of forms, genres, and media that extend from fairy tale and legend through political documentary to filmic quotations, musical numbers, call-and-response, stand-up, and sit-com. It is in turn wildly funny, horrific, warm, sensual, and celebratory, all in service of a powerful political critique that links overarching Native, feminist, environmental, anti-colonial, and class-based concerns with a specific and localized attack on systemic racism and sexism in a justice system that has consistently turned its back on the serial murder of women in Vancouver's downtown eastside since the mid 1960s. Her focus here is on a series of murders committed there between 1965 and 1987, all by the same man using the same *modus operandi*. His victims' deaths were nevertheless astonishingly ruled by the coroner, and reported in the press, to be "unnatural and accidental," finding "no evidence of violence or suspicion of foul play." What perhaps sets this play apart, however, is the way in which it offers a trenchant critique of state neglect and tacit approval of gendered and raced violence while at the same time celebrating the women, not as victims, but as vibrant, sensual, funny, and life-affirming individuals (even after death), and members of a loosely defined but deeply interconnected community of women. That community is perhaps best represented by Rose, one of the murdered woman and a kind of spectral telephone operator who stitches together the play's action simply by doing her job: "I am in between people," she says, "connecting."

There is something maternal about it, the wanting to help, the trying, going through the motions on the switchboard, but in the end just being there always it seems, just listening to the voices looking for connection, an eternal connection between women's voices and worlds.

The Unnatural and Accidental Women is also at once poetic, spiritual, and fanciful while remaining firmly grounded in its downtown eastside landscape and in the history of Vancouver, from the loggers' skid roads to the present day Skid Row, from trees to hotels, tree stumps to bar stools. The play is most obviously structured as a transformational collage, in which scenes blend and bend into one another with astonishing fluidity (as do people and furniture, material and spiritual realms), modelling transformation as at once a natural process and a template for change. All of this is grounded in what might be seen as a quest narrative, except that Rebecca's search for clarity and for her Native mother, "Aunt Shadie," is shadowed and complicated by Aunt Shadie's simultaneous search for Rebecca as the mixed-race daughter she had abandoned twenty years earlier to save her from seeing Native women the way her white father did – "the way white people look up and down without seeing you – like you are not worthy of seeing. Extinct, like a ghost." But Aunt Shadie really is a ghost now, one of the murdered women that form the play's central community and drive its other grounding structure, that of revenge tragedy. Like that of the Senecan tragedies of Shakespeare and his contemporaries, the action of *The Unnatural and Accidental Women* is prompted by murders that cry out for revenge, and like them its action is initiated and witnessed by a chorus of revenants. Unlike those sixteenth- and seventeenth-century dramas, however, the mood of this play's conclusion is celebratory rather than tragic, and the feast with which it ends is neither grotesque nor horrific, but healing, as the fulfillment of the quest and the achievement of revenge come together in a ritual "first supper – not to be confused with the last supper." Finally, as if these structural components—post-modern collage, pre-modern quest narrative, and early modern revenge tragedy—were not enough, the whole is framed and given extra depth and resonance by the story of the land, the tide, the wind, and the trees – the landscape from which the play emerged at the outset, and to which it returns at the conclusion.

CHARACTERS

REBECCA (ages 4 and 30): Mixed blood/Native – a writer searching for the end of a story.

ROSE (age 52): English immigrant – a switchboard operator with a soft heart, but thorny.

AUNT SHADIE (age 52): Native – mother qualities of strength, humour, love, patience.

MAVIS (age 42): Native – a little slow from the butt down, but stubborn in life and memory.

THE WOMAN (age 27): Native – looks and moves like a deer.

VALERIE (age 33): Native – a big beautiful woman proud of her parts.

VERNA (age 38): Native – sarcastic but searching to do the right thing, the right way.

VIOLET (ages 27 and 5): Mixed blood/Afro-Canadian – an old spirit who grows younger to see herself again.

The Barbershop Women: MARILYN (age 25): Native. **PENNY** (age 30): Native. **PATSY** (age 40): Native. A beautiful, sexy threesome that can move and sing.

THE BARBER (ages 30s and 60s): White – short, balding, nice and creepy.

THE LOGGER, THE MAN, THE ROMANTIC PARTNER, THE PILLOW, THE DRESSER, THE MAN'S SHADOW, THE AIRLINE STEWARD.

RON (age 35): A cop – handsome, with a nice body and a good sense of humour.

SFX voices: EVAN (age 8): Valerie's oldest son, wise and angry. **TOMMY** (age 5): Valerie's youngest son, naive and sweet. **THE OPERATOR**: A polite but repetitive telephone recording. **FATHERLY MALE VOICE**: The Woman's adopted father. **"Can I buy you a drink?"**: The Barber's Voice.

SETTING

ACT ONE: Scenes involving the women should have a black-and-white picture feel that is animated by the bleeding-in of colour as the scene and their imaginations unfold. Colours of personality and spirit, life and isolation, paint their reality and activate their own particular landscape within their own particular hotel room and world. Their deaths are a drowning-down of hopes, despairs, wishes. The killer is a manipulative embodiment of their human need. Levels, rooms, views, perspectives, shadow, light, voices, memories, desires. Rebecca's journey through Act One should be a growing up through memory. Being in a memory, but present in time. Walking. Seeing. Time going by. Life – colour of memory and the searching. Aunt Shadie and Rose are on the top level from the beginning. In their own spaces and places. They are in their own world. Happy hunting ground and/or heaven. Elements: Trees falling, falling of women, earth, water flowing/transforming.

ACT TWO: Scenes in Rebecca's apartment are present and in Kitsilano, but reflect the symptoms of urban isolation even without being on Hastings Street. Flow: Scenes of hearing, shadow-seeing, consciousness, unconsciousness of what is around us/within us.

THE UNNATURAL AND ACCIDENTAL WOMEN

MARIE CLEMENTS

DEATH BY ALCOHOL
THE VANCOUVER SUN
OCTOBER 22, 1988

"She was found lying nude on her bed and had recent bruises on her scalp, nose, lips, and chin.... There was no evidence of violence, or suspicion of foul play," noted Coroner Glen McDonald.

"...a native Indian, had been drinking continuously for four days before she died.... Coroner Larry Campbell concluded her death was 'unnatural and accidental.'"

"...drank enough to kill her twice. That's the conclusion of a coroner's inquiry into the native Indian woman's death. She was found dead, lying face down on a foam mattress with a blanket covering her, in Jordon's barbershop.... At the time of her death, Coroner Campbell said there was no indication of foul play."

"To get the blood-alcohol reading that... had at the time of her death, experts say she would have had to drink about 40 ounces of hard liquor all at once. The mother of four died at Jordon's barbershop.... Coroner Mary Lou Glazier concluded... death was 'unnatural and accidental.'"

"'She had the highest blood level-alcohol reading of all the women.' ...He believes Jordon was finally stopped because he killed his daughter, who was not an alcoholic and who has family that insisted police look into her death. 'He picked the wrong person. She was someone that someone cares about.' ...No coroner's report has been issued."

ACT ONE

SFX: A collage of trees whispering in the wind.

SLIDE: THE UNNATURAL AND ACCIDENTAL WOMEN

SFX: The sound of a tree opening up to a split. A loud crack – a haunting gasp for air that is suspended. The sustained sound of suspension as the tree teeters.

SLIDE: FALLING BACK – Beacon Hotel

Lights dim up on a small room covered with the shadows of tree leaves and limbs. Lights up on a LOGGER looking up at a tree, handsaw in hand. He shouts across time.

LOGGER
TIM-BER...

AUNT SHADIE
Re-becca...

A big woman suddenly emerges from a bed of dark leaves. Gasping, she bolts upright, unfallen. Nude, she rises leaving the image of herself in the bed. She follows the sounds and images of the trees.

SLIDE: Rita Louise James, 52, died November 10, 1978 with a 0.12 blood alcohol reading. No coroner's report issued.

SFX: Real sound of REBECCA slamming a glass of beer on her table.

SFX: The sound of trees moving in the wind increases.

SLIDE: TIMBER

Lights fade up on REBECCA as she sits, and thinks, and drinks at a round table with a red terry cloth cover. She takes her pen and writes in her journal.

The LOGGER continues sawing...

SFX: Sound of a long saw sawing under softly in lengths.

AUNT SHADIE walks through the forest, covered by the leaves/branches, in them.

REBECCA
Everything here has been falling – a hundred years of trees have fallen from the sky's grace. They laid on their backs trying to catch their breath as the loggers connected them to anything that could move, and moved them, creating a long muddy path where the ends of trees scraped the ground, whispering their last connection to the earth. This whispering left a skid. A skid mark. A row. Skid Row.

The LOGGER lays down his saw and picks up a chain saw...

SFX: Sound of a chain saw under.

Throughout – a blizzard of sawdust chips swarms the backdrop, covering AUNT SHADIE and tree parts. One by one, the trees have been carved into a row of hotels.

Hotels sprung up instead of trees – to make room for the loggers. First, young men sweating and working under the sky's grace. They worked. They sweated. They fed their family for the Grace of God. And then the men began to fall. First, just pieces.

AUNT SHADIE
Fingers...

REBECCA
...chopped down to the palm.

AUNT SHADIE
Legs...

REBECCA
...chopped up to the thighs.

AUNT SHADIE
Years...

REBECCA
...went by. You never knew what might be fallen. A tree. A man. Or, a tree on its way down deciding to lay on its faller like a thick and humourous lover, saying...

AUNT SHADIE
"Honey, I love you – we are both in this together. This is love till death do us part – just try and crawl out from under me."

REBECCA
Some of the men survived their amorous lover. Rows of men sweet-talked that last fallen tree into moving an inch to get that human limb out. Maybe just a leg – or part of it. Whispering...

AUNT SHADIE
"God, if you just do this for me. Jesus, just get this log off me... and...

REBECCA
Well, a whole crew of men sitting in their rooms drinking and thinking of the weight of that last tall love.

The LOGGER finishes, looks around and looks right at REBECCA. REBECCA mouths "I love you" to him silently.

The LOGGER cups his ear and shouts towards her.

LOGGER
Eh? (*He waves his hand "never mind" and continues.*)

REBECCA
Saying "Eh?"

The LOGGER continues the buzz with the chain saw. Wood chips blizzard on the backdrop. The chain saw buzzes under transforming to a bar saw.

AUNT SHADIE
(*laughs*) Saying "Eh?" a lot. Could you repeat that? Their voices yelling over the sound of the power saw buzzing thirty years ago, or was it last year? Never mind, the buzz rings in their ears just as the sawdust used to rest in their belly buttons after a hard day's work. Honest work. A tree for...

REBECCA
...a thumb.

AUNT SHADIE
A tree for a...

REBECCA
...leg.

AUNT SHADIE
A tree for their...

REBECCA
...hearing.

AUNT SHADIE
An honest trade made between a logger and his trees. No malice between the two – just an honest respect for the give and take of nature.

SFX: The full buzz of a bar under.

The woodchip blizzard clears, and crudely made stumps that look like bar stools remain behind her and deepen the look of the bar – The Empress Hotel. AUNT SHADIE walks across the bar but is also covered by it, in it.

REBECCA
Now the loggers sit like their lovers, the trees – they sit like stumps, and drink, and think. And think the world has gone to shit. They think of a time when cutting down a tree was an honest job, a time when they all had their good-looking limbs, a time when they were respected by the tallest order, a time when drinking was not an addiction.

AUNT SHADIE turns up a flight of stairs as we watch her shadow ascend.

AUNT SHADIE
And the woman. Oh the women strolled by and took in their young sun-baked muscles and happy cash.

REBECCA turns back to her journal.

REBECCA
If you sit long enough, maybe everything becomes clear. Maybe you can make sense of all the losses and find one thing you can hold on to. I'm sitting here thinking of everything that has passed, everyone that is gone, and hoping I can find her, my mother. Not because she is my first choice, but because she is my last choice and... my world has gone to shit.

She looks around the room and raises her glass.

Cheers...

Lights up on the same hotel room, as AUNT SHADIE takes two old suitcases out from under her bed. She lays them out on the bed and opens them slowly, hesitantly. Cree words spill out everywhere. She opens and closes the sound and begins to laugh. Affectionately, she snaps them shut, picks them up and walks towards the door and up. The suitcases get heavier and heavier as she rises.

SLIDE: THE SWITCHBOARD – Reception

AUNT SHADIE walks towards small lights that fade up and down. As she approaches, lights fade up on the back of ROSE sitting at her switchboard. Her lobby is a 1960s hotel. ROSE is dressed conservatively in 1960s attire. The switchboard beeps and lights. She connects throughout. AUNT SHADIE huffs herself forward.

AUNT SHADIE
Excuse me.

ROSE
(*not looking at her*) Can I help you?

AUNT SHADIE
Yeah sure. I'm looking for a place to leave my baggage for awhile.

ROSE
I'm sorry, I can't do that.

AUNT SHADIE
Why, because I'm In...

ROSE
...naked. Yes, that's it. You'll have to register first. I can't be taking just anybody's baggage now, can I? Can you write your name?

AUNT SHADIE
Listen, I'm naked not stupid.

ROSE
Oh. Well, I'm just trying to help you people out.

AUNT SHADIE
Why don't you look at me when you say that?

ROSE turns slowly around revealing a black eye and bruises on her face.

Wow, they sure dragged you through it.

ROSE
Humph. (*ROSE looks away from AUNT SHADIE's nakedness.*)

AUNT SHADIE
Haven't you ever seen anybody nude before ?

ROSE
Not up front.

AUNT SHADIE
I'm not sure if I should feel sorry for you or not. Well, I went to bed wearing clothes, and then I woke up naked as a jailbird.

ROSE
I woke up naked once.

AUNT SHADIE
What, a million years ago?

ROSE
Pardon me?

AUNT SHADIE
I said, good for you.

ROSE
Aren't you cold?

AUNT SHADIE
Of course, I'm cold.

ROSE
Here, put this on.

ROSE takes a big beige cardigan from her chair and hands it to her.

AUNT SHADIE
Now I feel ugly.

ROSE
It's from England.

AUNT SHADIE
Like I said, now I feel ugly.

ROSE
It's the same one the Queen wore on her inaugural visit to Canada.

AUNT SHADIE
Like I said, ugly. (*looking at the sweater*) Ugly. For a Queen, you'd think she'd dress better. It's almost like she's punishing herself. If I had all her money, I wouldn't be wearing all those dowdy dresses. Just once I'd like her to wear a colour. Something not beige or plaid. Something blue maybe. Something that gives her colour: Red!

ROSE
Mothers of countries do not wear red.

AUNT SHADIE
She's a mother alright. Always did love those white gloves though. They remind me of white swans, especially when she waves. It's kinda pretty actually.

ROSE
My mother always wore gloves. She used to say a lady wasn't a lady unless she wore gloves.

AUNT SHADIE
Hmm. My mother wore mitts. They were white though, and furry. Big rabbit mitts. When my mother waved, it wasn't so much pretty as it was sad.

ROSE
Waving can be sad.

AUNT SHADIE waves like a queen.

Where you going?

AUNT SHADIE
I'm dying for a smoke.

ROSE
What about registering?

ROSE watches as AUNT SHADIE signs her name.

Rita Louise James.

AUNT SHADIE
There, you satisfied?

ROSE
Just doing my job.

AUNT SHADIE
What's that?

ROSE
I'm taking account.

AUNT SHADIE
Reminds me of the government. Taking count but not accountable.

She picks up her suitcases and begins to leave.

ROSE
You're going like that?

AUNT SHADIE
(*looks down on herself*) Why not ?

ROSE
You sure you don't want me to find you some pants?

AUNT SHADIE
It's alright. There's a good draft...

ROSE
Oh please.

AUNT SHADIE
...and frankly, if the pants look anything like the cardigan, I might as well be dead.

ROSE
Suit yourself.

AUNT SHADIE
I always have.

AUNT SHADIE keeps on walking. Lights fade on ROSE. AUNT SHADIE stops and sits on her suitcases. She reaches inside one of them and pulls out a pack of tobacco and rolls a cigarette. She reaches in and picks up an outfit from when she was a housewife. She smells the material and closes her eyes in memory. The

*clothes talk to her and she to them. She drapes them over her body and smokes
her thinking smoke. Lights fade leaving a bright butt and smoke rising up.*

*SLIDE: Rose Doreen Holmes, 52, died January 27, 1965, with a 0.51 blood
alcohol reading. "Coroner's inquiry reported she was found nude on her bed
and had recent bruises on her scalp, nose, lips and chin. There was no evidence
of violence, or suspicion of foul play."*

*Lights fade up on ROSE, as she affectionately touches her switchboard. It
responds with light flashes and beeps and muffled voices.*

ROSE

I've always been right here. No matter where I am, I am in between people
connecting. I like to think I'm the one who connects them, but mostly
I like to think that they have to go through me. If nothing else, it gives me
a place. A place in the making, the flashes of being... the feeling of feeding
that beeping energy into a whole that understands it, and soothes it, into a
gentle darkness. A small whimper when it enters – a connection between
the here and there – a giant light it becomes. It begins and ends with the
beeping, but it goes through me. I wait for the cry like a mother listening,
hoping to slot the right thing into its void – hoping to be the one to bring
about the pure answer. Again, the pure gentle darkness that says I have
listened and you were lovely, no matter how loud your beeping cry
becomes, no matter how many times I wanted to help but couldn't. There
is something maternal about it, the wanting to help, the trying, going
through the motions on the switchboard, but in the end just being there
always it seems just listening to voices looking for connection, an eternal
connection between women's voices and worlds.

> *ROSE leans over and nosily watches AUNT SHADIE enter REBECCA's
> world.*

Everybody always thinks that the switchboard operator is listening in to
their conversations, and they're not always wrong. The tricky thing is to act
like you don't know a thing. I swear on the Queen, it's a tricky thing.

*AUNT SHADIE enters dressed as a young housewife. She is carrying her
suitcases and a folded piece of paper. She sets the suitcases down and places
a paper on the table. She turns to leave, but stops as REBECCA picks it up.*

SLIDE: RUNNING SHOES

SFX: Sound of wind in the trees.

*Backdrop gradually brings in close-ups of Hastings Street when it was the centre
of shopping. The Army and Navy, Woolworth's – late 1960s/70s.*

REBECCA
My dad – The Character was still full-limbed but hard-of-hearing when he died. Still asking "Eh?" after every sentence I spoke, but quick to hear the sound of change falling to the ground. Death was no big surprise for him. The thing he couldn't get out from under was the day she left. I found him holding a piece of paper she had put on the kitchen table. He held it for a long time and then simply folded it and put it in his pocket. "Where's Mom?" I asked.

SFX: Sound of tree falling and landing.

He said, "She went for a walk." I thought maybe she had gone to the IGA or something. Somebody was always having to go to the IGA. When she didn't return and he didn't move, I started complaining about the big fact that I was supposed to get new running shoes today. I was supposed to go downtown today. I was supposed to get a hamburger today... milkshakes, fries and ketchup at Woolworth's. It was supposed to have been a great day, and now we had to wait. I was getting pissed off, because I was getting tired of going to The Salvation Army for smelly clothes, and I felt like I was gonna be normal like everyone else when Mom said we could go to The Army and Navy and get something new, something that smelled good, something that nobody had ever worn. Blue suede running shoes – three stripes on either side. I had to have them. It was unbearable, and my dad just standing there, and my mom deciding to go to IGA. I thought it was a master plan. Both of them against me being normal. I started yelling – the injustice too great. My dad just stood there like he didn't hear anything. "Get in the truck," he said. We went. I ate hamburgers and floats and fries and everything I could see in the posters of food on the walls of the Woodworth's cafeteria on Hastings Street. We went to The Army and Navy. We went home. No Mom. Again.

"Where's Mom?" again. He said, "She left us. I didn't know anything was wrong." He sat down. I took my running shoes off. I would never wear them again. Nothing was going to be normal.

REBECCA takes the running shoes off and kicks them. AUNT SHADIE turns around and silently picks them up, putting them properly under her chair. She exits. Fade out.

SFX: Sound of car streams, transforming into the tide.

SLIDE: FOUR DAYS: DAY 1 – Glenaird Hotel

SFX: Sound of tide hitting the edge of the island/bed.

The hotel room is an ocean of blue. The bed an island. The lone woman sits on her island. She is wet and holds a white pillow that shapes her different needs. The comfort of a child, a lover. The woman reaches over and grabs a drink from the table beside her. She places it down and in... in her own drinking rhythm. The ocean gets deeper in its colour.

Rhythms of a drinking room: 1) Tide – Time. 2) Light vs. Shadow. 3) Drinking Rhythm.

SFX: Sound of the tide begins to increase and finally sprays to telephone static.

SLIDE: I'M SCARED TO DIE I

A click of light on. MAVIS sits in a huge beaten-up armchair. Her hotel room matches the chair. It is beaten and slightly tinged with hues of brown. As she sits, MAVIS leafs through her address book looking and reminiscing about each entry. She urgently picks up the phone and dials. A light flashes up on the switchboard, and we hear ROSE speak in the darkness.

MAVIS
Hi, Mona? It's me.

SFX: Weird static and otherworldly connection.

ROSE
I'm sorry, you've reached the operator.

MAVIS
The operator? I didn't want any operator. I dialed the numbers myself. I'm more than capable of calling a long-distance number.

ROSE
I'm sure you are. At any rate, you've reached the operator. *(very polite)* Can... I... help... you?

MAVIS
Well, I guess if you're just sitting on your ass you could put me through – save me the time of letting my fingers do the walking.

ROSE
I'm sorry, I can't do that.

MAVIS
Are you gonna help me or not?

ROSE
Well, to be honest... no one's ever reached me on the phone before, and I just don't know if it's house policy or not.

MAVIS
What kind of house are you in where people call and you don't help them?

ROSE

Don't raise your voice to me. I'm just following rules.

MAVIS

Whose rules?

ROSE

Management.

MAVIS

(*covers the receiver with her hand*) Bitch!

ROSE

Pardon me?

MAVIS

I said, isn't that rich.

ROSE

I'll put this call through just this once as a special favour, but this is highly unusual.

MAVIS

Sure... whatever.

SFX: Sound of real telephone connection.

(*ring*) Hi, Mona. I just thought... (*ring*) ...got to thinking of you and thought I'd call. Actually, I just thought I'd call cause (*ring*) I wondered if you and Bill might be coming into town sometime. You know, change of scenery and all.... (*ring*) Doing good here, though (*ring*) just would be nice to hear your voice. I'll try back later, okay? (*ring*) We'll talk about all sorts of things. What I need is a good laugh. (*ring*) You know, a laugh so hard liquid comes from your nose like that time.... (*ring*) Well, anyways, here I am going on.... Just would be nice to talk about some old times maybe. (*ring*) I'd like that. I'd... like... that...

She slowly places the receiver to her chest.

SFX: Sound of telephone ringing empty.

MAVIS looks back at her address book. Picks it up, and begins tracing names and thinking on each entry. Lights fade.

SFX: The telephone starts to buzz like a chainsaw under.

SLIDE: REBECCA – Hastings Street

The backdrop gives us a close-up of Pigeon Square. The buildings become smaller like stumps of logs. REBECCA sits at her table drinking. She holds a harmonica in her hand.

SFX: Sound of harmonica takes over the buzz of the chainsaw.

When she hears the sound of the harmonica, she gets up. A man enters and sits on one of the stumps. He watches her.

REBECCA
I'm dancing in Pigeon Square. It's not a dream, it's a memory. I'm four years old, and I don't have to ask why they call it Pigeon Square. There's pigeon shit everywhere. At four a genius... I know. A row of old men sitting like stumps... smoking, laughing, tilting their heads back in a chuckle or a slug of rum. They are talking to The Character – my dad. He's playing the harmonica. I'm pretending I'm a dancer. We don't know who's pretending more. Me, or him. But my feet are hitting the squares like I know what I'm doing, and he's hitting all the notes they can hear. They take their pennies out and splash them down around my dancing feet. The coppers fall... it is the most beautiful sound you can imagine, because you see I am very special, and talented, and the "poor bastards," as my father would say, are happy, clapping. I bow. My dad takes my hand. We say goodbye. Some of them touch my cheek like they remember a daughter, some smile and wave a mitt, not a glove...

The man finishes clapping, and reaches up to her...

...and one reaches his glove to surround my braid. My dad – The Character, takes his hand and says to the man in the clearest logger voice "I could kill you" "Enough." The man lets go of my braid. My father, in the clearest voice "I love you" squishes my shoulder in a hug and says, "It's time to get the chain for the power saw. It should be fixed by now."

REBECCA turns back to the table and takes a drink. The man gets up and leaves.

It should be fixed by now.

SFX: Sound of rhythmic clapping echoes, and start of laughing.

SLIDE: THE BARBERSHOP QUARTET 1 – Barbershop

SFX: The real sound of a man laughing drunkenly.

Lights up on the interior of a barbershop. It is old and worse for wear. Mirrors reflect back. MARILYN sits in one of the barber chairs, her back to us. Her hair flows over the back of the chair as the BARBER cleans and preps his utensils. He exits briefly. MARILYN looks closely into the mirror, as a reflection of herself as MARILYN à la Farrah Fawcett looks back at her, becoming larger and more beautiful in the mirror. MARILYN à la Farrah Fawcett begins to sing softly. She enjoys her hair dream. The BARBER enters dressed in hyper whites and drapes a white cape over her, and her hair dream. He turns the barber light on, and it begins to slowly rotate – a red and white swirl. He places a bottle between her legs and tenderly begins to braid her hair in one long braid. He suddenly grabs her braid roughly and takes his scissors to cut it. She grabs it back in a tug of war.

MARILYN
Enough.

He leans over her and grabs the bottle. He brings it to her lips tenderly. She drinks. It spills.

BARBER
Down the hatch, baby.
Twenty bucks if you drink it right down.
Down the hatch, baby.
Right down – finish it right down.

She gulps and they laugh. He starts to twirl the barber chair faster and faster.

Fade out.

SLIDE: ROOM 23, WHEN YOU'RE 33 – Clifton Hotel

Lights up on an old beat-up room. It is animated by an old DRESSER with an ugly personality. Small and battered, it has three drawers with a mirror on the top. VALERIE stands in front of the mirror thinking about 23-year-old tits and adjusting her tits in her shirt.

DRESSER
You have a nice set.

VALERIE
Oh, shut up.

DRESSER
Really.

VALERIE
Why... don't... you... shut up?

DRESSER
Why don't you make me?

VALERIE
Just shut your drawers.

DRESSER
Make me.

She takes her shirt off and is trying to get her bra off. It's stubborn.

VALERIE
If I have to tell you again, you're gonna get it.

DRESSER
Get what?

VALERIE
A big fat punch in the chest.

DRESSER
Valerie. Pick a drawer – any drawer.

The DRESSER displays each drawer.

VALERIE
Pick it yourself. Can't you see I'm busy here?

DRESSER
Too busy to pick a drawer.

VALERIE
Too busy to pick my nose.

DRESSER
Too busy to pick your ass.

VALERIE
Too busy to pick your ass.

They laugh.

DRESSER
Pick a drawer.

VALERIE
What do I get?

DRESSER
What do you want?

VALERIE
Nice lingerie.

DRESSER
What colour?

VALERIE
Red.

DRESSER
What do I get?

VALERIE
You get to watch me put it on.

DRESSER
Maybe you're not my type.

VALERIE
Eeeeee – an uppity dresser. I got a real problem if you're my type, don't I? What is your type, old squat one?

DRESSER
A tall chest with two big knobs.

VALERIE
You're a pig of a dresser.

DRESSER
You're a pig.

VALERIE
Come over here and say that.

DRESSER
You come over here and say that.

VALERIE
Pig!

DRESSER
Whore!

VALERIE
I'll knock your drawers off.

DRESSER
Why don't you just get my drawers off?

VALERIE
That's no way to talk to a lady.

DRESSER
What lady? I don't see any LAY-DEE.

The mirror of the DRESSER starts to reflect a man's face.

VALERIE
And I don't see any-BODY. So shut up!

DRESSER
Okay, baby. Okay. Do you want to see what's in my drawers?

VALERIE
Probably skid marks.

DRESSER
Come on, baby... take a peek.... Come on, baby. That's it, baby.

She draws closer to the top drawer. It slides open slowly. She leans over to look in. A hand comes out and squeezes her tit.

VALERIE
Fuckin pig!

DRESSER
Let go! You fuckin whore!

She squeezes the drawer on his hand.

VALERIE
Say Valerie is the prettiest one of them all.

DRESSER
Val-er-ie is the pretti-est? ...CHUG of them all.

VALERIE
That's a bad dresser.

She squeezes the drawer harder on his hand. He screams.

DRESSER
Valerie is the prettiest lay-dee of them all.

VALERIE
And smart.

DRESSER
...and smart.

VALERIE
And she still has a great set of tits.

DRESSER
...and she still has a great set of tits.

She lets go of his hand, and it shrinks back into the drawer. She turns.

VALERIE
I had two sons, you know... and I still have great tits.

DRESSER
Yah, you're a regular Hollywood dairy cow.

VALERIE
What did you say?

DRESSER
I said, you're a real Pocahontas.

VALERIE
Fuck you.

DRESSER
WHORE!

VALERIE
PIG!

She kicks him in the drawers. He groans. He moves towards her, they wrestle, and fall on the floor wrestling. Fade out.

SFX: Sound of the tide. A slower rhythm.

SLIDE: FOUR DAYS: DAY 2 – Glenaird Hotel

It is dark. The woman stands on her bed/island and clicks on the light hanging from the ceiling. A pillow is propped up like a person next to her. The light of the light bulb sways slowly, back and forth. As she listens, she lifts the drink to her mouth and places it down slowly in her drinking rhythm. Repeats gesture, listening.

SFX: Voiceover – a fatherly male voice.

VOICE
"Once upon a time, a very long time ago, there was a deer who lost its mother, because someone shot its mother. Something like the story of Bambi, except that the little fawn was adopted by a human family that

loved it. And then someone said that the fawn that grew to a deer should be with its own kind, so the father of the human family, who lived on the mainland, took a ferry and dropped the deer on an island miles away and hoped it would be happier. Well, the deer wasn't happy without the only family it had ever known, and it swam all the way back to its human family, and everything was going great, everything was going great, until it ate some lettuce from the neighbour's garden, and the neighbour shot it dead."

Rhythms of a drinking room: 1) Tide – Time. 2) Light vs. Shadow. 3) Drinking Rhythm. 4) Conversations – recent and past.

The hanging light stills. Fade out.

SFX: Sound of tide blends into the electronic sound of static.

SLIDE: I'M SCARED TO DIE II

Lights fade up on MAVIS sitting in her chair. She sits in the exact same spot and manner. She is leafing through her address book. She finds a name and stops and smiles. Slowly, she runs her hand over herself, not so much sexually but as if remembering sex. She picks up the phone and dials him. Lights fade up on ROSE's switchboard.

MAVIS
Hello, John... it's me...

ROSE
It's me, Rose – your operator. What number were you calling?

MAVIS
This is an emergency, if you have to know. Big Nose.

ROSE
You don't have to be rude – I was just trying to be helpful. I have a very demanding job, and I don't need this static from you...

MAVIS
Well, I have a lot better things to do than talking to people I didn't want to talk to.

ROSE
Listen, Madame.

MAVIS
Don't use that tone with me.

ROSE

Don't think that all I do all day is sit on my big fanny and wait for people
to talk to me like this – people who have no appreciation for the fine art of
communication.

MAVIS

It gets pretty damn bad when you can't even make a phone call without
having a conversation with someone you don't want to talk to. Nose.

ROSE

And about that nose business. I don't have a big nose. If the facts be
known, I have quite a fine upturned nose, and if you're referring to the
fact that I asked you who you were calling – well, that has nothing to do
with nosiness and everything to do with...

MAVIS

I'm asking you for nothing – but for you – to *shut up* – and put me through
to who I need to talk to – and not have to go through – this talk... talk...
talk. Cluck.... Cluck.... Cluck...

ROSE

Practically every time I pick up the phone...

MAVIS

...like a goddamn BEAKY chicken!

A long, hurt silence.

ROSE

I'll thank you very much to refrain from making comments about my
features.

MAVIS

Don't think that just because you use bigger words than me and you went
to reception school or something, that makes you better than me.

ROSE

I'm just doing my job, and that's all you can ask out of anybody – is a
person do the job they were meant to do, and I try to do my job a million
times a day.

MAVIS

Like you know it all, when you don't know me and you don't give a damn
how I'm feeling or what I'm worried about or why I can't get off my ass and
just leave my room.

ROSE

...a million times a day.

MAVIS
I'm so scared I can't move.

ROSE
...a million times a day...

MAVIS
I can't breathe.

ROSE
I get this static a million times a day...

MAVIS
I listen.

ROSE
...times a day...

MAVIS
I cry.

ROSE
...from the static of nothing.

MAVIS
A million times a day.

ROSE
I want...

MAVIS
I reach out for it.

ROSE
...and nothing.

> *ROSE plugs her through. A surprising click for everyone.*

> *SFX: Voiceover – "I'm sorry, the number you have reached has been disconnected. Please call your operator..."*

> *MAVIS tries to talk over the recording as if nothing is wrong.*

MAVIS
Hey, John. It's me. Remember me? Mavis. Mavis Gertrude Jones. Played baseball real good. You know, you used to say I had the best arm on the team. You know, you used to say I was the smartest person you'd ever met, because I was always reading those *Britannica Encyclopedias* with the letters

on them. You used to say I had the best body in town – just kidding... and a pretty good bannock maker too. The queen of bannock making.

> SFX: Voiceover – "I'm sorry, the number you have reached has been disconnected. Please call your operator and..."

I miss your smile. I remembered your smile the other day. Going into a piece of that bread and coming out all greasy, with butter and lard – all sassy. You could always make me smile... make me feel safe with those big brown arms of yours. John? Anyways, I remembered those big arms of yours, and I was thinking I'd really like to borrow them for a few weeks. I know, that seems silly, but I'd really like to have that feeling with me right now. Just until I can get away from this feeling. Shake it away with your big arms wrapped right around me. John? John.

> Arms of the brown armchair extend like real arms and curl around her. She hugs them and love-coos in comfort.

Thank you, John. You always were sweet to me. Sweet Johnnie.

> She love-coos to herself and Johnnie's arms, and finally falls asleep.

> SFX: Soft sound of pigeons cooing grows underneath.

> Pigeon wings mix and blur and land on the backdrop behind. AUNT SHADIE slowly emerges from them and walks towards REBECCA's table. She sits down silently.

> SLIDE: WHITE BIRDS – Hastings Street

> The Huge "W" of the Woodward's building is brightly lit red and appears above it all.

REBECCA
My mother. I see her in half-looks everywhere. I call it seeing the white bird look. This white is not the colour of skin, but the flutter of hope.

Women's white birds. Sometimes you witness it, and it makes you cry. Sometimes I see it across a coupled room, and when I do see it – I see my mother's chin bending down limp to her chest.

> A young AUNT SHADIE's chin drops down to her chest. REBECCA looks in her direction.

Not to look at me, though the crease in her neck makes it possible for her to look at me, with tenderness, or to look at her man with tenderness, or to look at anything smaller than her, with tenderness. But to bend that long neck down, till her beak reaches her collar bone, and sits for a long time before it comes up. It sits so long, you ask: "What's wrong, Mom? What's wrong?"

AUNT SHADIE doesn't answer.

So long that your heart starts to beat, because something is wrong, so wrong, and nobody will speak. Not your dad – The Character, who spoke words and made this bird-killing silence.... And finally, she lifts her head... finally she lifts her head, but something is gone. Something dead sits in her eyes, and rests itself on the tone of her voice, when my dad – The Character asks, irritated: "Jesus, Rita. What's wrong now?"

AUNT SHADIE raises her chin slowly. Smiles faintly.

She slowly smiles oddly. "Nothing." My dad – The Character continues talking, as if nothing has died. But I saw it flutter and die. "Are you alright, Mom? Mom?"

AUNT SHADIE rises and slowly walks away.

She is silent, and gets up and walks to the washroom, or we leave the restaurant, or she goes to the other room, and that hope dies without him even knowing it had anything to do with him. A man kills enough. A woman keeps on walking.

REBECCA gets up and watches her leave.

SLIDE: SWITCHBOARD – Reception

Lights up on AUNT SHADIE as she arrives at the reception counter. She is putting trapper clothes over her young housewife clothes. She leans on the reception counter, putting on a parka and rabbit mitts. ROSE's face is no longer bruised. AUNT SHADIE lays the sweater on the desk.

AUNT SHADIE
Thanks for the sweater.

ROSE
You're welcome, Rita.

AUNT SHADIE
You're welcome, Rose. Call me Aunt Shadie. Everybody else does.

ROSE
Alright, Aunt Shadie. Where did you get the clothes?

AUNT SHADIE
I found them in my baggage.

AUNT SHADIE begins to leave.

ROSE
Nice gloves.

AUNT SHADIE
Mitts.

She looks proudly at her mitts.

I used to be a real good trapper when I was young. You wouldn't believe it now that I'm such a city girl, but before when my legs and body were young and muscular, I could go forever. Walking those traplines with snowshoes. The sun coming down sprinkling everything with crystals, some floating down, and dusting that white comforter with magic. I would walk that trapline like a map, knowing every turn, every tree, every curve the land uses to confuse us. I felt like I was part of the magic, that wasn't confused. The crystals sticking to the cold, and the cold sticking to my black hair, my eyebrows, my clothes, my breath. A trap set. An animal caught. Red. If it squirmed, I would take my rifle and shoot it as fast as I could. Poor thing. I hate to see an animal suffer. *Meegwetch*, and thank you.

ROSE
It sounds barbaric.

AUNT SHADIE
Shopping at the Woodward's food floor is barbaric. You never know what you are eating. Even if it says ground hamburger meat on the package, how do you know it is ground hamburger? What is ground ham-burger? And why do they have to grind it? Everybody just eats it. No one questions where it came from. Must be the big hamburger animal. That big "W" in the sky doesn't stand for Woodward's, but for "what." WHAT did I just eat?

ROSE takes out a pair of long, white gloves and puts them on.

ROSE
I like that swan metaphor.

AUNT SHADIE
The what for? Swans are the great hamburger animal?

ROSE
Don't be silly. Gloves look like swans.

AUNT SHADIE
Well, actually, if I was to really think about it... probably more like skinned rabbit mitts.

ROSE
I like the swans.

AUNT SHADIE
Did you ever feel like hugging a swan?

ROSE
Yes, I have.

AUNT SHADIE
You? You have hugged a swan.

ROSE
Yes, I have. I have an appreciation for animals too, you know.

AUNT SHADIE
No, I mean. I'm sure you do in your own polite way, but... a swan.

ROSE
It felt good.

AUNT SHADIE
You got me kinda worried here. What kind of hug was it?

ROSE
Just a quick peck on the cheek. But it wasn't a kiss. I just walked up to it
real quiet, foot by foot, and placed my arms around it just for a second.
Nice swan.

AUNT SHADIE
Have you ever hugged a swan so much you almost squished it?

ROSE
No, I haven't actually. What kind of animal lover do you think I am?

AUNT SHADIE
Every time I see a swan, I feel like hugging it hard. The kind of hug where
you just can't stand how much you love it, or feel for it, and you're hugging
and hugging it, and you just get carried away.

ROSE
How many swans have you hugged?

AUNT SHADIE
I never hugged a swan. I just figured anything that beautiful wouldn't want
to be hugged. My nephews... yes... my daughter when she was small, my
parents when they were old, my pillow when I was lonely... myself when
I was stupid.

ROSE
How many things have you squished while hugging?

AUNT SHADIE
I never really squished anything. I was just trying to get across to you that feeling of loving something so much you could squish it. I think everybody should have that feeling at least once.

ROSE
Hugging till you squish, or being squished?

AUNT SHADIE
Both. But...

ROSE
What?

AUNT SHADIE
It makes you kinda want to be the squished one, doesn't it?

ROSE
Yes... yes, it does actually. Tea?

AUNT SHADIE
Sure.

REBECCA moves from her table and slots some coins into the juke box.

SLIDE: FOUR DAYS: DAY 3 – Glenaird Hotel – CONT.

As the lyrics of the song fade, the music remains under. She waltzes to it and to the voiceover of a conversation.

SFX: Sound of the tide fades up and eventually takes over.

SFX: In a convincing male voice, like music...

MALE VOICE
"You move so beautifully."

She steps.

WOMAN
Thank you. (*She stumbles.*)

MALE VOICE
"You have the most beautiful brown skin."

She steps.

WOMAN
Thank You. (*She stumbles.*)

MALE VOICE
"You don't have to be scared. I would never let anybody hurt you."

She steps and loses her balance. She takes her face out of her pillow's shoulder and looks down. She looks down at her legs as if something is wrong with them. The silhouette of a deer's legs and hooves look back from the floor. She begins to cry, confused. The pillow becomes a man, dressed like a pillow. He lifts her chin slowly, and dries her tears. Lights out.

Rhythms of a drinking room: 1) Tide – Time. 2) Lights vs. Shadow. 3) Drinking Rhythm. 4) Conversations – recent and past. 5) Music/Movement – romantic.

SFX: The phone rings.

SLIDE: I'M SCARED TO DIE III

MAVIS wakes in a start and picks up the phone.

MAVIS
It's okay, Johnnie... it's probably just my operator. You need your rest. Hello, who is it?

ROSE
It's Rose.

MAVIS
Rose who?

ROSE
Rose – you know very well, Rose who.

MAVIS
What do you want?

ROSE
I thought I'd call and check in with you. I heard somebody breathing funny on your line.

MAVIS
I just got company that's all.

ROSE
What kind of company?

MAVIS
Man company. He just kinda showed up out of the brown.

ROSE
Humph. I never did trust a man that just showed up.

MAVIS
Well, some of my best romances came from men that just showed up.

ROSE
Suit yourself... as long as nothing is wrong.

MAVIS
Listen, Rose, I appreciate your worry. It's just been nice and peaceful for a change. I just been having a creepy feeling, and that's why I don't go out much. But with John here it's not so bad.

ROSE
What kind of creepy feeling?

MAVIS
(*softly*) Death.

ROSE
Mavis, I can't hear you when you talk soft like that.

MAVIS
(*louder*) Nothing.

ROSE
Mavis, I think there's...

MAVIS
My sister. It's my sister.

ROSE
You're scared of your sister?

MAVIS
Isn't everyone?

ROSE
Why don't you to talk to her? I'm not doing anything anyway.

MAVIS
Sure. I'll be brave. (*She adjusts herself.*) Put me through, Rose. *Meegweetch*.

ROSE

Fine, just put me through... no, thank you... no, that's great of you, Rose... thanks for taking the time to.... Well, McWitch to you too!

MAVIS

Meegweetch, Rose. *Meegweetch*. It means "Thank You."

Click of call going through. It rings and...

Hi, Laverne. It's me... Ma...

SFX: Answering machine.

MACHINE

"Hi. You've reached Laverne..."

MAVIS

Laverne?

MACHINE

"We're not in right now, but if you leave a message we'll get back to you as soon as possible, or you can reach us on the pager at (204) 266-4325, or fax us at (204) 266-5646, or at work at (204) 456-1425, or just leave a message after the beep, I guess."

MAVIS

Gawd. Hi... it's me. Mavis... your sister. Yeah, it's been a long time, but I was thinking of you and... I'm doing real good. I just thought I'd call and say... it's good to hear your voice, even if it's on the answering machine. It sounds like you got a lot of stuff... Laverne. You know when someone wants your chair, your place? Not like our mother, or an elder, or someone we know, but when someone you don't like wants your place, and you can feel them thinking about it... just waiting for you to get up... concentrating on you getting up so they jump in your place, and never give it back. I can feel someone getting closer and closer, inch by inch, stepping closer, and pretty soon they'll be in my seat. Breathing where I should be sitting. I know that sounds weird, but it's just a feeling.

SFX: Answering machine clicks off.

ROSE

I wouldn't call if I'd been drinking or anything. I love you... I didn't mean to sound stupid.

SLIDE: THE BARBERSHOP QUARTET II – Barbershop

SFX: The sound of MARILYN singing softly.

*The interior of the barbershop flares up. The red and white swirl of the barber
light is twirling. PENNY sits drunkenly in the barber chair as a beautiful
MARILYN à la Farrah Fawcett emerges. Reaching her hands out to PENNY,
she begins to clear PENNY's hair from her face gently. PENNY looks into the
mirror and sees herself as PENNY à la Pat Benetar. They both laugh. The
BARBER enters dressed in hyper barber white. He places a white cape over
PENNY, and her hair dream. The BARBER takes the bottle and places it
between her legs and begins to braid her hair in one long braid. MARILYN's
song gets strained as she reaches for the bottle in an effort to take it from them.
The BARBER grabs it and raises it to PENNY's lips seductively. He moves to
climb on top of her.*

BARBER
Down the hatch, baby.
Twenty bucks if you drink it right down.
Down the hatch, baby.
Drink it right down.

Fade out.

SLIDE: KEEP ON WALKING – Hastings Street

*Lights up below on REBECCA as she walks. Backdrop of Hastings Street. Signs
in windows advertising for help. AUNT SHADIE's face appears in the images.*

REBECCA
Where do women walk to when they have been fallen? Sure, you could
say some of them walk on to something better. They leave their bastardly
husbands, get a job, and free themselves from suffocating domesticality.
They learn to type, or waitress, or become your chambermaid, your
housekeeper, your cleaner, your babysitter and pretty soon it feels like
this new-found freedom is not so free – the man's face has just changed.
If they can stand this, they stay. If not, one day they just keep walking.

SLIDE: THE WRONG ROOM – Balmoral Hotel

VERNA
...one fuckin day at a time.

*Lights up on VERNA sitting on her bed in the hotel room. A bottle of wine sits
on the bedside table eyeing her. She fondles the bottle wanting to take a drink but
touches a toy plane in her lap instead. She talks to her ex-husband on the phone...*

Yeah. I'm serious. I got a gift for him... for his birthday. If you come and
pick me up... maybe we could take the kid for Chinese food, and I could
give him his present then. Yeah, I'll be downstairs out in front waiting. I'll
be down there... I told you...

SLIDE: ROOM 23, WHEN YOU'RE 33 – Clifton Hotel

The room is dishevelled. VALERIE is lying on the floor, the DRESSER is lying on the floor. They are both trying to get themselves back together.

DRESSER
You have a nice set.

VALERIE
Oh, shut up.

DRESSER
Really.

VALERIE
Why don't you shut up?

DRESSER
Why don't you make me?

VALERIE
I made you already.

DRESSER
I made you already.

VALERIE
No reason to be a sore loser.

DRESSER
Pick a drawer.

VALERIE
Go away.

DRESSER
Go on, pick a drawer. I'll bet you'll like this drawer.

> *His bottom drawer slides open. The TOMMY drawer speaks.*

> *SFX: Voices of her two sons.*

TOMMY
Mommy?

VALERIE
Tomm...

TOMMY
Mommy.

VALERIE
Tommy.

TOMMY
Hey, Mom.

VALERIE
Hey, Tom. Tom... what are you doing in there?

TOMMY
Mom, I'm a real good dancer now. I can even dance better than Evan.

His second drawer opens. The EVAN drawer.

EVAN
Yeah, right.

TOMMY
I can.

EVAN
Like hell!

VALERIE
Don't swear.

EVAN
Don't tell me what to do.

VALERIE
I'm your mother.

EVAN
Yeah, right.

VALERIE
How are things?

TOMMY
Good.

EVAN
How do you think things are?

TOMMY
When are you coming home?

EVAN
Probably never.

VALERIE
Soon... real soon.

EVAN
Soon... liar.

TOMMY
When are you coming home? It's been a long time now.

VALERIE
It's hard to come right now. But soon. I'm gonna get this job and soon...

TOMMY
How soon?

EVAN
Soon. Liar.

TOMMY
How long is soon?

VALERIE
I can picture you in my head.

EVAN
Take a picture – it lasts longer.

VALERIE
Maybe, I could take a couple days off...

EVAN
...drinking.

VALERIE
...working. And we could get together...

EVAN
Soon.

VALERIE
Just me, and my two little men.

TOMMY
Mom?

EVAN
Mom?

VALERIE
Yeah?

The drawers don't respond. She gets real close to the drawers.

VALERIE
Yeah, I'm listening. I'm right here. I'M RIGHT HERE.

DRESSER
Yeah. Here you go, bitch!

> *The DRESSER lets her have it with the drawers. One of the drawers slams her head, the other her stomach and legs – it buckles her. It keeps punching her till she lies on the floor semi-conscious.*

> *The DRESSER slowly opens the TOMMY drawer.*

TOMMY
Mommy?

> *She barely wakes.*

VALERIE
I'm coming... I'm coming.

> *She crawls to the DRESSER. The top drawer slams her in the head. She slumps down, her head on the TOMMY drawer.*

> *The DRESSER's hand comes out of the top drawer and reaches down across her chest fondling her breasts. Lights out.*

> *SLIDE: Valerie Nancy Homes, 33. Died November 19, 1986 with a 0.04 blood alcohol reading. "Jordon arrived at the Vancouver police station with his lawyer to report the death. He said he and Homes had been drinking for two days."*

> *SLIDE: FOUR DAYS: DAY 4 – Glenaird Hotel – CONT.*

> *SFX: Sound of the tide starts under. The slowest rhythm. The distorted sound of love whispers between a man and a woman.*

> *The light bulb fades up slowly on the ocean that has become the room. The WOMAN is lying flat on her bed. A pillow lies on top of her. Her hand over the side of the bed holds a drink. She drinks and floats, making a slow swimming motion with her pelvis.*

SFX: Voiceover – A fatherly male voice- faster, more emotional.

FATHERLY MALE VOICE

"Someone had told her a story, a very, very long time ago, about a deer who lost its mother, because someone shot its mother. Something like the story of Bambi, except that the little fawn was adopted by a white family that loved it, and then someone said that the fawn that grew to be an Indian girl should be with its own kind, so the father of the white family, who lived on the mainland, took a ferry and dropped the Indian girl on an island miles away, and hoped she would be happier. Well, the Indian girl wasn't happy without the only family she had ever known, and she swam all the way back to her white family, and everything was going great... everything was... going... great..."

> *The pillow on top of her becomes the man dressed as a pillow. He grinds into her, adding a violence to the swimming sex rhythm. She is totally disconnected to what is happening, staring straight up to the story.*

WOMAN

...everything was going great, until she decided that she really didn't belong anywhere. So she decided it would be better to surrender to the ocean, to just let go, than to swim so hard, for so long, just to get to the mainland and be shot by a neighbour over a head of lettuce. (*She laughs.*)

> *Blackout.*

SFX: Sound of the glass hitting the floor.

Rhythms of a drinking room: 1) Tide – Time. 2) Light vs. Dark. 3) Drinking rhythm. 4) Conversations – recent and past. 5) Music-Movement-romantic. 6) Sex.

Lights fade.

SLIDE: THE BARBERSHOP QUARTET III – Barbershop

SFX: Sound of MARILYN and PENNY singing softly.

> *The interior of the barbershop flares up. The red and white swirl of the barbershop light is circling. MARILYN à la Farrah Fawcett and PENNY à la Pat Benatar reflect out towards PATSY as she falls from the chair and begins to crawl away. The BARBER dressed in whites follows after her with the scissors. The scissors make a chopping noise as he grabs her braid. The red and white swirl of light intensifies the struggle. The song of MARILYN and PENNY intensifies as they call to her.*

BARBER
Down the hatch, baby.
Twenty bucks if you drink it right down.
Down the hatch, baby.
Right down. Finish it right down.
Down the hatch, baby.
DRINK IT – DROWN.

> *The BARBER emerges from the swirl with PATSY's braid. He covers her body on the floor with his white cape. He turns and leaves, as WOMAN's reflections in the mirror begin to multiply and become surreal.*

> *SLIDE: KEEP ON WALKING – Hastings Street – CONT.*

> *The backdrop of windows of the hotel buildings. AUNT SHADIE's face appears in and out of the images.*

REBECCA
One might walk here. One story among a rooming house full of walking stories. I've come to find her story. My mother. My mother's one story. I walk through these streets. I walk through the women standing on legs like stilts. No pantihose, but varicose seams everywhere, blue and yellow on their plastic skin. Skirts hiked up and shirts hiked down, their faces hollowed to a pout.

> *SLIDE: THE WRONG ROOM – Balmoral Hotel – CONT.*

VERNA
I'll be down there – I told you. Okay, thirty minutes. Yes – I said thirty minutes. Right out in front. THIR-TEE minutes. (*She hangs up.*) Ree-tard. (*She starts talking to the plane.*) My son'll like you. Almost spent my whole skinny cheque. I hope he likes you. I hope he likes me. I hope he's not mad. My son has a temper just like his mother.

> *The plane lifts from her hand, and its wings wave a "yes." VERNA laughs. She takes the plane and opens the door to go out. She forgets her purse and lets the plane idle.*

> *SFX: Buzz of plane flying.*

You stay here.

> *She turns to get her purse, and the plane is flying down the hallway. She calls to it.*

It's not like you have to hold my hand – just wait up for me, will yah?

She loses sight of the plane as it descends down the stairwell. She follows it a flight behind. Floor 7.

SFX: Sound of plane descending.

SFX: A slight whispering. A male voice that grows louder under and...

MALE VOICE
"Can I get you a drink?"

SLIDE: I'M SCARED TO DIE IV

Lights up on MAVIS sitting in her chair with JOHN's arms wrapped around her tightly.

SFX: Sound of phone ringing.

MAVIS picks it up.

MAVIS
Rose?

Lights up on ROSE plugging into MAVIS' line but getting a busy signal.

SFX: Voiceover – the phone beeps an aggressive, electronic:

VOICE
"Can – I – get – you – a – drink?

Lights down on ROSE.

MALE VOICE
No. It's downstairs. I can't seem to transfer a call to you. She says she's your sister. Do you want to come and take it down here?

MAVIS
Laverne? My sister.

MALE VOICE
Do you want to come and take it down here?

MAVIS
(*puts her hand over the receiver*) My chair? Laverne. My chair? Laverne. Aahhh shit, I was just getting comfy. Okay, I guess I'll be right down.

She gently kisses Johnnie's arms and moves them gently to the side. She looks suspiciously around the room and murmurs under her breath.

MAVIS
You even think of sitting in my chair and I'll kick your ass.

She drops the receiver and runs for the door and exits.

SFX: Sound of quick footsteps down a flight of stairs.

(*offstage*) Laverne? Goddamn it! (*slams phone*)

SFX: Sound of quicker steps up a flight of stairs.

(*mumbling up*) My sister... my ass...

She emerges in the doorway. Her chair has been turned around to face her. A man sits in it.

Get out of my chair!

MAN
Can I get you a drink?

MAVIS
Where is John?

MAN
John who?

SFX: Voiceover – sound of static from the receiver and...

VOICE
"If you need help, just hang up and dial your operator... if you need help, just hang up and dial your operator."

Lights fade.

SLIDE: Mavis Gertrude Jones, 42. Died November 30, 1980 with a 0.34 blood alcohol reading. An inquiry concluded Jones' death was "unnatural and accidental."

Verna follows the plane down floor 6.

SFX: Descent of plane.

SFX: Louder. A MALE VOICE that grows louder and louder...

MALE VOICE
"Can I get you a drink?"

SLIDE: KEEP ON WALKING – Hastings Street – Cont.

Backdrop of close-up of grocery store. Faces/bottles. AUNT SHADIE's face appears and disappears.

REBECCA
I walk through the elderly and the mentally ill and people stir-fried on Chinese cooking wine. I walk, and when I get tired I stop for a pack of smokes at the corner store and look at the Aqua Velva people in front of me in line. They are not blue. I then look at the Aqua Velva bottles all lined up pretty on the shelf next to the Aspirin. The most normal of refreshments to sell. I look into the woman punching the figures into the till. She could be my mother except that she is Asian. I look for some kind of clue that allows a hard-working woman that's worked hard all her life to ring up a bottle of Aqua Velva and sell it to an old man who is not "The Aqua Velva Man" but "Man with Huge Red Nose." She rings it in, all business, no trace of remorse. She stocks it for him – refreshment meeting cologne. Seller meeting buyer. It stinks, and I need a drink that isn't blue.

REBECCA exits.

AUNT SHADIE stands in front of the barbershop mirror. Three slides emerge, and three women stand behind the images of their slides. They begin to emerge from the barbershop mirror as AUNT SHADIE calls to them in song and they respond, in song, in rounds of their original languages.

The women in the barbershop call to each fallen woman, in each solitary room. The women respond and join them in song and ritual as they gather their voice, language, and selves in the barbershop.

Throughout, the song floats in and out of each scene, submerging under some, and taking over others, flowing like a river. Each call and response a current. It grows in strength and intensity to the end of Act One where all their voices join force.

WOMEN
Do I hear you sister like yesterday today.
Ke-peh-tat-in/jee/ne-gee-metch
Das-goots/o-tahg-gos-ehk
Ahnotes/ka-kee-se-khak

SLIDE: Marilyn Wiles, 40. Died December 04, 1984 with a 0.51 blood alcohol reading. An inquiry at the time concluded Wiles' death was "unnatural and accidental."

Patsy Rosemary Forest, 25. Died July 03, 1982 with a 0.43 blood alcohol reading. At the time of her death, the coroner said there was no indication of foul play.

Penny Florence Ways, 45. Died June 08, 1985 with a 0.79 blood alcohol reading. The coroner concluded her death was "unnatural and accidental."

VERNA follows the plane down floor 5.

SFX: Descent of plane.

SFX: Louder. A MALE VOICE that grows louder under and...

MALE VOICE
"Can I get you a drink?"

Lights dimly up on VIOLET.

"Can I get you a drink?

WOMEN
Do I hear you sister like yesterday today.
Ke-peh-tat-in/jee/ne-gee-metch
Das-goots/o-tahg-gos-ehk
Ahnotes/ka-kee-se-khak

Under water – under time
Ee-tam-pehg/eetam-ehg
Te-pi-he-gun

SLIDE: VIOLET – Niagara Hotel

VIOLET, as she sits on the floor of her hotel room. Her focus upwards. The shadow of a man casts itself long on the walls. Her face reaches him mid-groin.

VIOLET
I've swallowed it all. I've swallowed it all... downtown, right between my lips. I didn't know if it was the neck of the bottle I was swallowing or his penis. Both have that musty kind of smell at the opening of it. Like it has been around for a while, waiting for the next set of lips but not cleaning in between deaths. Musty – you never know where it's been. I swallowed. Man's fingers weaved in my hair pulling down and up, down and up, down and up so many times I didn't know if it was the salt that filled me or the sting of the vodka. I don't even drink usually.

VIOLET's head falls down.

SLIDE: Violet Leslie Taylor, 27. Died October 12, 1987 with a 0.91 blood alcohol reading. "She had the highest blood alcohol reading of all the women." No coroner's report has been issued.

WOMEN
Do I hear you sister like yesterday today.
Ke-peh-tat-in/jee/ne-gee-metch
Das-goots/o-tahg-gos-ehk
Ahnotes/ka-kee-se-khak

Hear your words right next to mine
Ee-pee-ta-man/ke-ta-yaur-e
Win/me-too-nee/o-ta

> *VERNA follows the plane down floor 4.*

> *SFX: Descent of plane.*

MALE VOICE
"Can I get you a drink?"

WOMEN
Do I hear you sister like yesterday today.
Ke-peh-tat-in/jee/ne-gee-metch
Das-goots/o-tahg-gos-ehk
Ahnotes/ka-kee-se-khak

> *SLIDE: FOUR DAYS: THERE IS NO DAY FIVE – Glenaird Hotel*

> *SFX: No sound.*

> *The light bulb fades up. No movement. The WOMAN lays flat on her bed, alone in the hotel room. Clothes up when they should be down. No pillow. The light becomes brighter and brighter revealing an ocean floor in low tide.*

> *Light clicks out.*

> *Rhythms of a drinking room: None.*

WOMEN
You are not speaking and yet I touch your words.
Ee-ka/ee-I-am-e-en/maga-e-tagh-in-a-man/ke-ta
Ya-mi-win

> *SLIDE: Brenda A. Moore, 27. Died September 11, 1981 with a 0.43 blood alcohol reading. Coroner's report concluded her death was "unnatural and accidental."*

> *VERNA is on floor 3. She stops and listens for the buzz of the plane. Nothing but the sound of a man's voice coming from ROOM 315. VERNA approaches it slowly.*

MALE VOICE
"Can I get you a drink? Can I get you a drink – a drink? Can I get you a drink?"

WOMEN
So the river says to me drink me feel better.
Kwa-ne-ka-isit-/se-pe-h
Me-knee-qua-sin/me-thwa-ya

Like the river must of said to you first
Tas-koch-e-to-key/ka-key-e
Tisk/ne-s-tum

Below lights up on Rebecca as she sits at a table in The Empress Hotel.

VERNA enters room 315. The man dressed as an airline pilot seats her. Her son's plane buzzes around her head as he hands her a drink.

PILOT
Can I get you a drink?

REBECCA looks up from her small, red, terry-clothed table. She motions two glasses.

SFX: The plane sputters and sputters and smashes to the ground.

Lights out.

SLIDE: Verna Deborah Gregory, 38. Died September 25, 1986 with a 0.63 blood alcohol reading. Gregory's death was ruled "accidental as a result of acute alcohol poisoning."

WOMEN
Drink me – feel better.
Me-knee-qua-sin/me-thwa-ya

There is no sadness just the war of a great thirst
Moi-ch/ke-qua-eh/ka-quat-ta-keye-ta-mo-win

SLIDE: VIOLET – Niagara Hotel – Cont.

Lights fade dimly up on VIOLET as she detaches from her shadow. She leaves herself there with the man. She becomes smaller and more childlike, as she backs away and finally sits back on a swing and just stares, watching her woman self there with the man. Her body begins to become purple as AUNT SHADIE moves tenderly behind her and begins to swing her.

VIOLET
It was the back and forth of it. Like being on a swing when I was a girl. My father pushing the swing into the sky. Back and forth, that's where my mind went from the past and up from the past and up and up... I thought if I got any higher the swing would wrap around the pole and I would choke, but I went up after the last push, and after the last... my legs pumping the air for flight.

WOMEN
Do I see you sisters like yesterday today.
Ke-peh-tat-in/jee/ne-gee-metch
Das-goots/o-tahg-gos-ehk
Ahnotes/ka-kee-se-khak

> *AUNT SHADIE stops the swing and takes VIOLET's hand. They turn and begin to walk into a shadowy forest.*
>
> *SFX: Loud sound of pool balls being broken.*
>
> *The WOMEN suddenly turn their attention, song and focus on the bar. VERNA leads them into the bar.*
>
> *VIOLET suddenly turns with the sound of the pool balls being broken and looks towards all the WOMEN walking in the bar.*

VIOLET
Can I go with them?

AUNT SHADIE
No, you're too young. Besides, I need someone to walk with me.

VIOLET
Heh? Who's that?

> *ROSE walks towards the two.*

WOMEN
See you as if you were sitting right here next to me.
Ee-wa-pa-me-tan/tas-koots
Ota-e-iy-ya-pee-in

> *Below, the BARBER gets up, and VERNA follows him as he walks towards REBECCA, who rummages through her purse, takes out some money and leaves it on the table. She looks for something she thinks she's lost and dismisses it. She grabs her journal from the table just as VALERIE goes to look through it.*

Under the water – under the earth.
Eetam pehg/etam-as-keke

AUNT SHADIE
I'll introduce you to uppity. That's Rose.

VIOLET
And I'm Violet.

AUNT SHADIE
Exactly. And I'm poopoo ka ka. Anyways...

ROSE reaches them and hugs VIOLET.

WOMEN
My bodies floating where all the days are the same.
Ne-eow/e-pa-pam-mau-ho
Tehk/eddie-tah-to-ke-sik
Kow/pe-ya-kwun-nohk

REBECCA walks towards the exit where RON is playing pool and MAVIS is making him look good.

Long and flowing like a river.
E-ke-knock/aqua/e-pe-mow-
Ho-teak/tas-kooch/se-pe-h

VIOLET
She's squishing me.

AUNT SHADIE
She's hugging you.

VIOLET
No, she's squishing me.

AUNT SHADIE
Hugging – squishing. It's all the same thing.

VIOLET
The same what?

AUNT SHADIE
Love.

MAVIS bumps RON and he stumbles into REBECCA, who drops her journal. Newspaper clippings of the WOMEN fall to the floor. The WOMEN slowly pick them up, look at themselves and then slowly place their clipping back into REBECCA's journal.

WOMEN
My root – my heart.
Weh-geese/ne dee

> *The BARBER reaches her table and looks down, as VERNA places REBECCA's wallet on the table. He looks around and puts it in his jacket. He watches as REBECCA begins to exit.*

> *The WOMEN shift all their energy towards the BARBER.*

> *Lights begin to fade.*

My hair drifts behind me
Nes-ta-ga-yah/e-pim-mow
How-te-key

> *Lights out.*

ACT TWO

SFX: A distorted radio-sounding version of "Natural Woman" by Aretha Franklin drifts in and through. The WOMEN's voices pick it up softly.

SLIDE: THE MORNING AFTER – Rebecca's Apartment – Kitsilano

It is dark in the bedroom. The neon face of the clock on the bedside table shows 4:08. It clicks.

A figure stirs in bed. A blue hue splashes down on white sheets and a figure underneath. REBECCA awakens.

REBECCA
I remember drinking something blue, or was it thinking something blue? All I know right now is... I have to pee. That means I have to get up, which means you have to... get up. Get up, I dare you. Get up.

Her body doesn't move.

I'd like to lay here for an eternity, but I feel like I've eaten a squirrel and I need something to wash it down, and something to scrape it off my tongue. Don't feed the squirrels – eat them. Brilliant. Okay, I'm getting up, which means we're getting up.

The WOMEN sit or stand in the darkness. They can be vaguely seen, but REBECCA cannot really see or really hear them. MAVIS her Chair Ass sits.

REBECCA's body gets up, protesting. She stumbles through her bedroom. She makes walking, stumbling curses. She stubs her toe on the foot of the bed.

REBECCA
Ahhwww... fuuuuuuuuuck, that hurts. Fuck you, bed.

MAVIS
Watch where you're going, big feet.

REBECCA
(to herself) Big Foot.

She walks through her bedroom into the hallway, not turning the lights on but doing the blind wall-feel.

VERNA
Right on my little toe. Not this way or that, but right on my baby toe.

VALERIE
This... is a handicapped zone.

MAVIS
Well, you better hope she doesn't park on your toe.

VALERIE
Oh yeah. Too late – she just parked on my toe with the corn. What the hell is this?

VERNA
It's the fuckin toe walk.

REBECCA walks into the wall, forehead first.

REBECCA
Fuuuuck ouch.... Fuck you, wall.

ALL
Fuck you, big head.

REBECCA
(*to wall*) What did you say?

Nothing. Silence.

That's what I thought you said.

VALERIE
(*mimicking*) That's what I thought you said.

REBECCA reaches the fridge and opens the door. A bright light filters through like a tunnel, revealing the insides of the fridge and the inside of her apartment. The WOMEN are all seated in a line. They are in various hues of shadow and dressed in white. Their hair is short.

REBECCA
Ouch! Shit, that hurts.

VALERIE
Wow, let there be light.

VERNA
And there was light... I remember that.

REBECCA squints inside her fridge. Picks up a carton and tilts it back in a drink. Picks up another carton and another and another.

VALERIE
Let there be skim milk.

VERNA
And there was none.

VALERIE
Let there be orange juice.

VERNA
And there was none.

VALERIE
Let there be water.

VERNA
And there was none. Shit, she's making me have to go to the bathroom.

REBECCA closes the fridge door. Darkness. She stumbles along to the bathroom. She sits down on the can and takes a pee. The sound of a long pee.

MAVIS
You think she could close the door.

VERNA
You think she could go for me?

REBECCA
Oh, that feels good.

REBECCA flushes the toilet.

MAVIS
At least she didn't do number two.

VERNA
At least she didn't do number two while reading a newspaper.

VALERIE
Only men do that.

VERNA
Women read novels.

MAVIS
Like what?

VALERIE
Well, real smart novels. They leave it in the can so they can make themselves look good.

MAVIS
Like what?

VERNA
I actually finished the whole AA bible. Not one day at a time but one shit at a time. It took me a year... if you were going to ask.

MAVIS
I wasn't going to ask, but since you answered – why did it take you so long?

VERNA
I kept having to introduce myself. There was always a big silence after I said, "Hi, my name's Verna." It left me kinda empty.

ALL
Hi, Verna.

VERNA
Thanks.

> *REBECCA gets herself to the front of the sink. The loud sound of her brushing her teeth. The sound of her taking a drink from the tap. She reaches over to turn the bathroom light on. When the bathroom lights blast on, the images of all three WOMEN reflect back in the mirror. REBECCA looks closely in the mirror. The WOMEN scream in horror.*

REBECCA
Wo-ow... I look like shit.

> *REBECCA turns off the light.*

ALL
Speak for yourself.

> *The sound of REBECCA returning on her journey back to bed in the darkness.*

MAVIS
Ouch...

VERNA
Ouch...

VALERIE
Fuck! Oh yeah... right on the same toe, why don't yah!

> *REBECCA crawls into bed. Grabs her pillow and pulls it closer to her. She pulls it closer and feels it. She feels it harder, her hand exploring it. IT has legs. IT has a butt. IT has a penis. IT moans. REBECCA screams.*

IT
> Hey...

REBECCA
> Oh, fuck me!

VERNA
> Too late.

VALERIE
> The penis talks.

> *REBECCA jumps out of bed and turns on the bedroom light.*

IT
> Hey, what did you do that for?

> *They squint at each other.*

REBECCA
> It's time to get up. I mean... I mean... it's time for you to get out. Leave.

MAVIS
> That's cold.

VERNA
> I like it. Thanks, and it's time to get up. Get in, get out... and it's time to leave. It's to the point. Move on.

REBECCA
> Listen. I'm having a really bad morning.

IT
> Well, you had a really good night.

REBECCA
> If you say so.

IT
> You said so.

REBECCA
> That's really... special... but I have um... I have to get myself together here pretty soon and go to work. Work is good. Work.

IT
> You don't work.

REBECCA

Everybody works. You're right. I don't work. I write. Writing is work, and I really should work or write and um... it's not easy to write when...

IT

You have a strange man in your bed.

REBECCA

I was going to say, when there are people around.

IT

Oh.

REBECCA

Are you strange?

IT

Okay... I'm not strange. I'm a stranger.

REBECCA

That's better. At least you're not weird.

IT

Who's to know?

REBECCA

Okay, if you weren't a stranger, would I know you were weird even if I knew you? I mean, does anybody ever know anybody's true weirdness?

IT

This is weird.

REBECCA

This is hurting my head, Ted.

IT

It's Ron.

REBECCA

I know... it was just a rhyming thing. Yeah, Ron... Ron (*to herself*) ...Ron with the nice butt leaning over the table.

MAVIS

Turn over, Ron. Turn over a new leaf.

REBECCA

You were playing... we ended up playing pool.

RON
You're surprised I'm here.

REBECCA
Well, no. I mean, yes... I mean, who wouldn't be surprised? A guy like you. A girl like me. Listen, I'm swimming here. Let's just call this a day. Okay, Ron. Thanks, it was great. Really. Ron. It was great. Great.

RON
What was great?

REBECCA
Oh, you know – the conversation, the beautiful dinner, your great car... your great suit, how you put yourself together, your great words, your greatness, your all-over greatness... your money... your tireless dick. Is that good? You are great. Great.

WOMEN
Tireless dick? Let's see the great dick.

RON
We didn't do it.

REBECCA
O-kay... it just looks like we did.

RON
Well, there was a point when that was an option, but...

REBECCA
What?

RON
You started crying.

REBECCA
People do that sometimes.

RON
When they're making love?

REBECCA
No, when they're fucking and it reminds them of love.

RON/WOMEN
Ouch.

REBECCA
Sorry.

Silence.

Listen... I don't mean to be rude...

MAVIS
...maybe just a little peek...

REBECCA
...but I'm really not at my best right now, and maybe you should just leave.

RON
What's your best?

REBECCA
Coffee, fresh-squeezed orange juice, eggs benedict, morning sex.

RON
Do you bring a lot of men home?

REBECCA
What, to mother? No, *Ron*, I don't bring a lot of men home. Actually, you are the first man I've thought to bring *home* in ten years. And really, what if I did? What if I liked sleeping with men? What if I enjoyed sleeping with men so much I slept with men? What then, *Ron*... would that make me a slut? Or better yet, maybe I should've let you buy me a steak and potato and a bottle of plaid wine, and you could at least feel decent...

He buries his head in the sheets.

Don't go to Sunday mass on me now, Ronny. (*He looks up.*) I would get a good meal and a plaid wine, and you could feel like you deserved to fuck me. Fuck you, Ronny, and fuck the full meal deal.

RON
Are you finished?

REBECCA
I'm tired. I need a nap.

RON
Come here.

REBECCA
It's okay.

RON
Come here.

REBECCA
It's okay, I said.

RON
It's o-kay.

She goes towards him.

REBECCA
Okay. Don't you have a job?

RON
A day off.

REBECCA
Off?

RON
I'm a cop.

REBECCA
A cop.

RON
A problem?

WOMEN
A problem.

REBECCA
No, just weird. I don't usually do men with badges.

REBECCA and RON settle into each other and fall asleep. The WOMEN turn the lights off and walk into the living room. Lights up in the living room.

MAVIS
A cop.

VALERIE
You ever do a cop?

VERNA
Well, if I would have known they have nice butts and tireless dicks, I would've reconsidered.

MAVIS
A dick is a dick.

VALERIE
...is a dick.

VERNA
Is a prick.

MAVIS
I always kinda fantasized about it though... kinda like a Harlequin
Romance set in Canada. The Mountie, the horse and the Indian maiden.

VERNA
Exactly – the horse and the Indian maiden.

VALERIE
The Mountie would probably just be watching.

VERNA
You'd probably have a better time with the horse anyways...

MAVIS
You ever seen a horse's di...

VALERIE
Too much of a good thing.

MAVIS
You said that kinda fast.

VERNA
Maybe a Mountie with a dick the size of a horse.

MAVIS
Dream on.

VALERIE
I am.

VERNA
Thanks... now I'm getting all horny here. Let's make some tea and talk
about our ex's or something... that should calm us down.

*They follow each other into the kitchen. A kettle is set down and begins to heat.
Lights out. Steam forms.*

SLIDE: VIOLET DREAMS

*Lights slowly up on a figure above REBECCA's bed. The lights are different
hues of violet. VIOLET is on a swing, slowly swinging back and forth above
REBECCA's bed. She drops small pebbles over them as she talks.*

VIOLET

She's sleeping. Dreaming parts of worlds, yours and mine and hers. Dreaming and pressing into things... old memories and loves and waking in moments wondering where people ended and why even in sleep it hurts. Even in sleep, it occurs and reoccurs and you wake half here, half there, everything separated.

REBECCA

Everything not quite there, because you can't quite touch your own loss. Because it is so hollow.

VIOLET

So...

REBECCA

...So far away – when you scream, it echoes.

VIOLET

Oh, Jesus, we have all died for our sins.

REBECCA

...Oh, Jesus, you say...

VIOLET

...We have all died for our sins.

REBECCA

There are great days when everything is perfect. Cool days on your skin, when the breeze hits you just right and you can touch and taste the lips of those you loved. Cool, beautiful days when a tint of colour touches you... just so. Just so.

VIOLET

...Just so lovely.

VIOLET places a petal on REBECCA's lips.

REBECCA

You want to feel it on your lips forever. Just so. Just so until it ends, and all you can do is put your hand over your mouth. Gulping down the loss. Gulping down... down until you eat the scream. Blood vowels getting stuck between the sheets and pillows, between his legs and your throat, and all you want to do is say: Please help me. Please help me. Do you remember me? Because I remember me. I remember everything. Everything. Everything. And I can't breathe. And I would gladly die if I knew any better, but there is nothing to do but keep gulping silently. And it hurts my throat and God I want everything. I want to place my face in my mother's palm and say... and feel my lips on her lifeline and palm softness and whisper... I love you, you fucking bitch. I love you and where is everyone?

SFX: The WOMEN's kettle screams from the kitchen.

The violet lights slowly fade and cross-fade, bringing purple on...

SLIDE: SWITCHBOARD – Reception

AUNT SHADIE and ROSE move around a large family table, setting it for tea. They stop to notice the switchboard and get caught up in its flashing beauty. The calls are lighting up different hues of purple.

ROSE
It's so beautiful.

AUNT SHADIE
It gives me a headache.

ROSE
If you sit in a room and sit in a room... pretty soon... (*She listens.*) you can hear noises and voices coming through the wallpaper like a whole bunch of flowers sitting on a kitchen table. You become a part of that family of sounds just by hearing them. You can hear them eating and arguing, loving and fighting and breathing.

AUNT SHADIE
And snoring.

ROSE
And... snoring.

AUNT SHADIE
Is that why you became a switchboard operator?

ROSE
Partly.

AUNT SHADIE
The other part?

ROSE
It was a job, but after a while it made me a part of something bigger than my own loneliness. As if every time I connected someone I had found an answer.

AUNT SHADIE

I've heard her voice through the wall. As if I've had my ear to her as she's grown up. Just listening, not touching. Not able to soothe her, even when she was a child, because I wasn't there.

ROSE

Maybe she was listening back to you.

AUNT SHADIE

I didn't want her to see me the way he began to look at me. It wasn't that he said anything cruel, but men can be cruel with the twist of their face. I could feel myself disappearing, becoming invisible in his eyes; and when I looked in the mirror, what I held good like a stone deep inside was gone. I could no longer see myself. In life, you see yourself in how the people you love see you, and I began to hate seeing myself through his eyes. I began to hate my reflection. The stone though... loved his strong arms and body, loved the way his body tanned to meet mine in the summer times, loved the way he used to love me. I thought my silence complimented his voice, thought my redness, my stone, gave him weight. I have this child – light and dark, old and new. I place my stone in her and I leave. I was afraid she would begin to see me the way he saw me, the way white people look up and down without seeing you – like you are not worthy of seeing. Extinct, like a ghost... being invisible can kill you.

ROSE

I see you, and I like what I see.

AUNT SHADIE

I see you – and don't worry, you're not white.

ROSE

I'm pretty sure I'm white. I'm English.

AUNT SHADIE

White is a blindness – it has nothing to do with the colour of your skin.

ROSE

You're gonna make me cry.

AUNT SHADIE

You better make us some tea then.

ROSE

That will help?

AUNT SHADIE

No, but it gives you something to do.

ROSE goes through her serious ritual of making tea. The violet lights fade and cross-fade to REBECCA's bed. They light up the bed like the bottom of a river, rocks scattered, rocks curled. VALERIE and VERNA have come back to the bed riverside. They are sitting around drinking tea, looking like large boulders. They laugh and sing softly. VIOLET eventually comes down from the swing, childlike.

SLIDE: *SHE SLEEPS LIKE A ROCK*

REBECCA
My heaviness has shifted – I'm all lopsided. Right now, I am deep down laying between friends, tumbling over each other, because we are round and hard and loving every minute of it, because it is so far down the only language we have to know has moulded from the earth – its tears and blood, its laughter and love – gone solid. I hold it in my heart, it keeps me attached to the gravity of a perfect knowing.

VALERIE
A mother opens the heart of her child and places her rock inside the flesh. Inside, so no one – no man, no ugliness, will ever place its grabby hands on it.

VERNA
A mother buries its knowledge inside the child. *Kiss-ageeta-ooma.* (*Salish*) It drops inside the eternity of blood and earth. *Kiss-ageeta-ooma.* (*Salish*) I love you, silly face.

REBECCA
It makes me hit the riverbed like a rock. Water shining over me new, over me new, a new reflection of my true self, knowing I am heavy.

VALERIE
A mother opens the heart of her child and places her rock inside the flesh. A growing child takes a rock from the earth it walked from and places it in a leather pouch and hangs it around her neck. A woman walks heavy.

VIOLET
She sleeps like a rock.

VERNA
She sleeps like a rock.

VIOLET
She dreams like a rock.

VERNA
She dreams like a rock.

VALERIE
A woman walks heavy. A woman walks heavy. Like a rock molded from the earth – its tears and blood, its laughter and love – gone solid.

SLIDE: THE LIVING ROOM

MAVIS her Chair Ass is at REBECCA's desk. She goes through her phone book and dials a number. AUNT SHADIE picks up the phone from the switchboard.

MAVIS
Hi, Aunt Shadie.

AUNT SHADIE
Verna?

MAVIS
No, it's me... Mavis. We're a little late.

AUNT SHADIE
Get your ass home.

MAVIS
Don't yell at me – I'm the one who's considerate.

AUNT SHADIE
I tell you, Rose is making tea for everyone...

MAVIS
(*pinched operator's voice*) "To continue your call, please deposit more coins in the telephone or we'll have to..."

AUNT SHADIE
Don't even try that with me.

VERNA walks in from the bedroom.

MAVIS
Pardon me. You want to talk to Verna?

VERNA shaking her head – no, no, no.

Aunt Shadie wants to talk to you. Seriously.

VERNA
Hi, Aunt Shadie.

AUNT SHADIE
Like I was telling Mavis, get your asses home.

VERNA
We just got caught up. Like I told you, we'll be up there in thir-tee minutes. Seriously. Thirty minutes.

She screams out for VALERIE.

Hey, Valerie it's Pizza Hut. What kind of toppings do you want on your pizza. Here, you talk to them... I don't get what they're saying. They're talking too fast. Like you said, us Salish girls aren't so bright.

VALERIE marches in and grabs the phone. VIOLET follows.

VALERIE
We want everything. We want the special. Give us the special. Give us two specials. Hey, do you have any two-for-one specials?

VIOLET walks in from the bedroom.

VIOLET
Ham and pineapple.

AUNT SHADIE
You're gonna get something real goddamned special when you all get home.

VALERIE puts the receiver in her chest.

SFX: Muffled voice blabbing away.

VALERIE
I don't think this is Pizza Hut.

VIOLET
Why?

VALERIE
Because Pizza Hut just swore. You can never make Pizza Hut swear.

VIOLET
How do you know?

VALERIE
Because, sometimes when I'm bored, I phone them up and play with them.

VIOLET
Like how?

VALERIE
Well, I ask what they got and then I ask 'em if they have any pizza made with bannock and then I pretend I forget what they got and then I ask them what they got, what certain toppings are, and then anyways it goes on quite awhile. Indians aren't as much stupid as they are aggravating.

VERNA
It's not Pizza Hut, stupid. It's Aunt Shadie.

VALERIE
I thought I recognized her voice.

VERNA
Here, you talk to her. She won't yell at you, because you're a baby.

> *VERNA picks up the receiver, listens to it and pushes it on VIOLET. VERNA goes into another room.*

VIOLET
Hi, Aunt Shadie. It's Violet. How are you? We're fine. We're all good. No, we're just hanging around. You know, talking and stuff. How's Rose?

AUNT SHADIE
Save it.

VIOLET
She said save it.

VALERIE
She's pissed.

AUNT SHADIE
Rose made tea for everyone, and now it's cold and...

VIOLET
(*to VALERIE*) Rose made tea for everyone and now...

VALERIE
Who cares? She's a weird duck anyways... she can take the Red Rose manifest destiny and shove it up her ass...

VIOLET
...a teapot.

VALERIE
Exactly. Free the leaves, baby. Free the tea leaves of Canada. Say goodbye already... we'll be there as soon as we can.

VIOLET

Goodbye already... we'll be there as soon as we can. Aunt Shadie, sorry about the tea...

AUNT SHADIE

Just you hold it a...

Click of phone.

VIOLET

Sorry.

VALERIE

Where's Verna ? She's awfully quiet all of a sudden.

VIOLET

She's always quiet.

VALERIE

Just because a person doesn't say anything doesn't mean they're quiet. I can hear her thinking all the time. Where's Mavis? Now, her silence scares me. You know there's something wrong when you can't hear her talking.

They tiptoe around and peek in the bedroom. MAVIS is on the bed just about to pull the sheet off of RON's ass.

Mavis, you pervert.

MAVIS

I was just lookin', it's not like I was going to touch it or anything.

VALERIE

Go ahead, I dare you.

MAVIS

I dare you.

VALERIE

Shit, I wouldn't touch anything that beige.

VIOLET

Why?

VALERIE

Jesus, Violet, you don't want to be lookin' at that.

VIOLET

Why?

VALERIE
You might go blind.

MAVIS
I thought that's what happened when you masturbated.

VALERIE
Well, you should know.

MAVIS
Like... I... said. I thought that's what happened when you masturbated –
I never heard of anyone going blind by touching a white ass.

VALERIE
You shouldn't say masturbate in front of the kid.

MAVIS
Masturbate, masturbate, masturbate. Why?

VIOLET looks at VALERIE intensely.

VALERIE
It's a big word... with a... lot of responsibility.

MAVIS
Number one, she's not a kid – she just seems like one.

VALERIE
Well, maybe this isn't an ass – it just seems like one.

MAVIS
Only one way to find out. Touch it.

VALERIE
You touch it.

MAVIS
No, you touch it.

VALERIE
Scared of the real thing? You've been dying for it for so long. Go crazy.

MAVIS
You go crazy.

VALERIE pinches it hard.

RON
Oh!

RON wakes up and looks around. The clock neons 6:30. He crawls out of bed. Walks around the living room, picks up a newspaper, walks to the bathroom and shuts the door.

MAVIS

Now he's gonna take a shit and stink up the place.

VALERIE

Let a guy into your bedroom, and he thinks he can take a big dump in your can.

MAVIS

I bet he turns on the fan.

Sound of the toilet flushing and bathroom fan turns on.

VALERIE

Like that's gonna help.

They wait. Silence. Smell. They both start waving their hands in front of their face like a fan.

Shiiiiiiiiiiiit...

VIOLET starts looking for VERNA. VERNA wants to be alone and is sitting slumped down against a wall. VIOLET sits down next her.

VIOLET

Why do you think we're here?

VERNA

Is this the BIG question? Because, if it is... I'm not up to it, okay? Why don't you go ask "know it all" Mavis or something?

VIOLET

I'm asking you.

VERNA

And I'm telling you I don't know. I mean, why is anybody anybody? Why does anybody end up anywhere? Why does... I never figured it out, okay. I just don't know... if I knew I wouldn't be here or maybe I would. I just don't know.

VIOLET

Why don't you know?

VERNA

Why don't you shut up?

VIOLET
You don't have to be mean.

VERNA
(*in a whiny voice*) Why is the world mean? Why doesn't Mommy love me? Why is Daddy touching me there? Why? Why? I don't know. Why me?

VIOLET
Why aren't you nice ?

VERNA
(*raises her voice*) Why aren't you in bed?

VIOLET
Why are you yelling?

VERNA
I'm not yelling.

VIOLET
Why are you mad?

VERNA
Because I'm dead, and I'm still thirsty.

VIOLET
Thirsty?

> *VERNA leans over and screams at her silently.*

VERNA
THIRSTY, you fuckin parrot. I'm thirsty for... for... my kids, my man. I'm thirsty, thirsty, thirsty, THIR-sty, THIRSTY, dehydrated, dry, parched, thirsty. Get IT?

VIOLET
You didn't have to get mad. (*She puts her head down and pouts.*)

VERNA
(*lowers her voice and gets up*) It's the only way I know how to get from here... to there.

> *VIOLET looks up, and VERNA has disappeared. VERNA makes her way to the Empress Hotel.*

> *RON walks through all the WOMEN with coffee. They all stop and look at his parts.*

SLIDE: THE MORNING AFTER – CONT.

RON walks into the bedroom with two cups of coffee. He hands one to REBECCA.

RON
I made some coffee. You don't have any cream. You have a carton, but you don't have any cream.

REBECCA
That doesn't surprise me.

RON
So.

REBECCA
So. Ron. How are you this morning?

RON
I feel like shit.

REBECCA
Well, since we're doing the true confession part of the morning – me too .

RON
You were talking in your sleep... and you pinched my ass.

REBECCA
I talk in my sleep, but it wasn't me that pinched your ass.

RON
I pinched my own ass.

REBECCA
Stranger things have happened. Maybe you were feeling hard done by.

RON
I am actually, but that's another story. What were you doing down there?

REBECCA
The Empress? Thinking and drinking. What were you doing down there?

RON
Drinking and playing pool. We usually go in after work and have a couple of beers. Why do you drink there?

REBECCA
Well, I don't always drink there, but it's a good place to go and think, and I can usually have a drink in quiet without some suit coming up and trying to dazzle me. The worst thing that can happen is an old beat-up suit will sit down and try and dazzle me, which is usually more sad than it is offensive. Besides, I am looking for someone.

RON
Who – Mr. Right?

REBECCA
I married Mr. Right. And divorced Mr. Right. So, now I'm looking for Mr. Fun.

RON
So, who are you looking for really?

REBECCA
I'm looking for my mom. She went for a walk twenty years ago, and I haven't seen her since.

RON
And you think she's down there.

REBECCA
Yup.

RON
Why?

REBECCA
She was last seen down there.

RON
Why now?

REBECCA
Why now what?

RON
Why do you want to find her now?

REBECCA
I'm not mad anymore.

RON
Remind me not to make you mad.

REBECCA

Well, sometimes it helps to be mad.

RON

You think she's down there. Like living down there? It's not the greatest place to live.

REBECCA

No, really?

RON

I'm just saying the people that live down there are mostly drunks and junkies and Ind... First Na...

REBECCA

And what? You were going to say Indians. Oh, don't get all politically correct on me now...

RON

Okay, Indians. You got a thing for Indians?

REBECCA

Yeah, I got a thing for Indians. You got a thing against Indians?

RON

No, I was just saying...

REBECCA

Never mind. Save it for your job.

RON

What's that supposed to mean?

REBECCA

Listen. I'm not really into Education 101 this morning. So why don't you take your pale bum home.

RON

Let me guess... you're Indian.

REBECCA

Part Indian.

RON

Which part?

REBECCA

The good part.

RON

I thought you were Italian or something.

REBECCA

I thought you were white or something. And I was right. So we both win.

RON

It's just that you don't seem Indian.

REBECCA

That begs the question – what does an Indian seem like? Let me guess – you probably think that, if an Indian goes to university or watches TV, it makes them the same as every other Canadian. Only less. The big melting pot. The only problem is you can't melt an Indian. You can't kill a stone. You can grind it down to sand, but it's still there sifting through everything forever. There, you got it.

RON

Wow, and it's not even nine o'clock in the morning.

REBECCA

I haven't even finished my first cup of coffee.

RON

Since you're there, why do you think so many end up down there?

REBECCA

Since you asked, I don't think so many of them end up down there. I think so many people end up down there. Period.

RON

Why?

REBECCA

It's an accident. Something heavy falls on them. It might just be one thing... one thing and then everything seems to tumble down and pretty soon there is no getting up.

RON

What do you mean?

REBECCA

Like an accident – people drive by in their nice cars and stare at people on those streets, because they realize for a moment it could happen to them. So they might be saying "poor bastards," but what they're really thinking about is themselves and their own potential tragedy.

So these nice people finally look away and—to console themselves from that one conscious thought—think it couldn't happen to them. It's happening to "those" people. Even better if "those" people are mentally ill or brown or addicted to one thing or another. Because these nice people can park their nice cars in their nice driveways and open the doors to their nice homes and take a couple of nice valiums, or call up that nice Betty Ford and go for a nice little vacation "just to get away." They think they are safe. It doesn't matter where your room is – you still have to face the face.

RON
The room?

REBECCA
Yourself. Alone.

RON
So you're saying that's why people end up there.

REBECCA
Yes, they're alone and they know it but there's nothing more comforting than being with a group of people that know they are alone...

RON
...It's like going to hear the Blues when you're feeling like shit. It makes you feel better.

REBECCA
(*She looks at him.*) Yeah...

RON
Gotcha.

REBECCA
Well, this has been a lot of fun, but I really have to get a move on.

RON
That means I have to leave.

REBECCA
That means – yeah... you have to leave. I have to get dressed. Day stuff.

RON
Can I give you a call?

REBECCA
Mmmmm?

RON
Maybe I could take you out for supper.

REBECCA
Steak and potato and a good red wine.

RON
Sure... make me an honest asshole.

REBECCA
Make me an honest woman. My life is kinda clustered right now but...

RON
But...

REBECCA
Yeah... maybe... I think I've told you too much.

RON
I don't think you've told me enough.

REBECCA
Well, I wouldn't have told you anything, but I didn't think I'd see you again.

RON
And now?

REBECCA
I've probably said too much.

> *RON starts to get his clothes together and puts them on. He leaves. REBECCA rolls over to sleep.*

> *SLIDE: THE LIVING ROOM – CONT.*

> *The WOMEN are in different areas of the apartment touching and using REBECCA's things. VALERIE is going through REBECCA's laundry that's lying in a basket. She's pulling out different pieces of underwear and trying them on. MAVIS is sitting at REBECCA's desk playing with the phone. VIOLET has been in REBECCA's bedroom swinging on her swing and playing with REBECCA's pretty things. Gradually, the WOMEN pick what they want of REBECCA's clothing and make-up, and put them on.*

MAVIS
She's gonna know you were in her drawers. Women always know when someone's been in their drawers.

VALERIE
So. Like, what's she gonna do about it?

MAVIS

The point is – you shouldn't be wearing her underwear. It doesn't even fit you.

VALERIE

It fits parts of me. And why don't you get off your ass and find out where Verna went?

MAVIS

I will after... I finish this one last call.

VALERIE

Who the hell are you talking to anyways?

MAVIS

Talked to my Aunt Bertha. She died when I was eight. She thought I'd forgotten all about her, but I said I always remembered her on account she told me I was beautiful when I was little. I always remember people who said I was beautiful.

VALERIE

Well, that's got to be real hard on your memory.

MAVIS

What?

VALERIE

I said, are you going to see where Verna is or do I have to?

MAVIS

You have to.

> *VALERIE doesn't leave but eavesdrops on MAVIS' conversation.*

Hi... Dad. It's me. Mavis. Well, I just thought I'd call and say "hi." No reason. Like I said, I just got to thinking about you and thought – what the hell, I'll just give the old man a call just out of the blue. How have you been? (*She shrugs.*) How do I think you've been? Well, good I guess. Dad? Geez, he hung up on me.

VALERIE

What did you expect?

MAVIS

I thought he would've mellowed a bit in death.

> *VALERIE sniffs the air, and VIOLET tiptoes back into the room.*

VALERIE

I think she's been into the perfume.

MAVIS

How do you know?

VALERIE

Can't you smell her coming?

MAVIS

Geez, she smells like an old whore.

VALERIE

What's that supposed to mean?

MAVIS

Just that she stinks I guess.

VIOLET

She's got lots of perfume.

VALERIE

We know.

VIOLET

I love perfume. I always wanted lots of perfume. That a drop could make you smell good all over, feel good all over, is kinda amazing.

VALERIE

That's the way I feel about lingerie. I got my first real bra when I was 12, you know one of those God-ugly white things from the Sears catalogue. The first day I come to the city, I went into a lingerie store – it was the most beautiful thing. Red and silk and satin and nylons and things that went up your butt and things that went down your butt and pulled things together and separated other things. That's a fuckin miracle happening if you ask me. I guess lingerie was my downfall.

MAVIS

How so?

VALERIE

I always wanted to show it to people.

MAVIS

Give me a pair of clean cotton undies any day.

VALERIE

What do you know about lingerie? You never get off your ass to appreciate anything on your ass.

MAVIS
Listen, Valerie... enough about my ass, okay?

VALERIE
Okay, okay – touchy, touchy.

MAVIS
...and since you're worried about everybody's ass, go and see if Verna's in the can.

VALERIE moves towards the bathroom.

VALERIE
Probably reading her one-shit-at-a-time AA book. A capital-letter SOB story if you ask me.

VIOLET
She's not in there.

MAVIS
So now what?

VALERIE
Well, I guess we look good enough to go look for her.

They stop and look in REBECCA's mirror. They put on the finishing touches of make-up and scarves, etc. They look good. They turn to go.

Ready?

MAVIS
Ready.

They leave. VIOLET picks up some red lipstick and puts it on.

The phone rings. Lights up on REBECCA, as she mutters and gets up and picks up the phone. Lights up on AUNT SHADIE at the switchboard.

REBECCA
Hello?

AUNT SHADIE—recognizing REBECCA's voice—stops, breathes slowly and sits down, not able to answer, cradling the phone.

Answer, why don't you?

Nothing.

(*sarcastically*) I love you too.

> REBECCA *places the receiver down. Lights out on AUNT SHADIE.*
> REBECCA *enters the bathroom and starts the shower and gets in.*

> *The phone rings. She wraps herself and stumbles towards it, dripping. She picks it up.*

> SFX: *A male voice talking under.*

Ahhhh... enough already. (*picks up phone*) Hello? Am I missing something? (*to herself*) Well, why don't we just play a little game. I'm not sure yet – why? Why didn't you just say that? I must've lost it when I was down there last night. Yeah, I'll be down this afternoon. How will I know you? Okay, yeah. I'll ask the bartender. You can tell me by the picture on my driver's license, or at least I hope you can. Thanks... yeah this afternoon. I'll be there – I told you. Thanks.

> *She hangs up the phone.*

(*to herself*) Weirdo.

> REBECCA *searches through her laundry basket for her new underwear. She looks under things, the search continues.*

Oh, that's great. I finally get a set of great underwear, and the dryer eats it. Here, underwear. Oh, this is not a good day. I should just go back to bed. Go back to bed. Okay, I can do it. Seventy dollars worth of gonch disappeared... feeling like shit.

> *The phone rings. It's RON.*

Hello. I mean... (*sexy*) hel-lo. Just kidding. How you doing? I haven't seen you for at least a couple of hours. Dinner? What do you feel like eating? Steak. Perfect. No, great choice. How can I refuse when you say it like that? I have some running around to do today, but later tonight sounds good. Okay – see you then... there... whatever. Bye.

> *She gets up, walks past a mirror and looks in.*

Feeling good... looking like shit... lost my wallet... talking to myself... and a slut to top it off. Perfect.

> *She walks into her bedroom. Stops suspiciously and looks at the bed's toes.*

Don't even think about it if you want to live.

> *Lights down.*

VIOLET makes her way slowly up the stairs.

SLIDE: SETTING THE TABLE

ROSE is going around the table placing plates.

ROSE
You smell pretty. Do you want to help?

VIOLET
Okay.

>*VIOLET picks up a pile of cutlery and begins handing it to her. AUNT SHADIE sits quietly by herself weaving snowshoes. She places her feet in each, testing them out. ROSE and VIOLET place the silverware in a setting ritual.*

Why do you think we're here?

ROSE
That's a big question.

VIOLET
That's a big question – that's what everybody says.

ROSE
I spent most of life waiting for the big answer. Waiting to fall in love, waiting to have children, waiting to give.

VIOLET
Waiting for the right things to happen that would make everything alright.

ROSE
Waiting.

VIOLET
(*more like a woman than a child*) But not making a choice.

ROSE
Sometimes the right moment in time...

VIOLET
The right waiting is our own making...

ROSE
...our knowing that everything has a time and a place.

>*AUNT SHADIE puts both snowshoes on and is practicing. Proud of her limbs and her snowshoe expertise.*

AUNT SHADIE
That we've never forgotten.

> *VIOLET holds the last knife for a moment and then places it on the table in its setting. She turns to look at AUNT SHADIE. AUNT SHADIE nods and VIOLET walks back down like a woman.*

> *SLIDE: THE EMPRESSES*

> *The BARBER sits at a red terry-cloth table sipping beer. He is dressed in a suit, though shabby around the edges. VERNA is seated beside him, leaning into him, talking. The BARBER is scoping out the place and oblivious to her chatter.*

VERNA
Listen, you moron. I'm talking to you. Oh bald one. Don't think I even went around with you because you are good-looking or nothing – you're ugly. Ugly... look at those glasses – four eyes – big eyes bulging out like you're looking at headlights or something. Big dumb.... Stupid.

> *VERNA slaps him upside the head. His glasses fall off. He picks them up and places them back on his head. The slap changes his focus. He looks through the bar where his barbershop slowly lights up. In a hunting hallucination, his instinct sharpens as he sees a flash of brown moving. He attempts to stumble up. VERNA sits him down roughly.*

Not so fast, ree-tard. I got a few more things to get off my chest.

> *He staggers back down, his eyes fixated on an image coming through the mirrors of his barbershop. A forest forms in the mirrors. The flashes of brown become closer, getting clearer.*

GILBERT
Okay, baby... that's it, baby... that's it.

VERNA
Nee.chin whikth quan.knit to squaw.kwaw – I already took the liquor.

> *He concentrates single-mindedly on his vision.*

GILBERT
Oh, it is brown – the colour of my thirst.

VERNA
It's my drink – *tay squaw.kaw*

> *The brown blurs form into a beautiful projection of MARILYN, PENNY AND PATSY, who are dressed in their hair dreams, seductive and sensual. The projections accent their legs and limbs and eyes. VALERIE and MAVIS step*

into the image and slowly emerge from the mirror, beautifully in deer-like grace, in unison – part woman, part animal seduction. As they emerge, VIOLET follows behind them – high woman vogue. The following is a collage of images, song, language and movement. Intoxicating and potent.

Quaw.swhat.tus.at.na.ay.quee.quaw – as it reaches my stomach, *Yoh hat.toe.know.a.tone.nas.new.whakt* – of my sacred beliefs.

VALERIE and MAVIS get closer to him, moving slow and sensual. They stop to apply lipstick seductively, suggestively, for him.

Thirsty for living.

GILBERT
I watched.

They stop mid-lipstick.

VERNA
Thirsty.

WOMEN
I held my breath.

GILBERT
Like animals before her, she was there when I needed to take.

VERNA
Hungry.

The WOMEN seductively pour beer down his throat.

WOMEN
He was afraid of making a mistake.

VERNA
Hungry.

GILBERT
Like animals before her, I wished to look in her eyes...

He tries to pull VALERIE closer. VALERIE places her lips on his and feeds him beer.

VERNA
Hungry.

WOMEN
I saw the smallness.

VERNA
...lies...

GILBERT
I took them before they could really see me.

VERNA
In desperation.

They sniff.

WOMEN
I smelled him.

VERNA
Hungry for me.

GILBERT
Like animals before her, there was a stillness.

He staggers for them. They pull away. Stop.

VERNA
My heart.

They stop and sigh.

WOMEN
...a stillness...

VERNA
The real me.

WOMEN
...a peacefulness...

VERNA
Waiting.

GILBERT
A gasp.

They pose and sigh.

VERNA
Waiting.

GILBERT
Expecting...

They moan seductively.

VERNA
...to laugh at...

GILBERT
...deliverance.

VERNA
...Salvation.

They walk away slowly, beautifully, eyes on him.

WOMEN
There was only my God laughing when he said...

GILBERT
"...There are more ways than one to skin an animal."

WOMEN
There was only my God laughing when he said...

GILBERT
"...Everyone thinks it, they just don't do it."

WOMEN
There was only me laughing when he said...

GILBERT
Die. Die.

WOMEN
Only me.

VERNA
Seeing...

GILBERT
...the look in their eyes.

VERNA
Pointing...

WOMEN
...back...

VERNA
Leaving you...

GILBERT
...wondering – can an animal laugh?

> *VALERIE and MAVIS and VIOLET slip back into the mirror and through the images of MARILYN, PATSY AND PENNY. The mirror reflecting many women.*

WOMEN
Oh yes. Oh yes. Forever

> *GILBERT starts pounding his drinks, shaken.*

GILBERT
I am a good and decent man.
I am a good and good-living man.

> *MAVIS Her Chair Ass and VALERIE and VIOLET appear behind VERNA. VALERIE places her hand on VERNA's shoulder.*

VALERIE
It's time to go, Verna – he's not worth it.

GILBERT
I am clean.

MAVIS
He's just a man.

GILBERT
I am.

VERNA
An ugly man to boot.

GILBERT
I am.

VIOLET
An ugly man to boot.

GILBERT
I am.

MAVIS
You should feel sorry for him.

GILBERT
Therefore, I am.

VERNA
Sorry? (*pause*) All I feel sorry for is his little dick and his ugly face. Besides, I'm tired of feeling sorry for white people.

> *GILBERT continues to get blasted.*

MAVIS
Okay, enough of this ugly.

VERNA
What? You got something for him, Mavis?

MAVIS
I never had anything for him, Verna. I thought he was someone else.

VERNA
Well, that's easy to say now...

VALERIE
That's enough, Verna. We all thought he was someone we knew. Someone we needed. Okay, leave it alone.

VERNA
Skinny bastard.

MAVIS
We should go, Verna.

VERNA
You go.

VALERIE
We're not leaving you here, Verna.

VERNA
Why the hell not?

VALERIE
It would be too pitiful.

VERNA
You wanna make something out of this, Valerie?

VALERIE
Verna, you know I could make you in a minute.

VERNA gets up from her chair to challenge VALERIE.

VERNA
Make this...

MAVIS
Hello – it's her Rebecca.

VALERIE & VIOLET
Oh shittttttttttttttttttt...

REBECCA approaches them. The WOMEN back away slightly.

REBECCA
Excuse me?

WOMEN
Ahhhh... yeah?

GILBERT
(*hazy drunk*) Yeah? What do you want? (*He looks at her intensely.*) I mean... how can I help you? Miss.

REBECCA
Umm... the guy at the front said you were the one that had my wallet. I mean you were the one that found it. Remember, you told me to get the bartender to point you out.

GILBERT
Right... right. Mind isn't what it used to be. (*laughs*) Have a seat.

REBECCA sits.

I saw you in here last night. It must of fell from your jacket or something. I'm just glad I could help.

VALERIE
Help this, you fuckin pig! (*She squeezes her boobs together.*)

REBECCA
Well, thanks. It's always a big hassle when you lose your ID.

WOMEN
I'll say.

GILBERT
What's a nice girl like you hanging around a place like this?

MAVIS
Oh, that's original.

REBECCA
Just playing pool.

GILBERT
Can I buy you a drink?

VIOLET
No.

REBECCA
No, it's okay.

GILBERT
Seriously, you look like a lady that was lookin' for something.

He hands her over a beer. She watches the beer slide over.

REBECCA
O-kay.... Well, it's a long story.

GILBERT
I got all the time in the world.

REBECCA
Really. I have been looking for my mother. She was last seen in this neighbourhood. Seems I just get close to where she last lived, or where she used to hang out, and I somehow miss her.

GILBERT
You gotta picture? I've been around here for a long time.

REBECCA shuffles in her purse and pulls a picture out. She shows it to him. All the WOMEN look at it.

VALERIE
Holy shit, she was beautiful.

MAVIS
Kinda looks like me when I was young.

VERNA
Yeah, right.

GILBERT
I think I know her. I think her name was – well... I don't know her real name, but they used to call her Aunt Shadie or something...

REBECCA
Aunt Shadie?

WOMEN
Aunt Shadie?!

GILBERT
Aunt Shadie. Come to think of it, I had a drink with her awhile back.

REBECCA
How long ago is a while back?

GILBERT
I lose track of time – you know how it is? Anyways, she left some things with me to hold for safekeeping... she said she was gonna try and look up a daughter she hadn't seen in awhile. I'm always tryin' to help some of these women out.

REBECCA
Really.

GILBERT
If you want, we can finish these off and head over to my barbershop. I think I got something of hers there.

The BARBER watches her as REBECCA downs her beer. They get up, and he stumbles and tries to pull himself together. REBECCA looks around, she stops.

WOMEN
It's alright.

REBECCA
(to herself, them) It's alright.

Lights down.

SLIDE: WHEN SHE WAS HORNY AND WANTED SEX – The Barbershop

They enter the barbershop. GILBERT walks around and shuts the blinds to his storefront. REBECCA walks around the shop, keeping her distance. He stares intensely at her.

REBECCA
It's a nice shop. Do you have a lot of clients?

GILBERT
Just my regulars. They like the service I've always given them.

REBECCA
I'm sure they do.

GILBERT
I'm good at my job. Been doing it for thirty years now.

REBECCA
Really?

GILBERT
You could say this has been my calling.

REBECCA
What do you like best about it?

GILBERT
I'm in control, and I know what they want.

REBECCA
What do they want?

GILBERT
That depends.

REBECCA
I love barbershops. Always loved them. Ever since I was a little girl I used to come with my dad and watch him get shaved and have his hair cut.

She touches his utensils.

GILBERT
You used to have long hair?

REBECCA
Yeah, but I cut it because I... you wouldn't understand. I cut it to my shoulders a couple of months ago. It will grow, and I'll braid it like I used to when I was a kid.

GILBERT
Braids?

REBECCA
My dad used to do it for me... he used to say I looked just like my mom when he finished. I used to love that.

GILBERT
Can I braid it? I like women in braids.

REBECCA
No, it's alright. Thanks...

He grabs her hair from behind. She grabs her hair back.

Enough.

GILBERT
(*He turns and says to himself:*) You fuckin uppity bitch.

REBECCA
Pardon me.

GILBERT
Pardon me? (*mimicking her*)

He gets out a bottle from his cupboard.

Do you want a drink?

REBECCA
Sure, I guess. Shouldn't you be working?

GILBERT
I am.

Long awkward silence.

REBECCA
So... can I see what you have of my mother's? I don't usually drink in the afternoon, so this is really a special treat. It really goes straight to my head...

GILBERT
Here, I'll just top you up.

REBECCA
Yeah...

She watches him pour the drink.

GILBERT

I'm just gonna go freshen up a bit. Don't want to be in the company of a beautiful young woman looking like I need to brush my teeth.

GILBERT exits to go to the bathroom.

REBECCA

And you're only worried about your teeth... fuckin scary.

She goes to pull out a drawer and then stops and looks at the red and white barber light. She stops for a long moment and breathes. She walks directly towards it, taking the bottom off the light. A handful of long black braids fall to the floor. She gasps and touches each one until she gets to her mother's. She picks her mother's braid up and buries her face in it and sobs. REBECCA hears GILBERT approaching. Shaken, she takes her jacket off and covers the braids and tries to get herself together.

Here, Gilbert, why don't you have a seat. I always found shaving men sexy. It makes me horny. Can I shave you, Gilbert?

GILBERT

I don't know... it's not usually how things work.

REBECCA

Things they are a changin'...

GILBERT

What?

REBECCA

Just a song I had in my head. Oh, come on.

GILBERT

Okay... you have to be careful.

REBECCA

I'll be gentle.

He reaches up to touch her. She grabs his hands.

You have beautiful hands. I've always loved men's hands. How they move. Your hands are so soft and white. I bet you've loved a lot of women.

GILBERT

I've had my share of women.

REBECCA

You're being modest.

GILBERT
Women have always taken to me. I know how to make a woman happy.
I know what they want to hear.

He places his hands on her breasts.

REBECCA
Slow down, Gilbert. Slow down, we have lots of time. Would you like a
drink? Can I buy you a drink? Can I get you a drink?

GILBERT
What do you mean?

REBECCA
I mean, can I pour you a drink?

GILBERT
Sure, I guess.

REBECCA
Here you go. You sure you don't want more? You look like you can handle
your liquor.

GILBERT
I'm not scared of anything.

She pours him a heap.

REBECCA
Of course not. Okay, baby. Can I shave you?

GILBERT
You have to be very careful.

REBECCA
I'd never do anything to hurt you. Do want your bottle? Here, why don't
I place it right here, so it can be close to you? Do you like that? It's right
here so it can be close to you. Do you like that?

She grooves it into his crotch. He moans.

I'll just place this over you now. Like this?

She places his barbershop cape over him. It covers his body.

GILBERT
That's right.

REBECCA

That's right.

He grabs her hand. She keeps him from forcing her hand down.

GILBERT

That's right. Right down here... you fuckin...

REBECCA

Gilbert. Shhhhhhhh... just wait... just wait. Close your eyes and relax. Relax. I'm here, baby.

GILBERT

Yeah. I'll relax when I'm stuffing you with my...

REBECCA

Should I use this? (*She grabs the shaving cream bottle.*) So, I take it in my hand... spray it out like this? You tell me, you're the professional.

GILBERT

That's it. That's it. Jesus Christ, just do it.

REBECCA

Just close your eyes – let me do all the work.

She smoothes the foam over his face sensually.

GILBERT

Mmmmmm.

He closes his eyes. As she spreads the foam on his face, a forest reflects in the mirrors as it is being covered by billowing snow. A beautiful, crystallized snow scene.

A voice from the dark approaches through the landscape. It gets closer and closer. At first, just a movement and glimpses of brown.

AUNT SHADIE

I used to be a real good trapper when I was young. You wouldn't believe it, now that I'm such a city girl. But before, when my legs and body were young and muscular, I could go forever. Walking those traplines with snowshoes. The sun coming down, sprinkling everything with crystals, some floating down and dusting that white comforter with magic. I would walk that trapline...

REBECCA

I would walk that trapline...

AUNT SHADIE
...like a map, my body knowing every turn, every tree, every curve the land uses to confuse us.

REBECCA
...like a map, my body knowing every turn, every lie, every curve they use to kill us.

REBECCA & AUNT SHADIE
I felt like I was part of the magic that wasn't confused.

REBECCA
The crystals sticking to the cold and the cold sticking to my black hair, my eyebrows, my clothes, my breath. A trap set.

REBECCA braces herself. She takes the razor and is about to cut his throat.

An animal caught.

The BARBER's eyes suddenly blaze open. He grabs her hand and they struggle with the blade. The blade draws closer to her neck and is about to cut her open. AUNT SHADIE emerges from the landscape as a trapper. She stands behind REBECCA. She puts her hand over REBECCA's hand and draws the knife closer to the BARBER's neck. He looks up and panics as he sees AUNT SHADIE and the WOMEN/trappers behind her. Squirming, they slit his throat.

AUNT SHADIE
Red.

They look at each other. Blood seeps on his white gown.

REBECCA
Red.

AUNT SHADIE
If it squirmed, I would put it out of its misery as fast as I could.

The trappers follow through, as REBECCA and her mother stare at each other. The trappers take the razor, wash it and replace it. REBECCA hands each woman her braid. The WOMEN leave in a line. Her mother remains standing. REBECCA reaches in her pocket and hands her mother her braid of hair.

Re-becca.

AUNT SHADIE raises her hand and touches her face.

REBECCA
Meegweetch and thank you.

AUNT SHADIE hugs her and falls behind the line of WOMEN/trappers. She falls in behind the rest of the trappers, as the lights fade on the landscape and the WOMEN tracking their way back.

SLIDE: THE FIRST SUPPER – NOT TO BE CONFUSED WITH THE LAST SUPPER

REBECCA watches the long line of WOMEN as they take their heavy trapping clothes off, their long, long hair spilling everywhere. They begin to sit down to a beautiful banquet à la the Last Supper. Lights fade on them, and the sound of their voices becomes the sound of trees.

SFX: Sound of tree leaves moving in the wind.

REBECCA exits from the barbershop. She walks in the wind and trees.

SFX: The loud sound of a tree falling...

She stops and listens to the sound.

The barbershop is empty except for the BARBER in his chair. Barber lights swirl red and white throughout the barbershop. The red light intensifies and takes over the room. Fade out.

SFX: The sound of the tree hitting the ground with a loud thud.

REBECCA closes her eyes for a moment and then continues walking.

Fade out.

The end.